Musical Theatre Histories

Musical Theatre Histories

Expanding the Narrative

Millie Taylor and Adam Rush

methuen | drama

LONDON • NEW YORK • OXFORD • NEW DELHI • SYDNEY

METHUEN DRAMA
Bloomsbury Publishing Plc
50 Bedford Square, London, WC1B 3DP, UK
1385 Broadway, New York, NY 10018, USA
29 Earlsfort Terrace, Dublin 2, Ireland

BLOOMSBURY, METHUEN DRAMA and the Methuen Drama logo
are trademarks of Bloomsbury Publishing Plc

First published in Great Britain 2023

For legal purposes the Acknowledgements on p. viii constitute an extension of this copyright page.

Cover design by Rebecca Heselton
Cover images: *Ragtime* © STAN HONDA/AFP via Getty Images. *Hamilton* © John Paul Filo/CBS
via Getty Images. *Evita* © Hulton Archive/Getty Images. *Blood Brothers* © Anthony Barboza/
Getty Images. *Shuffle Along* © Anthony Barboza/Getty Images. *Oklahoma!* © Susan Biddle/for the
Washington Post/Getty Images. *Hair* © Ray Fisher/Getty Images. *Mamma Mia!* © jejim/ Shutterstock.

A catalogue record for this book is available from the British Library.

Library of Congress Cataloging-in-Publication Data
Names: Taylor, Millie, author. | Rush, Adam, author.
Title: Musical theatre histories: expanding the narrative/Millie Taylor and Adam Rush.
Description: [Original.] | London; New York: Methuen Drama, 2022. |
Includes bibliographical references and index. |
Identifiers: LCCN 2022016042 (print) | LCCN 2022016043 (ebook) |
ISBN 9781350293755 (paperback) | ISBN 9781350293762 (hardback) |
ISBN 9781350293779 (epub) | ISBN 9781350293786 (pdf)
Subjects: LCSH: Musicals–History and criticism. | Musicals–New York (State)–New York–History
and criticism. | Musicals–England–London–History and criticism.
Classification: LCC ML2054.T35 2022 (print) | LCC ML2054 (ebook) | DDC 782.1/409–dc23
LC record available at https://lccn.loc.gov/2022016042
LC ebook record available at https://lccn.loc.gov/2022016043

ISBN: HB: 978-1-3502-9376-2
          PB: 978-1-3502-9375-5
          ePDF: 978-1-3502-9378-6
          eBook: 978-1-3502-9377-9

Typeset by Integra Software Services Pvt. Ltd.
Printed and bound in Great Britain

To find out more about our authors and books visit www.bloomsbury.com
and sign up for our newsletters.

Contents

Illustrations

Acknowledgements

This book would not have been possible without the input, insight and support of our colleague Matt Lockitt. This publication began with three authors, and when Matt sadly had to step away from the project, he continued to support us with ideas and enthusiasm. Matt, like several other of our colleagues, has been instrumental to seeing this book into fruition.

Secondly, this book has been developed with and by several cohorts of students on the BA Musical Theatre degree at the University of Winchester. As a research-informed teaching project, every task and discussion topic, plus many other sections of the book, have benefited from the generosity of our students' ideas, excitement and discussions. We must particularly thank Hannah Thomas and Megan Selley for their excellent work as student interns, helping us both in the classroom and in contributing to the research.

The book has also benefited from conversations and interactions with other scholars in our community. Sections of this work have been presented at the annual Song, Stage and Screen conference and for the IFTR Music Theatre working group. The work was always met with support and intrigue and followed by productive discussion. In addition, we would like to thank the anonymous peer reviewers and colleagues who have provided feedback on the work in development, in particular Dominic Symonds. This insight has helped craft the work and push it in several new and contemporary directions.

We must also thank Dom O'Hanlon and the editorial team at Bloomsbury Methuen. After several years in development, we are thrilled that this book has found a home with such a supportive publisher looking to develop new research in musical theatre studies. Thank you to Dom and his team for all their hard work.

One further person to thank is Martin Nangle for some of the photographic images, and finally, we would like to thank our friends and family for their continued love and support.

'Why we tell the story': Introduction

In the age of social media, global television and online communication, musical theatre remains an art form that has, for most of the last century, been associated with two physical locations: the West End and Broadway. On either side of the Atlantic Ocean, over 3,000 miles apart, these two epicentres in London and New York have been considered the 'home' of musical theatre. Despite the form's genesis as an amalgam of European and American influences, the impact of immigration and colonization, and the traffic of shows and practitioners across the English-speaking world, musical theatre remains Broadway and West End centric. This also remains true despite the form's current importance as a globalized product that has stimulated nationally significant productions in countries as diverse as China, South Korea, Austria, Australia, the Netherlands, Canada and Germany. American scholars tend to favour stories of the American or Broadway musical, and vice versa in Britain, yet the development of this popular form is arguably stimulated by a series of transatlantic interactions between these two centres and beyond.

Some of Gilbert and Sullivan's operas, for example, opened almost simultaneously in London and New York, despite this writing team sometimes being considered the British musical's equivalent to Shakespeare. They, like many musical comedies in the nineteenth century, also travelled to the former colonies, spreading musical theatre around a large portion of the globe. Jump forward to Lin-Manuel Miranda's megahit, *Hamilton* (2015). The musical was developed in New York, is a self-described 'American musical' and depicts America breaking away from British rule during the American Revolutionary War (1775–83) and the early Republic (the musical concludes shortly after founding father Alexander Hamilton's death in 1804).

Nevertheless, the musical contains references to – or certainly resembles – earlier British megamusicals such as *Les Misérables* (1985) (Magee, 2018; Rush, 2021b) and has opened replica productions in many international cities. The labelling of a production as either distinctly British or American is thus extremely complicated.

What defines a work's national identity, then? Is it the nationality of the musical's cast, creative team or producer? Is it the show's content, setting or themes? Might it simply be where the production first opened or where it was produced and developed? If we pinpoint any of these suggestions as the exclusive answer, we are in rather complex territory. Historically, and in a less mobile world, it was easier to define who the producer of a production was, and where it opened gave a strong sense of derivation from one centre or the other. Once the originating point is established it is then possible to analyse the performance's narrative as deriving from that context, though patterns of influence confuse the issue even then. However, as the traffic in musical theatre performers, productions, creative teams and, most recently, finance has increased, it becomes increasingly difficult to differentiate between British, American and indeed other globally produced musicals.

An example of this is the 2012 stage adaptation of *The Bodyguard*. The musical is based on the 1992 American film, features the music of American singer Whitney Houston, was written by an American scriptwriter (book) and opened with Heather Headley, a Broadway star, in the lead role. However, the production first played in the West End and had a British director and producers; it has yet to play on Broadway. Is it therefore a British or American musical? A significantly more complicated example is Disney's *The Lion King* (1997). The stage production is based on a 1994 American animated film and is produced by an American corporation. It is set in Africa, however, with a predominantly African American cast, while also having an internationally diverse production team (with members from countries as widespread as Germany and Jamaica). Stylistically, the production incorporates a global myriad of theatrical styles, from Japanese Bunraku puppetry to Indonesian shadow theatre. The musical has played in New York, London, Tokyo, Hamburg, plus countless other cities, and has become a central part of each city's theatre industry and tourist trade. Whatever the ethics underlying some of the appropriation that has taken place, it is undeniably a cross-cultural work that plays around the world. Despite this, most scholars consider *The Lion King* to be an American text. It is the landmark work of Disney Theatrical Productions, a subsidiary of The Walt Disney Company, that opened in New York where it has played for over two decades. Likewise, *The Bodyguard* is considered a British musical, despite its predominately American content. British audiences might have assumed that it was a Broadway transfer, one that brought its star, Headley, to London, yet this was not the case.

With the incorporation of increasingly diverse production teams, performers and locations of development, musical theatre must now be considered transnational, despite many of its canonic works arising largely from the axis between Britain and America. Most of the chapters that follow focus on this axis, therefore, in the awareness of the much greater diversity that still needs to be thoroughly explored. Nonetheless, we maintain this focus because the transactions between Britain and America provide the dynamism from which the contemporary musical emerged as a transnational phenomenon. We do not answer the question about a work's national identity in relation to musicals, but rather we problematize the question by drawing attention to the transatlantic and global interactions out of which, and within which, musical theatre evolves.

Historiography and context(s)

This book, therefore, explores some of the interactions between London and New York as central to understanding the development of musical theatre. It does not consider the history of these centres in isolation, as many existing accounts of musical theatre history do, but as a series of journeys, overlaps and interactions. We question the gaps, the inconsistencies and the moments of domination or passivity in each centre's creation of musical works, to identify how contemporary musical theatre often results from transatlantic interactions or transnational collaborations. We also refer to other centres so that while the book does not attempt to tell a global story, it acknowledges and extends its focus beyond this binary axis, especially in the later chapters. The aim of the book is thus to rethink the telling of musical theatre history, primarily as a transatlantic form. Rather than continuing to privilege the conventional positions of power, however, we hope to unsettle the conventional narratives that are traditionally told by adding further stories. We also hope to gesture towards new stories that are yet to be told of the impact of international interactions on the global form, as well as within local sites. We are optimistic that this project will motivate our students and other researchers to explore the many other interactions that have had, and continue to have, a transformative effect on the diversity of musical theatre.

The book, in turn, looks to question the 'historiography' of musical theatre or, simply, how the history of the form is told. Often musical theatre history is framed in ways that are long-standing and widely accepted, which tend to privilege certain people or stories, and forget others; the work and contribution of white, middle-class, English-speaking and heterosexual men tend to feature more prominently than that developed by creatives of other identities. Richard Rodgers and Oscar Hammerstein II's *Oklahoma!* (1943), for example, is widely cited as one of the first 'integrated' or 'book' musicals that combined song, dance, dialogue and design to tell a cohesive story. The example appears in nearly every account of musical theatre history, certainly those focused on Broadway musicals, and is a widely accepted landmark among scholars (we include it in Chapter 1). However, what if we consider the history of musical theatre not from the perspective of form or integration, but in relation to the representation of gender or the global distribution of stage productions? What is *Oklahoma!*'s significance then?

R. G. Collingwood notes that the 'reenactment of the past in the present is the past itself so far as that is knowable to the historian' (quoted in Schneider, 2014). They suggest that the historian, which could be anyone telling a particular history, plays a vital role in constructing what is told and what is remembered. *Oklahoma!* is only significant, therefore, if historians keep recycling the same stories and assuming its place within a predefined narrative. This is echoed by the ensemble of *Hamilton*, for instance, who question 'who lives, who dies, who tells your story?'. In the musical's closing number, the various characters directly address the audience and consider who or what has been left out of the 'narrative'. Eliza, the titular character's wife, describes working tirelessly to protect Hamilton's legacy and closes the musical by noticing the theatre audience; she gasps in delight that, centuries later, her husband's story is still being told (note that her own story is not expanded upon – but we digress). In terms of *Oklahoma!*, Rodgers and Hammerstein are no longer alive to reinforce the importance of their work and thereby rely on others to tell their 'story'.

It is important to consider at this point that determining the context in which events took place, and the context in which they are described, or history is told, is also fundamental to understanding the event itself. Indeed, the extensive and continuing performance history of *Oklahoma!*, for instance, suggests that the work resonates beyond its original performance context. As Tony Bennett notes, 'neither text nor context is conceivable as entities separate from one another'; they are intrinsically linked (quoted in Jackson 2010, p. 245). Tracy C. Davis, however, reflects that 'a problem with "context" is that it is provided for the sake of "completeness," [... and] may be another's idea of irrelevance' (2004, p. 204). For example, a scholar like Tim Carter (2007) might consider the fact that *Oklahoma!* opened amid the Second World War central to understanding it as a key development in the integration of musical theatre form, where the broken nature of many American families, with sons and fathers off at war, is counteracted in the show's story of unity and the conscious integration of song, dance and dialogue. Another scholar, say Susan C. Cook (2009), might be drawn to the representation of masculinity in the show (drawing parallels between soldiers and the onstage cowboys), while Raymond Knapp (2005) might consider it helpful in determining how the musical reflects American national identity in the mid-1940s. This combination of history and context, like all well-constructed historical accounts, is central to the forthcoming pages. We consider musical theatre as a cultural artefact, produced in one environment and understood in many others. Musicals reflect and respond to the world around them, whether they are developed in one location (such as Broadway) or through interactions between and beyond multiple locations.

Deciphering multiple histories

For the reasons discussed above, this book does not present a single linear history. Instead, we introduce multiple histories that can be read in isolation, one after the other, or in any order the reader chooses. There are obvious connections and crossovers, but each chapter starts a new history; the clock resets and a 'history' unfolds. This does not mean, however, that every story is the same length or starts in the same place, before diverting into new territory that is unique to that discussion. The opening chapter, 'From Operetta to Poperetta', explores the development of musical theatre form in relation to other theatrical forms that are now several centuries old. The final chapter, however, 'From Revival to Revisal', contains a much shorter history. Although reference is made to earlier trends in reviving and reperforming works throughout the book, the first landmark in this final history is as recent as the 1970s. Not all histories are the same, especially in terms of time, place, political and social context, length or detail, yet all are significant and valid.

A way we might envisage these interlocking histories is like the various 'lines' or routes on a London Underground or New York Subway map.

Passengers can ride the Central line from East to West London, or from West to East, and therefore cover a broad stretch of ground and potential places to stop. Likewise, passengers can join the Waterloo and City line, between Bank and Waterloo station, for a much shorter and targeted journey across the capital. These two journeys are joined, however, by a common station: Bank. They may be different routes with different names, even represented by different colours on a map, yet they share a common destination or stop. This is the same in musical theatre history and the way such history is presented in this book. Key musicals, creatives, producers and more do not belong to isolated, singular histories but appear as connecting points across a myriad of related histories, 'lines' and chapters. This point was raised above in relation to *Oklahoma!*, which is included as a case study in Chapter 1, where it is addressed as significant in the development of musical theatre form, but it is also referenced in other chapters (on other 'lines') as a major work. The eight chapters or histories contained in this book therefore resemble different 'lines' on an Underground or Subway map. Whether a physical train journey or a chapter in this book, each line takes passengers into the heart of London and New York to discover the excitement of musical theatre. Each 'line' follows a different route, with different stops along the way, yet each takes passengers (or readers) on one of many possible journeys across the city – or, in our case, musical theatre history. Each chapter can be read in isolation but is also written to identify the multiple other avenues and routes through our 'city'. There is no singular or overarching route through the history of musical theatre, especially since the form is created transnationally, and this multiplicity is reflected in the forthcoming chapters.

It is worth noting that however multilayered and overlapping the following histories may be, there are other 'lines' not covered in this book, meaning that not every significant musical, production or creator is addressed, and some themes are represented across several lines. The representation of racial identity, for example, appears in several locations, rather than in a single chapter, and appears mostly in relation to non-white musical styles (Chapter 2), national identity (Chapter 6) and revivals of musicals – some of which are now considered problematic (Chapter 8). This is also the case with sexuality, which, as in many other histories of the form, is addressed in relation to gender (Chapter 5) and revisionist revivals (Chapter 8). Religious identity is similarly not covered in an isolated form, though the Jewish heritage of musical theatre is acknowledged, as are musicals that depict Christian themes or stories (such as *The Sound of Music* [1959] and *Jesus*

Christ Superstar [1971]). Further lines or stations are therefore implied, but yet to be fully drawn. In particular, the global context and wider interactions that have also contributed to this vibrant form are only a small part of this book. That said, the structure of this book also allows for a combination of both traditional and more unique histories. Some of the forthcoming narratives of form, gender or national identity are well-trodden ground, yet stories of censorship or Black musical styles are not. We take moments that appear as footnotes or isolated events in other publications and reposition them as histories in and of themselves, thus challenging the idea that musical theatre is the product of a single line of development and that its works can only be seen from one perspective.

How to read this book

This book contains eight different chapters or 'histories'. Chapter 1 opens the book with perhaps the most widely told and traditional narrative: that of the typically white men who altered how musical theatre works are structured and their stories told. This history addresses how musical theatre developed out of interactions between various highbrow and lowbrow art forms, including opera and melodrama, to create the integrated or quasi-operatic works of the contemporary period. Chapter 2 inverts this by exploring the influence of popular and racially marked musical styles like ragtime, jazz and, later, hip-hop. The chapter focuses on the contributions of African American creatives and is a history that is typically lost or hidden beneath the more dominant history told in the preceding chapter. Chapter 3 extends this interest in the interactions between high and lowbrow culture by considering musical theatre as a central facet of popular culture. This chapter traces an intermedial history in which musicals adapt and reference other texts and media, while also being adapted for film, popular music, television and social media.

Chapters 4 and 5 then consider two contextual factors that limit and determine which (and how) stories are told in musical theatre. Chapter 4 outlines the history of theatrical censorship, drawing attention to how productions have been altered by specific laws or, more recently, to remain inoffensive and acceptable within social norms. Chapter 5 then addresses the development in representations of gender in relation to the contexts in which they were written and performed. The chapter traces how representations that reflect a distinct masculine/feminine binary have more recently incorporated greater gender diversity and fluidity. Chapter 6 continues the theme of identity as it considers the representation of nationhood on either side of the Atlantic. It addresses how each nation has traditionally presented itself and its opposite number in musicals (Britain and America, London and New York), before considering more recent depictions of ethnic hybridity and interculturalism.

Most of the book is focused on the original contexts in which musicals are created and performed, whereas the final section considers how such texts play in new settings and contexts, exploring the movement and fluidity of musical theatre productions beyond the transatlantic partners. Chapter 7 considers how productions have, since the nineteenth century, travelled beyond their originating 'home' in licensed or franchised productions. This chapter explores the evolutionary story of globalization, examining how musicals interact with a world that is increasingly interconnected and even homogenized. The final chapter looks at a history of musicals repeating beyond a show's original production. It addresses why certain musicals have been revived at certain times, but also how they have been altered and revised to suit a new context. The book overall, then, largely journeys between two nations, exploring how productions and individuals in both Britain and America have altered the form, while also considering musical theatre as a form in a constant state of flux that responds to contextual, political and cultural challenges within and beyond this crucial axis.

Each chapter also contains recommended tasks and discussion topics. These might be activities that you complete in a classroom environment, with a tutor's input, or might be activities for you to consider as homework tasks that will help cement your understanding of a topic. Further reading suggestions are also included at the end of each chapter to guide any future interest you might have in a topic or a particular 'history'. These are divided into 'conceptual' suggestions, meaning scholarship that engages with the chapter's broader themes, and 'case study' suggestions that address specific musicals and/or productions. An example of this can be found below, where we suggest further reading regarding the issues and contexts raised in this introduction.

You have your ticket, your luggage is packed, you are now ready to go forth and discover the history of musical theatre – one of the world's most popular art forms – as a web of overlapping histories. The journey is complex, the interactions are diverse, yet the musical continues to grow and develop in light of numerous exchanges between Britain and America, and increasingly beyond. Bon voyage!

Further reading – conceptual

Davis, T. C. and Marx, P. W. (eds) (2021) *The Routledge Companion to Theatre and Performance Historiography*. London and New York: Routledge.

Schneider, R. (2014) *Theatre and History*. Basingstoke: Palgrave Macmillan.

Whitfield, S. (ed.) (2019) *Reframing the Musical: Race, Culture and Identity*. London: Red Globe Press.

Further reading – case study

Bennett, S. (2020) '*The Lion King:* An International History'. In J. Sternfeld and E. L. Wollman (eds) *The Routledge Companion to the Contemporary Musical*. London and New York: Routledge, 445–53.

Galella, D. (2018a) 'Being in "The Room Where It Happens": *Hamilton*, Obama, and Nationalist Neoliberal Multicultural Inclusion'. *Theatre Survey* 59/3: 363–85.

Harbert, E. (2018) '*Hamilton* and History Musicals'. *American Music* 36/4: 412–28.

1

'Putting it together': From operetta to poperetta

In Stephen Sondheim and James Lapine's *Sunday in the Park with George* (1984), the song 'Putting It Together' describes how one might make a work of art. The protagonist, George, sings 'bit by bit' and 'piece by piece' as he is surrounded by art curators and other viewers of his latest work. History, too, is made up of fragments, elements that come together and are later perceived as a coherent narrative. Some of the fragments of history are described in subsequent chapters to add nuance and context to the story we will tell in this chapter. When considering where to start telling such a story, however, George (via Sondheim) also has some advice: 'First of all you need a good foundation / Otherwise it's risky from the start.' Consequently we must ask, where do the foundations lie when studying the evolution of Western musical theatre? How do we decide where to begin? Is it 1943 and the arrival of the supposed integrated musical with Rodgers and Hammerstein's first collaboration, *Oklahoma!*? Perhaps we can slip further back to Hammerstein and Jerome Kern's 1927 landmark musical, *Show Boat*. Could it be the American musical comedies of the early 1900s, or Gilbert and Sullivan's operettas in Victorian London, or even perhaps *The Black Crook* (1866) in New York?

This chapter creates the foundation for the subsequent chapters by outlining the canonical history of musical theatre. It traces a journey that seems always to aim towards a new and better combination of the disciplines, such as song and dance (as defined differently in different eras by different creatives), which will ultimately produce a more credible or coherent performance of the drama. This trajectory is known as 'integration'. Rather problematically, all the key figures in this story tend to be white, Western, middle-class men. However, the tale recounts a journey from one possible starting point – nineteenth century European operetta – to the through-composed poperettas (also known as megamusicals) of the late twentieth century to document the evolution of the concept of 'integration'. There are detours to consider the more fragmented forms developed by Sondheim and Lapine, among others, yet this story documents the evolution of the formal structures of the work and the desire for ever greater 'realism' and 'integration' in the process of 'Putting It Together'.

European origins

In order to set the scene, we will take a short detour back to the Florentine Camerata in the late 1500s. Based in Renaissance Florence, Italy, there were two main groups (or salons) of writers, poets and musicians experimenting and discussing ancient Greek music and drama as a reaction to the excessive polyphonic writing of madrigals (a secular composition for several voices). One group's work resulted in a collection of songs by Giulio Caccini in 1602. In these songs, polyphony (two or more melodic lines played simultaneously) was abandoned in favour of a single vocal melody, with simple word setting, accompanied by bass line and harmonies improvised by the instrumentalist. Word setting for clarity and intelligibility was of primary importance. However, in 1589 the two groups had combined to mount a comedy called *La Pellegrina* by Girolamo Bargagli for the wedding of Grand Duke Ferdinand de Medici to Christine of Lorraine. There was music, choreography and a spectacular production of six *intermedii*, which reflected on Renaissance thinking about music – but this was still not opera. It was a third group, under the patronage of Jacopo Corsi, which included Jacopo Peri and poet Ottavio Rinuccini, who produced *Dafne* in 1597 that was sung throughout and may be deemed the first opera. All these works, though, were steps towards setting words to music, and using action to express meaning or tell a story.

The next fully sung drama, for the wedding of Maria de Medici to Henry IV of France, was Peri's and Rinuccini's *Eurydice* in 1600, though Caccini tried to claim greater success with his and Gabriello Chiabrera's *Il Rapimento de Cefalo*. This battle continued as Caccini then set the same Rinuccini text as Peri, but history has favoured Peri's *Eurydice*.

It is likely that both composer Monteverdi and librettist Alessandro Striggio knew the works of the Florentine Camerata. Their collaboration resulted in a secular music drama, *L'Orfeo*, which was first performed in

Mantua, Italy, in 1607. This work added musical structure by way of the still-emergent tonal harmony into the song form. Monteverdi himself referred to *L'Orfeo* as a musical fable, a work that moved towards the direct expression of human emotion and experience (the Dionysian), that incorporated tonal harmony and dramatic structure (the Apollonian), so that the work represented a re-formation of Greek principles of balance, and a reflection of Renaissance ideals.

KEY CONCEPT: Melodrama and other terms

The term *melodrama* literally means music drama. The *melo* of the name is derived from the Greek word *melos* meaning song or melody. The term has the same elements as *melodramma serio* or *opera seria*, a through-sung form that dealt with serious subjects using aria and recitative (sung words, close to the pitch and rhythm of speech, in which one or more characters narrate or engage in dialogue). Melodrama dominated eighteenth-century Europe with notable works by Handel and Gluck. *Opera seria* contrasted with *opera buffa* (Italian comic opera), which featured quotidian settings, regional dialects and a less elaborate form of vocal writing, in which recitative was sometimes replaced by spoken dialogue. Mozart, Rossini and Donizetti provided key pieces to the *opera buffa* repertoire. In France, the *opéra bouffe* was more satirical and risqué developing into operetta and musical comedy, while romantic opera developed from *opera seria* in the works of Verdi and Weber. Richard Wagner brought the romantic movement to a close with the development of the *musikdrama* in Germany in the nineteenth century.

The term *melodrama* also refers to a highly emotional and extremely formulaic kind of nineteenth-century popular drama that was unsung but accompanied by emotionally stirring music that prefigured the music that was later improvised to accompany silent films. These works, which began in Victorian England and travelled to America, 'espoused democratic values, favoured action over character development, and obeyed an absolute code of moral conduct whereby vice would not go unpunished nor virtue unrewarded' (Stempel, 2010, p. 40). Among the best-known British melodramas were *Maria Marten, or Murder in the Red Barn* and *The String of Pearls* (which told the story of Sweeney Todd, as later depicted by Stephen Sondheim and Hugh Wheeler in their 1979 musical).

Over time, composers drawn to the challenge of telling stories through words and music, extended, expanded and developed the Renaissance experiments to establish what we recognise today as opera. By the mid-nineteenth century, opera had acquired various local qualities and forms in Italy, France, England and across Europe, and subgenres emerged. However, for our purposes, the form of operetta or *opéra comique* that emerged from the *opéra bouffe* in France provided the template for an incipient musical theatre form.

American origins

Before progressing further into the more substantial interactions between European and American operettas and musical comedies, we will identify a 'beginning' for American musical theatre.

During the colonial period (1492–1763), the New World (now the Americas) was settled by immigrants from Europe, including Britain, and for them life was hard. Entertainments were a luxury that were neither readily available nor a priority. However, in 1735, a performance of the ballad opera *Flora, or, Hob in the Well* in Charleston, South Carolina, proved so popular, the first theatre in the New World was built to house it, launching a nationwide obsession with the form. Following the War of Independence (1775–83), the United States sought to differentiate its national cultural identity from its European forebears (as somewhat depicted in *Hamilton* [2015]). As a result, more theatres were erected and local companies of actors were formed who performed plays and, more importantly, melodramas (the plays, rather than the proto-operettas), while variety shows provided popular entertainment in saloons.

CASE STUDY: Popular American variety entertainments

Similar to British music hall (discussed further in Chapter 5), American variety shows consisted of combinations of short acts, including comedians, acrobats, clowns and even animal acts with some singers and musical accompaniment from a small orchestra. In the 1880s, variety began to mature into a cleaner, family-friendly genre called vaudeville. Vaudeville survived until much later in the century on television, though the live form was killed by the 1930s due to the Great Depression and the growing popularity of radio and film.

American Burlesque was originally very similar to vaudeville, though additionally featured a female chorus designed to be ornamental, with burlesque shows being noted for their comedy, reliance on physical gags and skits about familiar real-life situations developed with quick-fire talk back in classic exchanges (British burlesque was different in form to this, as discussed below). Burlesque was the training ground for many performers, especially those who went on to star in vaudeville. It was only in the late 1920s, when the Great Depression hit, that the sexualized removing of clothes (stripping) was used to maintain audiences. By the 1930s, audiences were almost entirely male. This kind of performance is documented in *Gypsy* (1959) and, in a more modern format, in the film *Burlesque* (2010).

Minstrelsy, first performed by white performers in blackface make-up, later offered Black performers their only chance to appear on professional stages – which they, extremely problematically, had to do in blackface while performing racist stereotypes. Minstrelsy was an 'explicit "borrowing" of black cultural materials for white dissemination' that presented 'slavery [as] amusing, right, and natural' (Lott, 2013, p. 4). Minstrelsy was most popular prior to the American Civil War (1861–5), when debates about slavery dominated the national discourse, and the form later impacted on the development of popular music (see Chapter 2). It was also the first truly American theatrical form that had a defined structure, though it, too, was comprised of discrete sections with songs, dances, skits and short plays, rather than an overarching narrative.

The late 1800s also saw the arrival in New York of a French form of variety entertainment called *revue*. American revue shows that followed much later include the Schubert Brothers' *The Passing Shows* (1912–24), *George White's Scandals* (1919–39) and the *Ziegfeld Follies* (1907–31). Featuring songs by writers such as Irving Berlin, Richard Rodgers and Lorenz Hart, who later wrote hit Broadway shows, the best of these revues threaded a variety of acts together with a theme or topic and featured the comedy, spectacle and variety, as well as the satire, of all the previous popular forms of entertainment.

These many forms of entertainment developed over the next eighty years until, in the year following the American Civil War (1861–5), a theatrical event occurred in New York that has since become legendary. In 1866, *The Black Crook* (1866) altered perceptions about the degree to which a show might become a long-running commercial hit and, through its transatlantic collaborations, about the potential interactions between song, dance and music.

CASE STUDY: *The Black Crook* (1866)

Music: Thomas Baker, Giuseppe Operti and George Bickwell. Lyrics: Theodore Kennick. Book: Charles M. Barras.

Compiled by William Wheatley and loosely inspired by Carl Maria von Weber's German romantic opera, *Der Freischütz* (1821), the melodrama tells the story of two young lovers, the villagers, Rodolphe and Amina, and the Count Wolfenstein, who also loves Amina. Wolfenstein is in alliance with Hertzog, an evil sorcerer, the Black Crook of the title. Hertzog has made a pact with the devil and is required to provide a soul every year and currently has his sights set on Rodolphe. However, everything is put in balance by the Fairy Queen Stalacta and her subjects as they reunite the lovers and vanquish Wolfenstein and the Black Crook.

The show played at Niblo's Garden in New York for a record-breaking 475 successive performances. In 2016, a revival of *The Black Crook* was presented off-Broadway at the Abrons Arts Center to coincide with the show's 150th anniversary. Director Joshua William Gelb stated that the revival was 'about interrogating the idea of spectacle' and reduced the original cast of 100 to eight performers (Viagas, 2016).

The show resulted from the fateful confluence of two separate entertainments: a melodrama and a 'Féerie' (a French melodramatic fantasy that contained story, spectacle and dance). *The Black Crook*, a melodrama, was booked to play Niblo's Garden by the theatre's manager William Wheatley, supposedly, less because of the quality of the piece itself, but because its spectacle suited what was the best equipped stage in New York. While *Crook* was in preproduction, an imported production that combined the Féerie, *La Biche au Bois*, with spectacular scenery derived from British pantomime, was scheduled to open at the Academy of Music next door. Unfortunately, it burned down, leaving the production without a theatre. Henry Jarrett and Henry Palmer, the producers of the now homeless spectacle, approached Wheatley with the prospect of partnering. As this expanded production of *Crook* approached its September opening, Wheatley seized every opportunity to create hype around the show by sharing details with the press about various aspects of the lavish production and its cost. The critical reception of the play (or book) was negative and has been slated as a 'hotchpotch' of elements in more recent writing (Ganzl, 2018), but the play was not the thing. Rather, *The Black Crook* favoured the theatrical over the dramatic, embracing spectacular scenery and 'skimpy' costumes for the dancers (see Figure 1.1). It was the combination of Wheatley's savvy as a producer plus the introduction of new performers and new songs across the show's run, that enabled *The Black Crook*'s extraordinary commercial success. The show even garnered over a million dollars at the box office over its extensive run. This is even more remarkable considering that, in 1866, a run of twenty performances was considered a success (Viagas, 2016). The triumph of this production may even result from its merging of highbrow with popular forms (note the continuity of the aim for a balance between Dionysian and Apollonian elements developed by the Camerata).

Figure 1.1 The chorus of *The Black Crook*. © Billy Rose Theatre Division, the New York Public Library for the Performing Arts.

Two years after the opening of *The Black Crook*, Lydia Thompson and her British Blondes arrived in New York. Thompson's British-style burlesques (beginning with *Ixion* in 1868) were comic parodies of literary or theatrical works that contained existing songs with altered words, topical references, parody, cross-dressing and comic puns (and so differed from the American burlesque described above). Inspired by Thompson's burlesques, Edward E. Rice and J. Cheever Goodwin wrote music, book and lyrics for a burlesque of Henry Wadsworth Longfellow's poem *Evangeline* in 1874, establishing a local form of burlesque possessing a combination of American and British sensibilities.

Richard Traubner, while acknowledging the show's burlesque characteristics, suggests that *Evangeline* might rather be recognized as the first American operetta. The distinction, he proposes, is indebted to the show's original music, which has more continuity than other contemporary entertainments that featured cobbled-together scores (1983, p. 359). At a time when many American theatres housed European operettas, the American operetta gradually began to emerge. The contributions of three composers are central to establishing an American form: European-educated Reginald De Koven scored *Robin Hood* (1891), *The Fencing Master* (1892) and *Rob Roy* (1894), among others. American-born John Philip Sousa, while being famous to this day for his marches, also wrote for the stage, with *El Capitán* (1896) being his most notable operetta. Irish-born Victor Herbert wrote prolifically, with *Babes in Toyland* (1903), *Mlle. Modeste* (1905) and *Naughty Marietta* (1910) among his most successful outputs. Of these, and other operettas written at the time, *Naughty Marietta*, with a book by Rida Johnson Young and produced by the impresario Oscar Hammerstein I (grandfather of Oscar Hammerstein II, who will return to the story below), is significant in that it is set in an American location – New Orleans – rather than a European one.

From operetta to musical comedy

The operetta emerged in France in the 1850s as a reaction when the opéra comique began to treat increasingly serious subjects. Just as in England, the urban working classes were drawn to the cities for work where they were entertained by cafés-concerts – similar to music hall in Britain. Meanwhile, French composer Jacques Offenbach pioneered the development of operetta over the course of a career in which he produced almost 100 works for the musical stage. These works employed performers from the cafés-concerts, and librettists with a taste for the bizarre and the witty, especially Ludovic Halévy. Licensing restrictions had limited works to one act until this point, but the lifting of that restriction led to Offenbach, with librettists Hector Crémieux and Halévy, writing one of the most successful satirical operas of the period: *Orphee aux Enfers* (1858) – or *Orpheus in the Underworld* and *Orpheus in Hell* in English.

In keeping with the burlesque practice of parodying literary works and theatrical practices, this work created a satire of the myth of Orpheus and Eurydice and of the operatic form itself. Not only are the main couple unhappily married and involved in separate affairs, but the philandering Jupiter (King of the Gods) may have been a veiled comment on the womanizing behaviour of the Emperor, Charles-Louis Napoléon Bonaparte. The work was successful and entertaining, however, and it soon began to tour around Europe to Germany, Austria, France and London. *Orphee aux Enfers* arrived in New York in a German translation in 1881. Meanwhile, in Britain, the success of the comic operas of Gilbert and Sullivan (more below) encouraged the translation of French and Viennese operettas into English. Orpheus arrived back in London in 1882 as *Orpheus in the Haymarket*, encouraging many other European writers to follow, including the Austrian Johann Strauss whose *Die Fledermaus* (with Carl Haffner and Richard Genée, 1874) followed the international circuit.

Orphée aux Enfers, and Offenbach's follow-up, *La Belle Hélène* (Paris, 1864), with a libretto by Henri Meilhac and Halévy, both proved immensely popular in Britain towards the end of the century. So much so that the first collaboration between William Schwenk (W. S.) Gilbert and Arthur Sullivan imitated their Grecian mythological flavour. Invited to work together by the impresario John Hollingshead, manager of the West End's Gaiety Theatre, the duo authored *Thespis, or The Gods Grown Old* (1871). The plot concerns a troupe of actors, one of whom is the eponymous 'first' actor Thespis, who venture to the top of Mount Olympus for a picnic and end up relieving the weary Greek gods of their duties. While the libretto still exists, the score is lost. Were it not for the intervention of Richard D'Oyly Carte, who approached Gilbert about writing a one-act operetta as a companion piece to Offenbach's *La Perichole* (1868) in 1875, nothing more may have been heard of the new writing team. As it was, Gilbert and Sullivan's *Trial by Jury* (1875) was a great success and established the pair who went on to produce fourteen comic operas together.

The operettas of Gilbert and Sullivan are characterized by complicated farcical plots that satirize British class structure, politics and manners. They place the central romantic figures in different classes but give them similar upper-class sensibilities. A convenient plot twist reveals their births to be similar though their upbringing may have diverged. In this way class structures that rely on birth are revealed to be ludicrous. More importantly for this chapter, Gilbert, in particular, despite his 'topsy-turvy' farcical plots, was keen to promote a new kind of realism in acting and coherent characters in these musicals.

KEY CONCEPT: The Savoy Operas

The English operettas written by W. S. Gilbert and Arthur Sullivan are often collectively referred to as the Savoy Operas, though not all were written for the Savoy Theatre in London. Other writers were also commissioned by D'Oyly Carte to create work for his company, works that are now largely forgotten – so the term 'Savoy Operas' has become almost synonymous with Gilbert and Sullivan's joint output. After *Trial by Jury* in 1875, the writing team went into partnership with Richard D'Oyly Carte for *The Sorceror* (1877). 'The Triumvirate', as the three are sometimes labelled, continued working together on and off until 1896. Many of the same performers worked for the company from one work to the next, so the operettas reiterate similar character and vocal types in a formulaic combination. Meanwhile, separate companies were established that toured the English-speaking world.

In 1881, to house his newly formed D'Oyly Carte Opera Company, the producer built the Savoy Theatre, which was reputed to be the first theatre to use electric lighting. The Savoy Theatre remained under the management of the D'Oyly Carte family for over a century and was refurbished in 1929, before being rebuilt in 1993 following a fire. The current Savoy Theatre (attached to the Savoy Hotel) continues to house musicals in the heart of London's West End.

Gilbert and Sullivan's fourth collaboration, *HMS Pinafore* (1878), became their first international hit after it sailed into Boston six months after its London premiere. The comic opera proved so popular with American audiences that, by the following March, there were eight productions playing in New York and another six companies performing the show in Philadelphia. *Pinafore* certainly influenced the development of American musical comedy, not just in its mix of realistic characters and farce, but in its song and character types. European operettas such as these demonstrated comic plots with coherent characters accompanied by complex vocal music and, especially for the romantic leads, soprano and tenor ranges. Comedy characters had separate song types, such as patter and comedy songs, with a much smaller vocal range at speech pitch, whose delivery derived from popular traditions (such as the music hall) in Britain. These works were precursors to musical comedy in Britain.

Operetta in New York

Meanwhile, as transatlantic travel by liners became increasingly popular and straightforward, operetta, or light opera, continued to establish itself as a viable American commercial art form on Broadway. A significant influence on the American light opera was the international success of Franz Lehár's *Die Lustige Witwe* (*The Merry Widow*), which ushered in the 'Silver Age' of Viennese operetta. Following its premiere in Vienna in 1905, the work played in London in 1907, produced by George Edwardes and translated/adapted by Adrian Ross, and premiered in New York the same year. Immigration to America from Europe also contributed to the interactions between European nostalgia and American popular traditions, with Rudolf Friml (born in Prague) and Sigmund Romberg (born in Hungary) providing successful American works. *Rose-Marie* (1924), for example, a collaboration between composer Rudolf Friml and librettists Otto Harbach and Oscar Hammerstein II, tells the story of a French-Canadian singer who loves the miner Jim Kenyon, a man suspected of murdering a native American. The producers promoted *Rose-Marie*'s cohesion between drama and music, stating in the original programme: '[t]he numbers of this play are such an integral part of the action that we do not think we should list them as separate episodes' (quoted in Traubner 1983, p. 379). Note the use of the words 'play' and 'integral' here, eighteen years prior to *Oklahoma!* in 1943.

While Viennese operetta seemed to provide a balance between high art and popular culture in Britain, in America it served to simultaneously mock high-art pretensions and elevate the popular or mainstream traditions of early musicals (Knapp, 2006, p. 28). At the same time such works could be doubly read as serious and camp, musical drama and heavily coded performance (Ibid, p. 42). Many American operettas were set in an historical and irrecoverable nostalgic past or 'Other' place, removed from a real political context to focus on the personal individual stories especially of its women who control what is ostensibly a man's world (Ibid, p. 62). So, while operetta in Britain continued successfully for some decades, especially in the works of Ivor Novello and Noel Coward, by the Second World War it had become a nostalgic and increasingly dated form. Meanwhile a transformation occurred as the dramatic cohesion of operetta developed its comedy in a further negotiation between high and popular culture.

Musical comedy

The turn of the twentieth century, or what is known as the fin de siècle, saw the emergence of a new, modern popular entertainment: the musical comedy, though the form was slightly different in America and Britain. The musical comedy in Britain developed from British burlesque, music hall and operetta, when producer George Edwardes, needing a show to replace a cancelled burlesque, decided to experiment with form. The initial experiment yielded a structurally loose, not quite burlesque, not quite operetta, musical variety titled *In Town* (1892). A surprise hit in its premiere season, Edwardes set about refining and repeating the formula. To do this, he enlisted the talents of Owen Hall, Harry Greenbank and Sidney Jones, who delivered the book, lyrics and music, respectively, for a new show called *A Gaiety Girl* (1894). While *A Gaiety Girl* markedly improves on the structure of the book Adrian Ross and James T. Tanner provided for their prototype musical comedy *In Town*, it maintains and promotes its predecessor's thoroughly modern sensibility (Macpherson, 2018, pp. 16–17).

The modern – the anxieties of the new century, industrialization and the tensions between progress and tradition – sits at the centre of the new musical comedy. This sense of the modern, reflected through the urban settings (e.g. department stores), the representation of female occupations (e.g. shop girls), with the characters decked out in the latest fashions, distanced the new genre from the period aesthetics of operetta. Importantly, it theatricalized tensions between the urban (modernization) and rural (tradition). *The Arcadians* (1910), for example, features an airship landing in an arcadia untouched by the modern world and the consequences of the interaction of the two worlds.

The show also addresses this tension dramaturgically utilizing musical means. The score for *The Arcadians* is the result of a cumulative effort of two quite different writers: Howard Talbot, a classically trained composer, evokes the Arcadian world via pastoral, folk-like melodies and harmonies, often in triple time; whereas, popular songwriter Lionel Monckton depicts the modern world of the city through contemporary rhythms and harmonies in simple time (Macpherson, 2018, p. 36).

A considerable number of these modern musical comedies followed *A Gaiety Girl* across the Atlantic to America while, increasingly, there developed an equivalent traffic in the other direction. The young American composer Jerome Kern was brought to London to contribute songs to numerous Edwardesian musicals before contributing material to New York shows for Charles Frohman. Considering the degree of the transfer between Broadway and London, led by George Edwardes in London and the anglophile American producer, Charles Frohman (who preferred to import the 'genuine article from England' [Stempel, 2010, p. 136]), it is hard to establish a single historical origin or national format, and yet there are differences.

In America a tradition of rapid-fire crosstalk was developing from vaudeville comic sketches with inserted songs and dances that began to develop into longer pieces. Edward (Ned) Harrigan and Tony Hart developed a series of characters based on racial stereotypes from working-class neighbourhoods. Although not particularly innovative there was a sense of humanity in the representation, particularly of the Irish-American characters, and the shows were popular across classes. Joe Weber and Lew Fields developed two-act shows that featured sketches and burlesque parodies that focused on urban life and particularly the immigrant experience from their perspective as Polish-Jewish immigrants. The work that is most important for our story of mobility, though, is *The Belle of New York* (Morton and Kerker, 1898) which 'had been brought integrally from New York with a full American cast and Chorus – a novelty for the West End' (Ganzl, 2018, p. 662). Having not initially been a huge hit on Broadway it was bought by Australian producer George Musgrove for the Shaftesbury Theatre in London, where it was much more successful. Although comprised of which Kurt Ganzl describes as 'pretty and occasionally … very catchy' music, the performers, and particularly Edna May as Violet and the Casino Theatre chorus line who were 'bursting with obvious health', ensured the work ran for 697 performances before touring the provinces and, indeed, the world for decades to come (ibid.) with West End seasons both before and after the First

World War and even into the early 1940s. It made such an impact that, in London, it was followed by *The Belle of Mayfair* (Stuart, Brookfield and Hamilton, 1906) and *The Belle of Brittany* (Talbot and Greenbank, 1908). Meanwhile, the work some people regard as the first American musical comedy, Irish-American George M. Cohan's *Little Johnny Jones* (1904), gradually became a hit despite reviews commenting on its 'vulgarity', 'gimmicky patriotism' and 'mawkish' sentimentality (quoted in Wollman, 2017, p. 41).

As these popular entertainments transferred they brought with them their different approaches to comedy and music that reflected changing cultural contexts. There were many similarities since each evolved in contact with the other, but also differences that underpinned the next stages of this story.

Into the twentieth century

With the outbreak of the Great War (later known as the First World War) in 1914, the Edwardes and Frohman style of musical comedy waned in popularity in Britain. The revue, a fragmented and thematically threaded entertainment, proved a more relevant alternative to audiences at a time when social structures and the continuity of life were disrupted by conflict in Europe (Linton, 2016, p. 144). Meanwhile, across the Atlantic at a remove from the immediacy of the war, the foundations George M. Cohan laid for an American musical comedy were built upon by subsequent composers, lyricists and book writers. The next significant development towards an integrated form is reflected in a suite of six musicals, known collectively as the Princess Musicals.

Created between 1915 and 1918, the Princess Musicals take their name from the intimate Princess Theatre for which the shows were written. Elisabeth Marbury, a theatrical agent, was reportedly the instigator who established the Princess as a venue with producer Ray Comstock. However, the figures primarily associated with the Princess musicals have a transatlantic pedigree. The first show adapted for the Princess Theatre by composer Jerome Kern, an American who learned his craft working on the Edwardes/Frohman musical comedies partly in London, and Guy Bolton, an English-born American book writer, was *Nobody Home* (1915). The show was quite a drastic adaptation of Paul Rubens's *Mr Popple (of Ippleton)* (1905) that had opened at the Shaftesbury in London and then toured the British provinces before arriving in New York with its new name. Crucially, the idea of creating a musical farce was Rubens's development of a French vaudeville style (Ganzl, 1986, p. 904), though by the time it arrived in New York all its songs had been replaced, its spectacle reduced, and its book adapted for the 299-seat Princess Theatre and its meagre $7,500 production budget. The show was successful enough that Bolton and Kern were asked to continue in a similar style with *Very Good Eddie* (1915).

English lyricist P. G. Wodehouse joined the team, and together, they crafted *Have a Heart* (1917), *Oh, Boy!* (1917), *Leave It to Jane* (1917), *Oh Lady! Lady!* (1918) and *Oh, My Dear!* (1918). Although not all the shows played at the Princess Theatre, they retained an ethos informed by the intimacy of the space, which limited the scope of scenic opportunities and the size of the chorus and orchestra, and dictated that they focus on story, character, song and wit. To ensure musical coherence there were numerous reprises of songs, and dialogue was designed to transition smoothly into, and back out of, song. The shows retained the urban associations of musical comedy, while telling farcical stories about young couples in love set in contained locations, such as cruise liners or college campuses. While the era of the Princess Musicals only lasted for three years, their impact on what a musical could be resonated well into the 1940s.

It seems logical then that the first show to bridge the gap between musical comedy and operetta, the landmark *Show Boat* (1927), resulted from the collaboration between Jerome Kern and Oscar Hammerstein II. Kern was following his work on British musical comedies and the Princess shows, whereas Hammerstein's grandfather had imported many European operettas including *Naughty Marietta* and he had, himself, come of age as a collaborator on *Rose-Marie*.

CASE STUDY: *Show Boat* (1927)

Music: Jerome Kern. Lyrics and book: Oscar Hammerstein II

Beginning in 1887, the musical tells the story of a family of performers whose showboat (a paddle steamer with on-board entertainment), the Cotton Blossom, travels up and down the Mississippi River, stopping to give performances at towns on the riverbanks. Magnolia, the daughter of the boat's owners, Cap'n Andy Hawks and his wife Parthy, meets riverboat gambler Gaylord Ravenal, falls in love and marries him. Meanwhile, the leading man and woman of the showboat, Steve and Julie, are also married. Having been told that Julie is of mixed race, the police come to arrest her for being married to a white man – the crime of miscegenation. Steve drinks a drop of her blood so that they are both considered Black, but this means they both must leave the boat; the pair cannot perform for white audiences in the segregated Southern states. By 1903, both marriages have failed. Magnolia is left destitute in Chicago by Ravenal, with a young child to care for, while Steve has left Julie, who is now an alcoholic club singer. Magnolia is told of an audition by Frank and Ellie, the song and dance performers from the showboat who are now, fortuitously, working in a club in Chicago. Magnolia arrives to audition and Julie, the club's singer, leaves unseen, allowing Magnolia to get the job. That is the start of her rise to stardom. Twenty years later, Magnolia retires to the showboat, where her father invites Ravenal back to see her. They are reunited as 'Ol' Man River', one of the show's standout songs, is reprised.

The show is adapted from Edna Ferber's novel and has been revived numerous times in New York and London, and there are three musical film adaptations.

Show Boat's status is acknowledged by Joseph P. Swain, who designates it as the first maturation of the Broadway musical (1990, p. 15). It has a strong book that deals with serious subjects, including race relations, interracial marriage, alcoholism and failed marriages, combined with elements of traditional musical comedy (especially in the show-within-a-show sequences and the happy ending). The musical language adopts techniques from operatic composition, such as leitmotifs, where a musical motif identifies a specific character, place or moment. Kern also uses inversion: he turns the melodic statement associated with the fictional showboat Cotton Blossom upside down to create the melodic statement for 'Ol' Man River' (Block, 1997, p. 28–9). This technique creates a melodic mirror of the river flowing under the boat. 'Can't Help Lovin' Dat Man of Mine' alludes to Julie's African American heritage through her knowledge of this 'folk' song. When she sings it to Magnolia, Queenie (the African American cook) recognizes it and questions how Julie might know the song. This is prefigured during the opening sequence by the song's melody underscoring an earlier exchange between Pete and Queenie about Julie, further weighting the tune and connecting it to Julie and her racial identity. All these features demonstrate the increasing maturity of the musical language in these early works.

> # KEY CONCEPT: Diegetic and non-diegetic song
>
> A diegetic song takes place in the world of the play, an example being the performances that take place on board the titular *Show Boat*. Equally, a character singing a folk song they learned as a child, as with Magnolia, is a diegetic song for an acknowledged audience.
>
> A non-diegetic song is when characters sing outside of an acknowledged performance context, often expressing their thoughts or feelings, having a conversation or attempting to come to a decision (like Gaylord and Magnolia's love song, 'Make Believe'). The musical theatre canon includes a mixture of these types, though more often relying on non-diegetic songs, and *Show Boat* is an interesting early example of the use of both.

Show Boat is the earliest Broadway musical to become part of the standard repertoire and is still performed today, though the language and stereotypes it contains are now acknowledged to be controversial. Yet the musicals that followed in its wake did not immediately continue its innovations or continue to address contemporary American issues. In October 1929, the stock market crashed resulting in the Great Depression, a global financial crisis that lasted well into the 1930s. Economic conditions impacted on the desire of audiences to see 'serious' musicals and on producers being willing to take a financial risk on innovation, meaning familiarity of form provided comfort (Swain, 1990, p. 48).

Although the Depression impacted on the styles of musicals being produced through the 1930s, it must be noted that the decade was not entirely deprived of innovation and experimentation. George and Ira Gershwin revitalized the satirical operetta through a brash American lens with their political satire, *Of Thee I Sing* (1931), which they followed with the Broadway folk opera, *Porgy and Bess* (1935). Later in the decade, Rodgers, Hart and George Abbott's 1936 musical, *On Your Toes*, opened on Broadway. It featured an extended, twenty-minute diegetic ballet sequence, 'Slaughter on Tenth Avenue', which was staged by George Balanchine, the co-founder of the New York City ballet. Prior to Balanchine, ballet made its way into the traditional Broadway chorus line through the work of Albertina Rasch who blended '*pointe* technique with American jazz' (Genarro, 2011, p. 46). However, until

Balanchine insisted on being acknowledged as 'choreographer', the dances, which were generally entertaining diversions in musicals, were staged by 'dance directors'. The ballet 'Slaughter on Tenth Avenue' lays the dramatic narrative foundations for the dream-ballets of the 1940s that followed. A year later, Marc Blitzstein's *The Cradle Will Rock* (1937), aimed to put a Brechtian social critique of America on the Broadway stage (see Chapter 4), while Rodgers and Hart gave Broadway an unlikeable protagonist in *Pal Joey* in 1940. Each of these, and other small experiments, incrementally led to what would become known as the 'integrated musical' or the 'musical play'.

The musical play and beyond

Through the early part of the 1940s, while Britain bore the brunt of the Second World War in Europe, the Broadway musical became more thoroughly invested in the narrative and characters – the book – establishing the musical play or book musical. This was not an overnight innovation, as this chapter has attempted to articulate, but rather a series of small evolutions that arose out of a transatlantic history of migration and cultural exchange, and eventually manifested in what is now labelled the 'integrated musical'.

KEY CONCEPT: Integration

The term 'integration' is often used in the context of inequality: by promoting equality among different races, genders and cultures inequality is tackled. Similarly, the basic concept of the integrated musical is that each of the aesthetic elements, song, dance, dialogue, design, work together in equality to tell the story and develop character. Nevertheless, if we consider that 'integrated' is related to the word 'integrity' we can gain a deeper understanding of the aim. Firstly, the disparate elements supposedly become integral to the storytelling; if something is removed, the structural integrity of the piece becomes unstable. Secondly, musical theatre writers were artists who wanted to be taken seriously and to create musicals that spoke about the world. The move away from escapist musical comedy to a more integrated musical form marks a move by creators of musicals to attain a degree of artistic integrity. It was the development of these musicals that led to what is referred to as the Golden Age of American musical theatre.

However, labelling is complex and problematic. Richard Traubner asserts that the term 'musical play' is 'a euphemism for romantic operetta', maintaining a distinction between the dual genres of musical comedy and operetta (1983, p. 377). Conversely, shows that might readily be labelled as operettas have been identified by their authors as 'musical plays', 'musical romances' or 'musical adventures' (Stempel, 2010, p. 174). The Broadway musical play, however, while possessing qualities that might reflect the aesthetics of operetta, is akin to American musical comedy in that it directly addresses issues concerning American cultural identity. Moreover, the integrated musical of the 1940s and 1950s tends to have one foot placed in the operetta camp with the other firmly grounded in musical comedy, balancing the serious with the comedic, and drawing together high and popular forms in the narrative development of the work.

Richard Rodgers and Oscar Hammerstein II's *Oklahoma!* (1943) is another work that is often designated as a first – in this case, the first integrated book musical. But why *Oklahoma!* and not *Show Boat*, sixteen years prior? Or any of the other shows referred to? This may partly be the result of the public relations blitz led by Hammerstein in which he promoted the idea that this musical was different. As he wrote in *The New York Times*, the songs had a 'different function'; they were to 'tell our story and delineate characters' becoming 'a continuation of dialogue' – a feature that is true in 'any well-made musical play' (quoted in Block, 1997, p. 98). In his notes on the lyrics, Hammerstein described the 'well-integrated musical play' as a state of mind, 'an attitude of unity'. Rodgers also described how the 'individual parts complement each other'. So partly this designation results from the wording used and the widespread publicity about the work, but there are also innovations in *Oklahoma!* that demonstrate this new level of integration.

CASE STUDY: *Oklahoma!* (1943)

Music: Richard Rodgers. Lyrics and book: Oscar Hammerstein II.

Based on Lynn Riggs's 1930 play, *Green Grown the Lilacs*, the musical contains two love triangles: one dramatic, one comedic. Laurey, a modern heroine who runs a farm with her Aunt Eller in the American mid-West (Oklahoma) in 1906, is torn between the handsome and charismatic cowboy, Curly, and the lonely brooding farm worker, Jud Fry. Interestingly, Jud is represented in different productions as either the misunderstood loner and outcast (a psychological 'Other' who is outside the community, and therefore to be feared) or the archetypal villain. The separation of farmers and cowhands as discrete communities who come together through marriage is used as an allegory for the decision of Oklahoma Territory to become part of the United States in the formation of a national identity. At the start Laurey's indecision about who should take her to the box social (a community gathering) is partly based on having been invited by Jud, whom she is a little afraid of, but mostly just to tease Curly. The second love triangle is between Ado Annie, who, while Will Parker (her cowboy boyfriend) was away in the metropolis of Kansas City making enough money to marry her, has been dating Ali Hakim, a travelling peddler. Hakim not only represents Annie's inability to 'say no' but also signifies a concern about exotic (in this case, Persian) foreigners who are portrayed as sensually exciting and untrustworthy.

Laurey decides to go to the box social with Jud despite her fears. At the box social, Hakim ensures that Will and Annie are thrown together so that he is released from marrying her. She later agrees to stop seeing other men and marry Will. Meanwhile, Jud tries to buy Laurey's basket at the auction so that they can picnic together, but Curly sells his horse, gun and saddle to win – meaning he can no longer earn his living as a cowboy. Jud first threatens Curly and then, when he reveals his feelings to Laurey, she fires him. Curly and Laurey agree to marry and for Curly to work on the farm, only for Jud to reappear at their wedding and try to kill Curly. In the ensuing fight, Jud is killed, Curly is summarily declared to be innocent of murder and the two leave to live happily ever after.

Although this is clearly a simple love story, Rodgers and Hammerstein focused on ensuring that nothing would be extraneous to the plot. Initial drafts reveal how the authors attempted to open *Oklahoma!* with a traditional female chorus, echoing the conventional musical comedy chorus line. However, it became apparent that if an element was not serving the story – the show opening with a female chorus, for example – it needed to be removed. As is well documented, Hammerstein reverted to a simple, small-scale opening. Aunt Eller sits alone on stage churning butter as an *a cappella* male voice (Curly) intones the virtues of the morning, thus directly reflecting the opening of Riggs's source play (Carter, 2007, p. 80). This degree of focusing, in collaboration with director Rouben Mamoulian and choreographer Agnes de Mille, filtered through to all aspects of the musical. Humour and jokes are derived from character rather than being inserted gags (Stempel, 2010, p. 301). Likewise, the quantity of musical numbers is reduced compared to earlier shows, just as dialogue is interwoven through songs and social dance is employed to convey period and situation, rather than just as an entertaining diversion.

De Mille created diegetic dances in 'Kansas City' and 'The Farmer and Cowman', choreography that also establishes the idea of community. She also staged sequences that extend book songs into the non-verbal, as in 'Many a New Day', for instance. However, one of the musical's crowning achievements is the ballet, 'Laurey Makes Up Her Mind', which closes the first act (just under 15 minutes long in the film version). Commonly known as the 'dream ballet', the sequence reveals Laurey's dreams for the future and her fears of home and sexuality prompted by her indecision about which invitation to the Box Social she should accept. Through the dream Laurey confronts two imagined futures with her suitors, the idealistic union with cowman Curly and the darker, sexualized life with farmhand Jud Fry. The dream ballet, that used movements from contemporary as well as musical comedy dance, is significant for combining highbrow and popular dance and music to articulate the psychological impasse Laurey had reached in the narrative.

The musical was followed by a string of important 'integrated' musicals from Rodgers and Hammerstein that would include *Carousel* (1945), *South Pacific* (1949), *The King and I* (1951), *Flower Drum Song* (1958) and *The Sound of Music* (1959). Many other writers took inspiration from these successes and wrote book musicals, including Cole Porter (*Kiss Me, Kate* [1948]), Frank Loesser (*Guys and Dolls* [1950]), Alan Jay Lerner and Frederick Loewe (*My Fair Lady* [1956]). In 1957, composer Leonard Bernstein, librettist Arthur Laurents, lyricist Stephen Sondheim and director/choreographer Jerome Robbins developed *West Side Story* in which balletic choreography, symphonic music and a story of warring gangs were uniquely combined (see Chapters 6 and 8). All these shows toured to Britain where, though some had mixed responses given the different cultural context in the post-war period, they brought a freshness and vitality to the weary, rather nostalgic British stage. Musical comedy continued in parallel to these 'integrated' shows, but the next step in this history saw the disintegration or fragmentation of such linear narratives in the politically turbulent 1960s and 1970s.

Fragmentation and the concept musical

Perhaps the musical had reached the peak of integration at this point, though certainly creative teams such as Lerner and Loewe in America, plus Lionel Bart and David Heneker in Britain continued to write musicals with linear narratives that sought to integrate all the elements in the service of the plot. In 1964, Jerry Bock, Sheldon Harnick and Joseph Stein's *Fiddler on the Roof* opened on Broadway. The musical depicted life in a Russian Jewish *shtetl* at a time of change, where several traditions, as explored in the show's opening number, are being broken. Rather symbolically, this integrated musical could represent the end of the Golden Age era. Just like the lives of the characters in *Fiddler on the Roof*, musical theatre and broader society were rapidly changing. Campaigns against the Vietnam War and the Civil Rights movement were taking place in America, for example, while new British pop groups appeared who reflected youth culture (notably The Rolling Stones and The Beatles). Meanwhile, across the Western world, the feminist and civil rights movements were changing society. Relationships within communities seemed to be transforming, especially in urban settings, creating an exciting time to be young, since suddenly everything seemed possible.

In response to the splintering of society into identity groups, the rise of the counter-cultural movement and increased urbanization, the idea of integration no longer seemed to reflect the zeitgeist. A new breed of musicals emerged that embraced alternative formal structures and were politically aware. Known as concept musicals, these shows focus on a theme or concept, rather than being constructed as a linear narrative. Knapp describes the form as 'less about a particular narrative than about establishing perspective' (2005, p. 241). The term was first used in relation to the production concept of a director or designer, where it applied to specific productions rather than the structure of a work. In musical theatre, it is now generally used to form a loose classification of those musicals that have a meta-narrative interacting with the narrative such that an overall theme emerges or where the loose plot elements can be read as having a kind of narrative but remains open to interpretation.

Stephen Sondheim and George Furth's *Company*, for example, has a kind of plot that links moments in Bobby's life that he reflects on during his thirty-fifth birthday party, but it is more significant for the ways it deals with themes of love, marriage and coupledom. Although *Company* is generally regarded as a concept musical, there are arguments over which was the first concept musical – just as there are arguments over the idea of integration.

Geoffrey Block traces the idea of a concept musical back to loosely plotted revues built around a theme as early as the 1930s (2011, p. 105). He also describes how the concept musical, like the integrated musical, did not arise fully formed but developed out of early experiments (in this case, musicals like *Allegro* [1947] and *Love Life* [1948]). Later (and generally accepted) examples include *Hair* (1967), *A Chorus Line* (1975) and *Assassins* (1991), as well as several works by John Kander and Fred Ebb such as *Cabaret* (1966), *Chicago* (1975), *The Rink* (1985), *Kiss of the Spider Woman* (London, 1992) and *The Scottsboro Boys* (2010). It is notable that these are all American works that experimented with fragmented narratives.

CASE STUDY: *Cabaret* (1966)

Music: John Kander. Lyrics: Fred Ebb. Book: Joe Masteroff.

Adapted from John Van Druten's play *I Am a Camera* (1951), which is based on Christopher Isherwood's semi-autobiographical novel *Goodbye to Berlin* (1939), *Cabaret* is set against the rise of the Nazi party in Berlin. The narrative follows two love stories: Sally, an English singer, meets and moves in with the newly arrived Cliff, an American writer who is lodging with Fraulein Schneider; meanwhile Herr Schultz, a Jewish grocer, woos and becomes engaged to Fraulein Schneider. At their engagement party, Schultz's Jewish song is noticed by the Nazi, Ernst, and others respond by singing a folk song that becomes a kind of Nazi anthem ('Tomorrow Belongs to Me'). Schneider calls off the wedding after she realizes the threat she will face if she marries a Jewish man at this time. After this disappointment, and as a result of his grocery being attacked during Kristallnacht, Schultz leaves.

Sally works as a singer at the Kit Kat Klub, a Berlin cabaret that seems like a separate, licensed space, where there is freedom for subversion and all kinds of sexual, racial and gender difference (as can be seen in Figure 1.2). The Master of Ceremonies (Emcee) of the cabaret acts as a kind of narrator for the show, and the songs in the cabaret are a metatheatrical commentary on the events in the world outside. Meanwhile, Cliff has been earning a living by giving English lessons and carrying parcels in and out of Germany for Ernst, but, when he realizes they fund the Nazi party, he refuses to continue and, now that Sally is pregnant, decides to take her back to America with him. Sally refuses, has an abortion and buries her head in the sand, singing that 'life is a cabaret', while Cliff leaves on the train and starts to write the novel that will become this musical.

Figure 1.2 Joel Grey (top centre) and company in the stage production *Cabaret* (second photo call). Photo: Friedman-Abeles Collection. 1966. © NYPL.

Cabaret (1966), directed by Hal Prince, exemplifies many of the features of the concept musical, and it also has metatheatrical elements. Although there is a narrative, there is also a thematic concept that underpins the work that is variously adapted in productions. Ostensibly, the book deals with two failed love stories, but it also explores those lives within the context of the rise of Nazism in 1930s Berlin. Even this issue can be thematically expanded, and the rise of fascism and the persecution of Jewish and homosexual people can be allegorically associated with other times and places. For example, the McCarthy hearings (late 1940s–late 1950s) that were demonizing communists and homosexuals in America might be a potential allegorical reading of the themes of the work when it was first performed only a decade after these events. Equally, the narrative could be read in the context of the treatment of African Americans in the Civil Rights struggle. Recent productions have focused more closely on the holocaust itself, however. The point is that the narrative is intended to be read allegorically, and the framing of the show within the context of the Kit Kat Klub with songs like 'If You Could See Her Through My Eyes' (commenting on racial difference) and 'Two Ladies' (commenting on sexual difference) alerts audiences to this fact.

KEY CONCEPT: Metatheatre

The term *metatheatre* or *metatheatrical* is used to describe those aspects of a theatrical text that draw attention to it as performance, which remove it from the 'realistic' evocation of life. In contrast with integration, which seeks to create an illusion of realism, metatheatrical devices reveal the theatricality of a performance. Framing devices can be metatheatrical, such as the use of a narrator (the Emcee in *Cabaret*, the chorus in *Sweeney Todd* or the Narrator in *Into the Woods*). Performances of songs within the plot (diegetic songs), or shows within shows, are the most common kinds of metatheatrical device in musical theatre. They are tools through which writers can comment on the staged 'real' action outside the diegetic performance revealing the artifice of theatre to audiences. Kander and Ebb, for example, used the Kit Kat Klub performances in *Cabaret*, vaudeville routines to represent the media scrum in *Chicago* (1975), remembered film performances in *Kiss of the Spider Woman* (1992) and a minstrel show in *The Scottsboro Boys* (2010). These frameworks enable commentary on the 'real' action and on the politics of the world beyond the theatre.

Since this period there have been many (predominantly American) musicals that have explored alternative chronologies or fragmented and episodic narratives, such as *Nine* (1982) and *The Last Five Years* (2001). Stephen Sondheim, in particular, developed a variety of musicals that experimented with notions of time, including *Merrily We Roll Along* with George Furth (1981), *Sunday in the Park with George* with James Lapine (1984) and *Assassins* with John Weidman (1990). The diversity, complexity and innovation in his writing have established him as a leading figure of the musical. In Britain, Leslie Bricusse and Anthony Newley developed two concept musicals: *Stop the World – I Want to Get Off* (1961) and *The Roar of the Greasepaint – The Smell of the Crowd* (1964). The final part of this chapter, however, returns to Britain to continue the story of integration into a different incarnation.

The megamusical or poperetta

Two young British writers, Andrew Lloyd Webber and Tim Rice, were introduced to each other as a potential pop writing partnership in the late 1960s. Commissioned by a local school to write a musical, the pair produced a pop cantata, *Joseph and the Amazing Technicolor Dreamcoat*, that, while it has since become a longer piece, even at the start attracted enough attention to get the pair signed. Although *Joseph* only came to public attention in 1972, their next collaboration, *Jesus Christ Superstar*, which was released as a single in 1969 and a concept album in 1970, went on to enormous success on both sides of the Atlantic. Robert Stigwood recognized the album's potential as a stage musical, and the show opened in New York in 1971 and in London in 1972, soon to be followed by *Evita* (1978). Lloyd Webber and Rice soon went their separate ways. Rice wrote *Chess* with ABBA composers Bjorn Ulvaeus and Benny Anderson (arguably a concept musical) as well as contributing lyrics to other shows including several animated film musicals. Lloyd Webber developed *Cats* (1981) with input from director Trevor Nunn, choreographer Gillian Lynne and producer Cameron Mackintosh (also arguably a concept musical), followed by *Song and Dance* (1982), *Starlight Express* (1984) and *The Phantom of the Opera* (1986) and a number of other shows. Cameron Mackintosh also developed his own globally successful company at this time (see Chapter 7), through which he produced *Les Misérables* (1985) and *Miss Saigon* (1989), both of which were composed by the French writing team of Alain Boublil and Claude-Michel Schönberg.

Although Lloyd Webber has remained at the forefront of musical theatre composition and production in the intervening years, it was this initial group of highly successful musicals that became known as the 'British invasion'. This was not the first 'invasion', as we have seen, with numerous British musical comedies travelling to New York in the 1900s, but it is significant that these shows returned integration and operetta to American shores alongside the more fragmented works.

In respect of the development of the integrated musical, a key feature of *Les Misérables* is that the music is continuous and drives the action; it uses musical themes or leitmotifs to predict the action and reprises to link moments within the narrative, and since it is through-composed consideration is no longer needed to overcoming the jolt between scene and song. Unlike musical comedies, which contained dialogue scenes, songs and dances that interrupt the action, or book musicals that attempted to

CASE STUDY: *Les Misérables* (1985)

Music: Claude-Michel Schönberg. Lyrics: Alain Boublil (with Jean Marc Natel in French and Herbert Kretzmer in English). Book: Claude-Michel Schönberg and Alain Boublil (with Trevor Nunn, John Caird and James Fenton in English).

Adapted from Victor Hugo's 1862 novel, the musical depicts Jean Valjean on parole from prison, where he was held for nineteen years for the theft of bread to feed his family. Valjean tries to escape his parole and struggles to find work but is helped by the Bishop of Digne, from whom he steals. On being discovered and forgiven, he resolves to live a better life but must break his parole in order to achieve this laudable goal. As a factory owner some years later, Valjean meets Fantine, one of his workers who is trying to support herself and her daughter, Cosette. Cosette is lodged with the Innkeeper Thénardier and his wife, and their daughter, Eponine – for which Fantine must pay. Fantine is fired unjustly and finally resorts to prostitution as she can find no other work. She comes to the attention of Valjean's former prison guard, Javert, now a police inspector, and Valjean is noticed when he takes Fantine to hospital, where she dies having elicited Valjean's promise to adopt Cosette. Valjean comes to Javert's attention again when he saves a man trapped under a cart using his enormous strength, which Javert recognizes as unique. These characters struggle during the years of the French revolution as Javert righteously seeks to rearrest Valjean, and Valjean, the supposed criminal, lives a noble life supporting Cosette and her young lover, Marius. Javert finally sees his errors and commits suicide, while Valjean also dies leaving the survivors of the failed revolution to continue the fight for equality. *Les Misérables* played almost constantly in the West End from October 1985 until forced to close by the Covid-19 pandemic in 2020. It has elicited countless international productions and cast recordings in addition to a 2012 film version.

smooth the interruption between scene, dance and song with better books and underscoring, the characters sing throughout. Moreover, *Les Misérables* is a historical epic that spans generations and takes place at a time of political upheaval. It deals with epic themes of good and evil, religion, romance and war. These features of the megamusical are a continuation both of the story of integration and the operatic history of the musical. In many senses, then, *Les Misérables* is a contemporary updating of earlier forms of musical theatre, rooted in operetta, and travelling a similar transatlantic route.

KEY CONCEPT: The Megamusical

There is a group of musicals known as megamusicals, perhaps partly because of their epic stories, romantic sweeping scores and huge set designs. Many also have musical scores characterized by an almost operatic level of motivic continuity and a combination of orchestral and pop instruments and styles (the high art and popular culture combination appears again) (Sternfeld, 2006). They were also 'mega' in their level of spectacle and their global spread. These shows developed in London (or at least in Europe), though American megamusicals emerged later, including *The Lion King* (1997) and *Wicked* (2003). Many of these productions have international writing and/or production teams.

Conclusion

The megamusicals of the 1980s and 1990s are not the end of this story since the most recent American musical that deserves the title of megamusical (at the time of writing) is *Hamilton* by Lin-Manuel Miranda (2015). It tells the epic story of the founding of America before, during and after the American War of Independence through the lives of the founding fathers, especially Alexander Hamilton. It combines highbrow and popular art forms including rap, R'n'B and 1960s Brit-pop to tell a story through musical signification and the interaction of character motifs so that the action is driven by music and dance. It thematically focuses on romance and war, life and death, success and vengeance, as well as exploring the place of outsiders, marginalization and storytelling itself. In Britain, the megamusical lives on in works such as *The Grinning Man* (2016), which, like *Les Misérables*, is based on a Victor Hugo novel of romance and tragedy (though is arguably much more comedic). Meanwhile, in Europe the failed Broadway megamusical of 2006, *Tarzan* (by Phil Collins and David Henry Hwang), was turned into a surprise

European hit following its 2007 adaptation in Scheveningen (Netherlands) and later five-year run in Hamburg.

To return to the start of this chapter, and the foundations of our history of musical theatre, we have discovered that perhaps musical theatre is multiple, diverse and transnational – arising from many sources in several countries, but always exploring ways of telling stories through music and song that suited particular times and places. Many new forms of musical theatre have emerged, including not only those mentioned in this chapter, but others that will be introduced later in this book. More importantly, this story of the increasing integration of musical theatre is only one story, and one that has leapt over inconvenient digressions and inconsistencies to create a linear narrative like the ones in the musicals it describes. These stories demonstrate some of the transatlantic interactions through which it has evolved. Other stories will be told in the following chapters, but this story is the canonic starting point that explains how music and dance are woven into the plot to create a book musical, and how the integration of diverse popular and high art elements are put together to produce a commercial form of entertainment that has established a global industry.

Tasks

Take a recent news story and turn it into the plot outline for a new musical. Which elements of the story might you include? What kind of musical might you turn it into and why? What kinds of music might best be used to represent the key characters? Would you focus on themes or narrative drive and why?

Develop an outline for a burlesque of a popular television programme. What would you aim to burlesque and why? How would your work reflect the contemporary context?

Discussion topics

Select a Golden Age musical or a megamusical. How might its themes and its musical language speak to contemporaneous and current audiences differently?

Analyse the same Golden Age musical or megamusical as above. What techniques and devices did the writers and creative teams use to construct the perception of integration?

Further reading – conceptual

Cottis, D. (2016) 'Towards a British Concept Musical: The Shows of Anthony Newley and Leslie Bricusse'. In: Robert Gordon and Olaf Jubin (eds) *The Oxford Handbook of the British Musical*. Oxford and New York: Oxford University Press, 309–30.

Rebellato, D. (2009a) '"No Theatre Guild Attraction Are We": *Kiss Me, Kate* and the Politics of the Integrated Musical'. *Contemporary Theatre Review* 19/1: 61–73.

Taylor, M. (2009) 'Integration and Distance in Musical Theatre: The Case of *Sweeney Todd*'. *Contemporary Theatre Review* 19/1: 74–86.

Further reading – case study

Block, G. (1997) '*Carousel*: The Invasion of the Integrated Musical'. In: *Enchanted Evenings: The Broadway Musical from* Show Boat *to Sondheim*. Paperback issue [2004]. Oxford and New York: Oxford University Press, 159–78.

Edney, K. (2010) 'Integration through the Wide-Open Back Door: African Americans Respond to *Flower Drum Song* (1958)'. *Studies in Musical Theatre* 4/3: 261–72.

Linton, D. (2016) 'English West End Revue: The First World War and after'. In: Robert Gordon and Olaf Jubin (eds) *The Oxford Handbook of the British Musical*. Oxford and New York: Oxford University Press, 143–70.

2

'We are the rhythms that color your song': From ragtime to rap

When author E. L. Doctorow published *Ragtime* in 1975, which contained a combination of real and fictional characters, his novel found immediate success at a time when ragtime music – a historically Black musical style – was being revived in American popular culture. Interestingly, however, the racial connotations of ragtime music are not introduced in the 1998 stage adaptation of Doctorow's novel until most of the way through Act 1. As the musical's African American protagonist, Coalhouse Walker Jr., plays a wealthy white family's piano, entertaining himself as he waits for his lover, Sarah, the family's elderly grandfather interrupts Coalhouse to question, 'Do you know any coon songs?'. Coalhouse, not outwardly offended, replies, 'Coon songs are made for Minstrel shows. White men sing them in blackface. This is called Ragtime.' In this moment, Coalhouse rejects the racist terminology attached to the musical genre and introduces a musical style that is 'his' or, rather, a musical style that was developed from African American traditions by African Americans that is quite specifically not the same thing at all. This 'New Music', as the ensuing song is titled, alters each of the characters in various ways. Coalhouse is reunited with Sarah and their son, while Father (the head of the white household) returns from his travels to an unorthodox household that has accepted change and racial diversity. The characters sing of 'opening a door' and 'changing the world', as signified by embracing a new musical style. Ragtime music is thus introduced by an 'Other', ready to be consumed, and normalized by a white family (and a typical Broadway audience), just as African American music is considered fresh and vivacious and is appropriated into white culture.

This chapter explores the importance of African American musicians and their musical innovations on Broadway and the spread of those musical styles across the Atlantic to Britain (and elsewhere). It documents a time before African Americans had an equal voice, equal representation or equal power, yet their music influenced and informed musical practices around the world. This story is contained in the title of this chapter, which references a song from George C. Wolfe's jukebox-style musical *Jelly's Last Jam* (1992). The musical documents the life and music of Jelly Roll Morton, one of the key figures in the introduction of jazz to wider audiences and features tap dance to critique the appropriation of certain dance styles in musical theatre history.

The story told in this chapter traces how ragtime arose as a result of diverse European and African American influences. Although the music first arrived in vaudeville, music hall and revues, it very quickly spread into and influenced the music of musical comedy. Following the cakewalk (another racially marked genre) appearing in several other forms, ragtime was the first type of 'Black' music to appear on Broadway in the early twentieth century. Jazz and rhythm 'n' blues (known later as 'RnB') followed in the 1920s, which later influenced rock 'n' roll in the 1950s. This lineage then became rock and soul in the 1960s, followed by disco and funk in the 1970s. More recently, rap and hip-hop have been highly influential as the 'new' pop music of the millennium. In turn, all these musical forms appear in musical theatre, whether to tell the stories of African American music history or to represent characters of colour or just to revivify musical theatre with the fresh rhythms from popular music. This chapter, therefore, documents an important and often occluded history, that of the popular music of musical theatre, and this story documents a greater movement from West to East than in the previous chapter.

Ragtime and early African American music

The musical *Ragtime* is set amid the chaotic flux of immigration in New York City in the early twentieth century as three groups of fictional characters (plus several historic figures) interact. It also depicts the period when the music of ragtime was at its height (between 1896 and 1917), though the novel and musical are located more narrowly between 1906 and 1916. Furthermore, the musical fuses various musical styles and communities, as if weaving together the multiple 'rags' that formed modern America (these years were often referred to as a 'melting pot'). The musical also features an overtly theatrical framework, where characters directly address the audience.

CASE STUDY: *Ragtime: The Musical* (1998)

Music: Stephen Flaherty. Lyrics: Lynn Ahrens. Book: Terrence McNally.

The suburban white family is named only as Mother, Father, Younger Brother and so on, apart from the young narrator, Edgar, the son of the family. Father leaves Mother in charge of the household while he goes on an expedition to the North Pole. In his absence, Mother discovers an African American orphan child buried alive in her garden at the same time the police arrive with the baby's mother, Sarah. Mother decides to care for the destitute pair (note the naming of the protagonists with whom the audience should empathize). The father of the child is the successful ragtime pianist, Coalhouse Walker. He resolves to win Sarah back and even buys a brand-new Model T Ford (from Henry Ford) to go and visit her. At first, she refuses to see him, but he eventually wins her back through his ragtime music. Nevertheless, Coalhouse has enemies led by Fire Chief Willie Conklin, who targets the obviously successful African American and destroys his car. Sarah goes to petition for justice on his behalf at a vice presidential rally but is mistaken for an assassin and killed. In Act 2, Coalhouse, and many other disempowered people, seeks justice for Sarah's death by attacking firemen and firehouses. Finally, Coalhouse barricades himself inside New York's J. P. Morgan library, where Booker T. Washington, an African American presidential advisor he respects and admires, is brought to reason with him. After listening to ineffective advice from Washington, Coalhouse encourages his men to leave so that they can engage in peaceful protest and educate their children to change society. As Coalhouse is ushered out of the library by armed police, with the promise that both he and Conklin will receive a fair trial for their crimes, he is shot and killed. Elsewhere, the Jewish immigrant, Tateh, arrives empty-handed from Latvia on a 'rag ship' and, over the course of the musical, finds success as a street artist, then a movie director/producer, before marrying Mother (after Father dies in the sinking of the *SS Lusitania* in 1911).

The musical opened in Toronto in 1996, before moving to Broadway in 1998, where it was later revived in 2009. It played in London's West End in 2003 and was revived in an open-air production in 2012 and as an actor-musician fringe production in 2016.

The story centres on three groups of people. The first group is a settled white Anglo-Saxon protestant (WASP) family, who represent the communities that emigrated from Europe following the Founding Fathers in the seventeenth and eighteenth centuries. These are successful and wealthy families, who, while originally immigrants themselves, might also have owned slaves and earned their income from slave labour. *Ragtime* is mostly set in New York City, however, where society is perhaps among the most liberal in the country (though Father insists the family move to the calmer Atlantic City, New Jersey, in Act 2). The music of this community derives from a European history that included social dances like the waltz, religious hymns, choral music and the European masters of classical music. It is Edgar, the son of this family, who acts as the musical's primary narrator, as if the audience sees the story unfold through the most innocent, yet privileged, of eyes. Edgar is also the most far-sighted of the family, as supported by a subplot in which he can sense the future. He repeatedly shouts 'warn the duke', a phrase he does not understand, several years before the Austro-Hungarian Archduke, Franz Ferdinand, was assassinated in 1914 (an event that initiated the Great War 1914–18 – later referred to as the First World War).

The second group consists of an African American woman from Harlem, named Sarah, her baby and his father, Coalhouse Walker. They represent the many educated African Americans who moved from the southern states northwards in the hope of a better future during the great migrations of the late nineteenth and early twentieth centuries. This followed the end of the American Civil War and the abolition of slavery in 1865, which was itself amended by the imposition of the segregationist Jim Crow laws (which reinstated different racial divides in American society and culture). Coalhouse's music, derived from southern origins, is considered new and exotic and is the ragtime of the musical's title.

The pair end Act 1 singing the anthemic on the 'Wheels of a Dream' that references the American Dream and Martin Luther King's famous 'I have a dream' speech. In the absence of the dead protagonists, the show ends with this song being sung by the family who have adopted their child and their music. In this way the musical appropriation and the absent African American characters of the musical are paired in a political critique of the silences and absences in musical theatre history and performance. It is not surprising, therefore, that productions of this show have had mixed reviews from largely white audiences whose personal and cultural histories are being challenged.

It is also possible to relate the character of Coalhouse Walker to the history of African American musicians like James Reese Europe, who arrived in New York in 1903 and conducted at Carnegie Hall, a major New York concert hall, in 1912. Europe was a second-generation musically educated African American; his family moved from Mobile, Alabama, to Washington, DC, in 1890, when Europe was aged 10. He created the Clef Club Orchestra that, between 1910 and 1913, organized and professionalized labour standards for musicians of colour, promoted musical styles from classical to popular (all written by composers of colour), made early jazz recordings and boosted the cultural value of ragtime by mixing European and folk instruments in his orchestra. Unlike some of his contemporaries, however, Europe believed in combining the influences of Europe with African American musical genres to transform American musical identity. However, his insistence on the integrity of his orchestra as entirely African American led to a perception of essentialism among white audiences. Like Coalhouse in *Ragtime*, Europe's career exemplifies the difficult balancing act played by successful musicians when society and politics were the province of white men.

These changes were not only happening in America, since many musicians and performers of colour were welcomed to tour Britain (and indeed Europe). As early as 1837 a troupe of American performers of colour entertained in Britain, eventually arriving at Buckingham Palace – led by Frank Johnson (Riis, 1986, p. 51). There were banjo playing troupes, all kinds of musicians and singers as well as touring companies of minstrels (African American and white performers who all performed in blackface) who brought not only their voices but their music. Indeed, the number of all-African American shows, including several book shows, increased in New York between 1898 and 1906, which led to many new performers moving into the profession and receiving an apprenticeship on the road before moving to the shorter acts suitable for vaudeville in America, music hall in Britain and revue in both countries. Although many individual artists or groups had appeared earlier, the first complete African American variety show to reach England was *Oriental America* in 1897–8, directed by John W. Isham. This was followed by the first African American musical to cross the Atlantic, *In Dahomey* (Williams, Walker and Cook, NY 1902, London 1903). This show not only introduced the songs of Will Marion Cook, but it brought many performers to England, some of whom stayed to teach, set up companies or toured smaller acts in music hall or as concert performers. A complete ragtime show transferred to the London Hippodrome in December 1912, a piece entitled *Hullo, Ragtime*, preceded a few days earlier by a report in

Figure 2.1 Hattie McIntosh, George Walker, Aida Overton Walker, Bert Williams and Lottie Williams performing a cakewalk taken from the stage production *In Dahomey*. © Billy Rose Theatre Division, The New York Public Library for the Performing Arts.

The New York Age (a major African American newspaper) that London had gone ragtime crazy (ibid., 54). This attracted more entertainers to Britain and Europe and the music continued to spread.

Importantly, this musical style became linked for British and European audiences with the 'Americanness' of the performers. Instead of the 'strangeness, inferiority, special musicality, or the peculiarly racial stage business' that white Americans might focus on, European audiences discovered a unity in African American and white American style that they found exciting and modern (Riis, 1986, p. 56).

KEY CONCEPT: Racial segregation and the Jim Crow laws

Between 1861 and 1865, the American Civil War was fought because southern slave owners seceded from the union in order to preserve slavery (with enslaved Africans having been shipped across the Atlantic since the sixteenth century). The country divided and went to war, so strongly was this issue felt. Following the Emancipation Proclamations in 1862 and 1863, and the thirteenth amendment to the US Constitution in 1865, there was a dramatic migration north – the Great Migration. The 1866 Civil Rights Act gave citizenship and equal rights to men of colour (only men), guaranteeing equal treatment, but this was rarely upheld in practice. Many former slaves, who had neither education nor job prospects, continued as farm workers under a system of 'sharecropping' while the Southern Homestead Act enabled land reform to African American communities. Meanwhile, some of these newly released former slaves established their own churches (with their own music).

However, in practice there was still separation between people of colour and white communities, especially in the South, that was crystallized in the Compromise of 1877. A Republican, Rutherford B. Hayes became president from where he battled white supremacists in Southern states who were associated with the Democratic Party until a compromise, known as the Jim Crow laws, was reached. Named after an 1828 minstrel song called 'Jump Jim Crow', famously performed in blackface by (white performer) T. D. Rice, Jim Crow quickly became a derogatory term for an African American. The Compromise (or laws) allowed individual states, often former confederate states, to introduce racial segregation in all public facilities, including education, transport and accommodation, during the late 1870s and 1880s. Instead of the Civil Rights that had been anticipated in 1866, people of colour could be treated as 'separate, but equal' in certain states across America – though, of course, there was nothing 'equal' about it. It was not until 1955 that the segregation of public schools was declared unconstitutional, followed by Rosa Parks's refusal to sit in the 'colored section' of a public bus, plus many other acts of civil resistance into the 1960s. The Civil Rights Act of 1964 finally gave all Americans equal rights, in law, if still not in practice, since racism remains a contentious issue in modern America (with examples such as the 2020 George Floyd murder which triggered a dramatic rise in participation in the Black Lives Matter movement).

The third and final group in *Ragtime* are recently arrived European immigrants, fleeing poverty and persecution, as represented by a Jewish man, Tateh (Yiddish for 'father'), and his unnamed daughter. Immigration to the so-called New World (America) had been consistent since the time of the first colonists but rose markedly after the Civil War (1865 onwards), when colonists were first called immigrants. Tateh is introduced with Eastern European and modal-themed music, though he is quickly assimilated (both culturally and musically), which is notable because, crucially, he can pass as white – something which is not possible for Coalhouse Walker. Mother first meets Tateh as an immigrant when her son, Edgar, is fascinated (and confused) by Tateh tethering his daughter to him with a rope. They meet again in Act 2, however, when Tateh has reinvented himself as the successful Baron Ashkenazy and the pair sing 'Our Children', as if from the same class and cultural background.

These three stories of migration and integration are the context and background of the musical *Ragtime*, but they demonstrate the politics of the work, and the difficult conversations that are needed about the importance, and appropriation, of Black music in the development of musical theatre. This is particularly difficult since, as Eubie Blake, one of the creators of the early Black musical *Shuffle Along*, argued, there was no single place of origin of ragtime. Blake had first heard musicians playing ragtime in churches, syncopating the music of Verdi and Chopin (Gilbert, 2015, p. 26). Scott Joplin, who became the most famous composer of piano rags, suggested that syncopated rhythms had gone unnoticed by white people until the 1890s, since segregation had kept 'Black music' separate from white people.

Musically, ragtime piano tunes consist of quick syncopated melodies in the right hand, with a straight, even rhythm stressing the beat in the left hand. By the 1890s to rag a piece of music meant to play it with this type of syncopated rhythm, leading to musicians of all races ragging well-known classical and popular melodies in performances on the vaudeville and minstrel circuits. Increasingly, as more musicians of colour, like Joplin, Cook and Europe, had access to musical education, they were able to transcribe, then publish and record, their music for everyone to purchase and play. As ragtime was embraced in Britain and Europe in musical theatre shows and vaudeville acts, a young generation of Europeans danced to the same beat and composed following the same patterns until the outbreak of the Great War. Ragtime was replaced by jazz, and other musical genres after the war, but was revived in the 1970s, but this story demonstrates how the music of musical theatre has the history of slavery right at its heart.

Early African American musical theatre

African American composer Will Marion Cook was born in 1869, after the emancipation of slaves, and was one of relatively few African Americans of the time who had a classical music education. His parents were college-educated and, recognizing his talent, raised funds to support his musical education. After attending Oberlin Conservatory as a teenager, he was sent to Berlin, Germany, to continue his study of the violin. When he returned to New York, he switched to composition and began attending classes with Antonín Dvořák (though he disliked Dvorak and was soon barred from the class). Dvorak was an internationally renowned Czech composer who emigrated to New York in 1892 and became director of the National Conservatory of the Music of America, where he promoted the importance of incorporating national styles into a new type of American classical music. Rather than writing in the style of the European classical composers, therefore, Cook chose to develop commercial music based on his own culture and began composing ragtime songs and musical theatre. He believed that African Americans should capitalize on what they did best and, having seen stars like Bert Williams and George Walker performing their vaudeville patter and cakewalk, decided to adopt music from African American popular culture to create a show: *Clorindy*.

Clorindy; or the Origin of the Cakewalk (1898) was the first musical on Broadway to be written, produced and performed by African Americans. With music by Cook and lyrics (plus an eventually unused script) by Paul Laurence Dunbar, the musical was performed in the roof garden of the Casino Theatre, New York, late in the evening, where it drew much of its audience from those leaving the main theatre below, who heard the ragtime music of its score. Having discovered that the Roof Garden manager was looking for a show, and was auditioning an act, Cook gathered a cast together and gate-crashed the audition. The show had to be shortened and adapted, but it opened in July 1898 to much acclaim; it marked a new type of theatre on Broadway and it demonstrated the possibilities of the new syncopated music. *Clorindy* lasted just forty-five minutes and featured Ernest Hogan, an African American blackface vaudevillian and songwriter, performing ragtime-inflected music and so-called 'coon' songs to great success. Although this early Black musical might suggest progression in the representation of African American identities, the performers still wore blackface make-up and played the stereotypical characters that had been performed in vaudeville. However, writers Cook and Dunbar, plus the star performer Hogan, had entered into the cultural revolution that was just beginning and opened up further opportunities for themselves and other African American artists.

Importantly, Hogan had sold the publishing rights to one of his first songs, 'La Pas Ma La', which featured heavy syncopation. It remains one of the earliest documentations of ragtime in published sheet music and is one of the first dance-instruction songs. 'La Pas Ma La' earned Hogan the title of 'Father of Ragtime' (Gilbert, 2015, p. 27), though Scott Joplin is now considered the most important and most famous ragtime composer of piano music. Hogan's later song 'All Coons Look Alike to Me' earned him $100,000 from sales both in America and Britain, where it was advertised as a 'ragtime arrangement'. Many similar styled songs were also popularized by white female performers on the Broadway stage, meaning the minstrel stereotypes of African Americans as jovial, yet unintelligent objects of ridicule were quickly reinforced by new performers, many of whom were white. African American men, in particular, were portrayed as lazy and criminal, while broader racist stereotypes portrayed both sexes as immoral and over-sexed. Despite this extremely ugly character and book content (by contemporary standards), then, the ragtime style infiltrated the mainstream cultural industries in America and Britain. It did this through live performances in vaudeville and variety in America and music hall and concert performances in Britain, as well as song interpolations into musical comedies in both countries, and sales of sheet music, such that the genres called 'coon songs' and 'ragtime' were often virtually interchangeable. At the turn of the twentieth century, ragtime music introduced syncopation, raised interest in African American music, was the most important commercial product on Tin Pan Alley, and became the first nationally and internationally popular genre of the twentieth century.

CASE STUDY: Tin Pan Alley

The name Tin Pan Alley originally referred to West 28th Street between Fifth and Sixth Avenues in Manhattan. Publishers based here offered paid employment to young musicians and singers who performed songs to catch the ear of potential buyers of sheet music and, later, record buyers. Songs were performed in vaudeville, musical comedy and in other leisure spaces – known as song plugging. Meanwhile, young composers also came to sell their material to the publishers as a way to break into the music business, including for traveling black vaudevillians from throughout the United States who dropped off recent compositions 'to try their luck at a "hit"' (Gilbert, 2015, p. 23). Importantly, given the rise of ragtime and later jazz and blues, there was no legal colour bar or segregation, though de facto behavioural separations were evident. Fats Waller was one of the alley's leading songwriters (whose music is showcased in the musical revue *Ain't Misbehavin'* [1978]). Other (white) songwriters including George Gershwin and Irving Berlin had early successes through Tin Pan Alley. Although this was a comparatively unsegregated space that gave considerable exposure and financial return to composers of colour, they made less money than their white counterparts and were not given the same access. Meanwhile, the result was the assimilation of their music by mainstream (white) musical theatre, and the retention of earlier racist stereotypes, especially since some of the most offensive songs were still promoted by African American writers.

Cook followed *Clorindy* with the far less successful *Jes' Lak White Fo'ks* (1899), also at the Casino Roof Garden Theatre, and soon began writing songs for other peoples' musicals (including songs for both white and African American Broadway stars). He also became the resident composer for the Williams and Walker entertainments, *In Dahomey* (1902), *Abyssinia* (1906) and *Bandanna Land* (1908). Although the characters retained some of the stereotypes of minstrelsy in *Clorindy*, Williams and Walker's next work, *Abyssinia* (1906), reversed the trend with the African characters representing ancient culture and the Americans being a target of humour. After their third collaboration, *Bandanna Land*, Walker suddenly died. Williams was invited to perform in the *Ziegfeld Follies* from 1910 until 1919, followed by *Broadway Brevities of 1920*, which effectively broke through a notable race barrier, although he was one of a tiny group of performers in this category. Moreover, he had already written one of the first racially integrated musicals, *The Southerners* (1904). Here, right at the start of the twentieth century, then, the influence of ragtime syncopation and racial integration was beginning on Broadway, though not without significant power imbalances.

At around the same time, Bob Cole began an African American production company and mounted his first full-length musical comedy, *A Trip to Coontown*. The musical opened in 1898, the same year as *Clorindy*, but had a complete book (rather than a variety of acts). That said, several specialty acts and performers incorporated their own material, such that the show often seemed like many earlier revue shows. It played briefly on Broadway before touring America and then returning to New York.

Following their first attempt at writing a musical comedy, brothers John Rosamund Johnson and James Weldon Johnson moved to New York City in 1899. Publisher Isadore Witmark and theatrical producer Oscar Hammerstein (grandfather of the later composer) were impressed and helped establish the pair, ending both the colour bar and the stereotyping of African Americans in their work. With Bob Cole, the pair began writing for other performers and, since the team needed funds, Rosamund and Cole established a hugely successful vaudeville act that was unlike anything previously performed by men of colour: they performed in the style of a classical concert and included many of their own songs. The pair toured to Britain in 1906 to play a six-week run at the Palace in London – reporting that the city seemed to offer them 'a personal welcome' (Riis, 1986, p. 54). The racial tolerance and critical praise were reported back so that 'at least two-dozen major black acts or stars toured in England during the first decade of the twentieth century' (ibid., 54). Although these were not necessarily in musical theatre shows, the performers were bringing song, dance and new popular music, and many stayed for a number of years.

While James Weldon Johnson returned home and established a music school John Rosamund Johnson and Cole both stayed in New York where they wrote and starred in their own musical comedy, *The Shoo-Fly Regiment* (1907), putting to rest many of the stereotypes and taboos that limited how African American performers had hitherto been seen. As Henry D. Miller notes in *Theorizing Black Theatre*, Cole, in particular, pursued more genuine and authentic representations of African Americans, rather than replicating how white artists had depicted them (2011, p. 21). The pair later wrote and starred in *The Red Moon* (1908), before Cole's early death left Johnson working as an actor again in musicals like *Porgy and Bess* (1935) in the 1930s and 1940s.

Although the deaths of Cole and Walker and the move of their erstwhile partners to mainstream performance meant a hiatus in the development of Black musical comedy, further racial integration of performers had begun, but more importantly the assimilation of African American music into musical theatre was now unstoppable. It is this history to which the musical *Ragtime* refers through its central character, Coalhouse Walker. It is not just the history of blackface performance, but the history of real people, composers and musicians, singers and dancers, who made careers in vaudeville and on Broadway, and who were welcomed and praised for their new and dynamic popular music and dance in Britain and Europe.

Shuffle Along and all that jazz

From 1910 to 1920, most of the new works of Black musical comedy were performed for racially diverse (though still segregated) audiences either across America or in Harlem, New York, rather than on Broadway. Beyond Broadway, African American performers played all kinds of roles, rather than the stereotypes and caricatures that were still being adopted on Broadway. It was in Harlem, therefore, that Flournoy Miller and Aubrey Lyles, both African American writers, developed the comic characters that were to appear in the next landmark Black musical: *Shuffle Along*.

CASE STUDY: *Shuffle Along* (1921)

Music and lyrics: Noble Sissle and Eubie Blake. Book: F. E. Miller and Aubrey Lyles.

Two grocery store owners, Sam Peck and Steve Jenkins, originally played by Lyles and Miller, living in Jimtown, USA (note the connection to Jim Crow laws in this name), both run for the office of mayor with the promise that whoever wins will make the other his chief of police. With the help of some crooked campaigning, Sam wins and appoints Steve as promised, but the two start to argue, resulting in a comic fight (one of the signature vaudeville routines of Miller and Lyles). However, the virtuous third opponent from the mayoral race, Harry Walton, promises to end their corrupt regime. With the help of the townspeople, Walton wins the next election and the girl (Jessie). Act 2 was then interrupted so that Noble Sissle and Eubie Blake could perform a short concert derived from their vaudeville act (Wollman, 2017, p. 67), just as Miller and Lyles had the opportunity to insert their comedy fight in Act 1. These insertions would not have been unexpected to audiences of the time in shows where plots were much looser frameworks containing material from other sources.

The musical was revived on Broadway in 1933 and 1952. George C. Wolfe (who also wrote the book of *Jelly's Last Jam* referenced in our chapter title) adapted the musical in 2016, as *Shuffle Along, or, the Making of the Musical Sensation of 1921 and All That Followed*, which focused on the creation, success and aftermath of the original production.

According to *Time* magazine, *Shuffle Along* was the first Broadway musical to prominently feature syncopated jazz music and the first to feature a chorus of professional female dancers (though professional female dancers had already featured in revue). Although some reviewers suggested that the crooked leading characters relied too heavily on dated racial stereotypes (Zoglin, 2016) this show was important as the first Broadway show written and performed by African Americans in over a decade; it provided opportunities for many African American performers, and it boosted the careers of others. Following their successes in this musical on Broadway Josephine Baker and Paul Robeson, for example, both travelled to Europe, where Baker became famous at the Folies Bergère in Paris, adopting France as her home. Robeson toured Britain in 1922, and repeatedly thereafter, settling in London for several years as an actor and singer, where he performed in *Show Boat* on stage. In common with the earlier wave of entertainers, he reportedly found the acceptance there more comfortable than the segregation at home. He recorded spirituals, European folk songs, as well as classical music, and even made several films – including his iconic portrayal of Joe in *Show Boat* (1936) – all of which popularized both Black and white music.

Shuffle Along also provided a catalyst for the gradual desegregation of performing companies and audiences, shattering the assumptions that white audiences would not enjoy African American shows, and contributed to the ending of the minstrel stereotypes (Wollman, 2017, p. 70). Famously, and most importantly, when thinking about the influence of African American music on musical theatre, it was the jazzy syncopated songs of Eubie Blake and Noble Sissle, rather than the thin plot, that attracted audiences. George Gershwin, Al Jolson and Langston Hughes, among others, flocked to see the show and, in turn, the musical helped unite Broadway communities, encouraged diverse audiences and influenced mainstream popular music.

The score contained blues, ragtime, barbershop and jazz, as well as operetta-style ballads. Here we see the transatlantic influences reappearing as European styles are mixed with African American and Broadway genres to produce a multifaceted musical theatre score. The voices and singing were also commented on by critics, including Alan Dale who noted in the New York *American* that Lottie Gee, the 'singularly pure soprano', sang with 'taste, discretion and distinction' (in Woll, 1989, p. 70). Since the show was a huge success, producers jumped on the bandwagon to develop other musicals, such that there were nine new African American musicals in the next three years. This bolstered the careers of African American performers and creators, but the requirement that these shows imitate, or at least follow the formula of, *Shuffle Along* tended to limit innovation in character and plot. This was not necessarily the case with music, however, since the jazz style and the mix of genres flourished in musical theatre. Ragtime, and then jazz, became ubiquitous in musical comedy with such innovations inspiring notable white composers like Irving Berlin, Jerome Kern and George Gershwin.

The rise of minstrelsy

So far, this chapter has explored how ragtime arrived on Broadway and then developed into jazz both of which forms spread through Britain and Europe. Nevertheless, every innovation arises from somewhere and the development of ragtime is particularly notable in that it incorporates earlier forms like minstrelsy and vaudeville (as addressed in Chapter 1). To tell this story, we look at a recent musical, *The Scottsboro Boys* (2010), which controversially told a story of racial injustice through the tropes of a (similarly racist) minstrel show.

When *The Scottsboro Boys* opened at the Lyceum Theatre, on Broadway, in November 2010, over thirty people, most of whom had presumably not seen the musical, protested against the show's racist use of blackface and minstrelsy (as organized by the Freedom Party). Its white director, Susan Stroman, spoke out in the following days, claiming that the production used the tropes of minstrelsy to critique systematic racism in the American justice system, not to celebrate a racist art form (see Cohen, 2010). Indeed, the musical incorporated the grotesque stereotypes of African American performers to highlight the injustices in the young people's treatment. Led by

CASE STUDY: *The Scottsboro Boys* (2010)

Music: John Kander. Lyrics: Fred Ebb. Book: David Thompson.

The musical documents the true story of nine African American teenage males travelling to Memphis in 1931. They are riding the railroad train illegally when two young white women, who are also taking the train illegally, accuse them of rape to avoid being accused of prostitution. The male adolescents are then prosecuted in a hostile courtroom, defended only by a drunken lawyer, and sentenced to death. Just before they are due to be executed, they are granted a reprieve by the Supreme Court on the grounds that they were not well represented, and now face a new trial. This time, the teenagers are represented by a New York lawyer and one of the young women recants her story. She is believed to have been bribed, however, and the innocent young men are convicted once again. Their lawyer continues to appeal and the teenaged men are repeatedly found guilty, even after the second young woman begins to buckle (though she never recants her story). Eventually the four youngest are released – the youngest was only thirteen at the time of the supposed crime. Another is shot in prison and left brain-damaged. Haywood Patterson, arguably the musical's main protagonist, is finally brought up for parole but refuses to plead guilty and dies in prison twenty-one years later.

The musical opened off-Broadway, before a Broadway transfer, in 2010. It also played at the Young Vic Theatre, London, in 2013, followed by a limited West End run in 2014.

In the true account of the 'Scottsboro boys' – a reference to the city in which the male adolescents first stood trial – all of the prisoners were released or had escaped by 1946. Clarence Norris, for example, who had been sentenced to death, skipped bail and went into hiding until he was granted a full pardon in 1976. The last surviving defendant died in 1989. In 2013, three years after the musical had opened in New York, all of the men who had yet to be pardoned were pardoned posthumously. However, the story was a cause célèbre at the time, causing scandal in the liberal North and instigating changes in how criminal trials could be conducted across America.

one white performer, the Interlocutor, the predominantly Black cast reframe such stereotypes to provide social critique. Moreover, towards the end of the show the African American actors challenge the white interlocutor, turning the minstrel tradition on its head, and so the form of the show becomes a direct critique of racism. The protesters may have been ignorant of this context, simply taking production images of characters like Mr Bones or Mr Tambo at face value, without considering that the creative team sought to remind audiences how much, or how little, society had really changed. This broader context is also highlighted by the musical beginning with Rosa Parks waiting for a bus and ending with her boarding the bus but refusing to sit in her assigned section at the rear.

Over 150 years before *The Scottsboro Boys* opened on Broadway, between the 1840s and 1890s, minstrel shows became highly popular across America. Although the practice of white performers using burnt cork to blacken their faces and create grotesque caricatures was common in circuses and travelling shows from the 1790s, they came to prominence in the 1820s and 30s. As noted above, white entertainer Thomas Rice created a blackface song and dance act in 1828, to the song 'Jump Jim Crow'. Many other solo performances followed until four blackface performers united as a troupe calling themselves the Virginia Minstrels. They developed a full-length performance in 1843. Soon, most major American cities had at least one minstrel troupe and the Virginia Minstrels toured to Britain as early as 1843. Although minstrel shows took many forms, most were organized into three parts (following Edwin Pearce Christy of the Buffalo-based Christy's Minstrels) (Knapp, 2005, p. 53). It was by appearing in such entertainments that many African American performers had their first opportunity to appear on stage as 'colored minstrels' wearing blackface make-up. Indeed, they did not have a choice about whether to use blackface make up – if they wanted to work in these shows that was required, and some African Americans even passed for Caucasian in mainstream minstrel shows. Crucially, this often meant that racial stereotypes were further reinforced by African American performers, though it also provided professional opportunities on the variety stage as the national circuit developed (as with Walker and Williams). These sketches and routines were then transferred to early musicals as described above. Professional minstrel troupes disappeared in America by the 1920s, though blackface performance continued in many Hollywood films, including performances by Fred Astaire (*Swing Time* [1936]) and Judy Garland (*Everybody Sing* [1938]), and on mainstream British television until the 1970s.

CASE STUDY: The minstrel show format

Before the war, minstrel shows often depicted plantation life. After the war, however, the format gradually became much more structured. In the first part, the troupe entered with a rousing opening number and then sat in a semicircle with a tambourine player (Mr Tambo – or Brudder Tambo) at one end and a bones player (Mr Bones – or Brudder Bones) at the other and a 'Master of Ceremonies', or MC, in the middle called the Interlocutor (often the only performer not in blackface make-up). The two end players performed comic banter, while others performed songs and instrumental performances. After the intermission, the Olio was a variety show consisting of dances, sketches and acts like juggling, similar to British music hall, which was concluded with a pastiche political oration by one of the comics. The final section or 'Afterpiece' was a short play with songs. This might consist of a sentimental plantation comedy or a pastiche of a popular performance (similar to the British burlesques). Notable, though, was the frequent inclusion in post-war years of two stereotypical characters: Jim Crow and Zip Coon. Crow was a country bumpkin, stupid and uneducated, while Coon was a city slicker who was arrogant and ostentatious, yet undermined himself with mistakes in his manners and grammar. Other stereotypes included Mammy, Uncle Tom, Pickaninny and Jezebel. The evening ended with a cakewalk dance, so named because plantation competitions had offered a cake as a prize for slave imitations of their white masters. Parts of this format are recreated in *The Scottsboro Boys*.

Several important musical styles arose from minstrel performances. Minstrel groups sang close harmony versions of plantation tunes, or mock plantation tunes, which ultimately led to the development of barbershop quartets. Meanwhile, so-called 'coon songs', including ragtime syncopation, pervaded variety shows and early musicals. A key step to popularizing these forms was the education of musicians so that song sheets could be written as well as, later, tours and recordings made. Oberlin Conservatory (established 1833) was always co-educational, and from 1835 admitted people of colour. Fisk University, in Nashville (established 1866), is perhaps the most famous institution set up to provide education to formerly enslaved people. To

support the school financially, tours were organized by the Fisk Jubilee
Singers from 1871. The group sang spirituals and songs by Stephen Foster
and toured America, as well as Europe and Britain, where they performed
for Queen Victoria. Although the membership of the group changed as
members left (and, indeed, some stayed in Britain), their influence meant
that similar groups were set up across both countries, many led by singers
from the group. This altered the perception of performers of colour and the
cultural awareness of Black music.

These histories indicate that there is no single source from which a new
musical style is created, or derives, but that it arises out of the interactions
between forms, cultures and circumstances. Ragtime stemmed from the
combination of the music of enslaved people, which may have arrived from
Africa and the Caribbean, and European musical forms that were perhaps
heard on plantations and in churches, plus the syncopations and stereotypes
of 'cakewalks' popularized in vaudeville. The kidnapping and imprisoning of
slaves, then later the Great Migration and the touring of shows and concert
parties transferred musical influences around North America and across the
Atlantic. The development of composition and publishing was supported by
the increased educational opportunities that appeared for African American
musicians, who began to travel to Europe and Britain with companies like the
Fisk Jubilee Singers, Minstrel troupes, variety acts and musical theatre shows,
as well as by the commerciality of Tin Pan Alley. It is this pattern that repeats
later with jazz, then blues, rock 'n' roll, gospel, soul and, much later still, rap
and hip-hop. There is no single point of origin, but a series of influences and
opportunities that lead to a gradual evolution that suddenly appears in the
mainstream at a particular time and place. However, it cannot be ignored
that there is a power imbalance in the transmission (or appropriation) of
musical styles that move predominantly from African American music to be
assimilated in commercial white theatres and popular music.

Meanwhile, in Britain, during the Edwardian period when revue
began to supplant musical comedy, there were many opportunities for
performers from all backgrounds, including Caribbean and African
American. *Eightpence a Mile* (1913), for example, 'mixed dances such as
"Russian ballet" with Latin tango or the African-American "cakewalk"
with Viennese waltz' in a way that supported London's claim to be at the
forefront of a contemporary cosmopolitan culture, even though the ideas of
nation and race were also problematic (Linton, 2021, p. 12). Innovations in
transport and travel as well as printing and recording technology meant that
performances, musicians and new genres spread rapidly and fluidly. Since

Black music had, by the 1920s, influenced most writers of musical comedy, it is not necessary to mention all of these developments. *Show Boat* and *Porgy and Bess* represent key moments of change in the interwar years, both featuring scores by white creatives and either largely non-white or integrated casts. There was a sense that Black music and African American performers might ultimately attain equality after the Second World War. More African American performers were working in mainstream shows, but this meant that the opportunities for African American creative teams and performers (other than stars) to create their own shows were reduced.

Langston Hughes tried to alter this pattern with a series of plays, musicals and operas, including a play with music, *Simply Heavenly* (1957), in which the African American characters retained their own culture (Woll, 1989, p. 239). The most important musical for this story of the development of Black music is *Black Nativity* (1961), which incorporated gospel music, and was followed by another gospel musical *Tambourines to Glory* in 1963 – though neither reached Broadway. These vocal performances brought a new approach to singing that moved to musical theatre with the musical style. Although *Black Nativity* may have been the first production to use this music and, according to scholar Allen Woll, to legitimize both Black and gospel music on Broadway, it was *Tambourines to Glory* that integrated gospel music into the dramatic structure, rather than as diegetic song (where characters overtly perform a number). Hughes's final musical *Jerico-Jim Crow* (1964) included traditional and modern Black music in a history of African American lives in America.

Following this several other Black musicals appeared, mostly off-Broadway, in a little burst that began to reflect the increasing integration of Black and white identities at the time of the civil rights protests (though many featured somewhat outdated representations of characters and topics). It was not until the late 1960s, then, that another group of Black musicals were produced in New York that seriously addressed race relations, some of which, by the 1970s, even made it to Broadway. This group began with *Purlie* in 1970, *Raisin* in 1973, followed by *The Wiz* in 1975. Finally, writers of Black musicals were allowed to convey social messages, voiced by characters and performers of colour, on a mainstream stage. This was then followed by several musicals, largely created by white writers, that referenced the history of Black music, many of which were jukebox musicals that transferred to London, demonstrating the interest of British audiences in this music and the history associated with it. Shows included *Bubbling Brown Sugar* (NY 1976, London 1977), *Ain't Misbehavin'* (NY 1978, London

1979), *Eubie!* (NY 1979) and *Sophisticated Ladies* (NY 1981, London 1991). The most important book musical of this time was *Dreamgirls* (1981), though, interestingly, it did not arrive in London until 2016.

Dreamgirls and Motown

Dreamgirls is set in the 1960s and tells the story of a three girl group similar to The Supremes or The Shirelles who found fame at Tamla Records with producer Berry Gordy. Gordy, who also produced records by Stevie Wonder, James Brown and Marvin Gaye, formed Tamla Records in 1959 and then changed the name to Motown Record Company in 1960 (though Tamla Motown remained one of the company's labels). The significance of this company, among the many others in popular music, was that it was an African American–owned record company that became successful across white and Black charts and radio stations, which had, until this time, been separate. African American songs were often rerecorded by white artists for white consumption, meaning it was very difficult for African American performers to break into the mainstream popular charts or achieve nationwide success (as depicted in the 2009 musical, *Memphis*). Motown Records, however, represented many performers of colour who achieved significant crossover success in the popular music charts and so came to the attention of audiences in Europe and Britain as well as America.

The musical style had originated in gospel music, especially the call and response antiphonal singing in church groups and the use of backing singers. Soloists incorporated an excess of ornamentation, free improvisation in the melody line and the full timbral range of the voice. Rather than the tradition of bel canto, which moderated the tone of the voice so that it was consistent throughout, and attempted to hide the effort of performance, the vocal sound of blues, gospel and soul all incorporate a full-bodied sound; the belt, the shouts and screams and instrumental sounding syllables all actively expose the effort of performance (as depicted in Figure 2.2, where the backing group and instrumentalists are imagined as equals in accompanying the soloist). This transforms the listening experience from something aesthetically pleasing that supports verbal communication into something that articulates the raw emotions and the body of the singer. It was this emotional musical and vocal language that has featured in many shows, especially *Dreamgirls* and, more

Figure 2.2 Cleavant Derricks, Loretta Devine, Sheila Ellis and Sheryl Lee Ralph in a scene from the Broadway production of the musical *Dreamgirls*. 1983. Photo: Swope, Martha. © NYPL.

recently, *The Color Purple* (2005), but has actually become widespread in contemporary musical theatre.

Interestingly, soul music became enormously popular in the North of England, where it was known as 'Northern Soul'. This became the music of a youth movement known as mods in the 1970s who danced athletically to the music of African American artists. The fictional story of a Dublin band playing this music is told in the novel *The Commitments* (1987), which became a popular film in 1991 and a stage musical in 2013. The popularity of this story alone demonstrates the easy transatlantic reach of this musical style and its incorporation by other minority communities.

Meanwhile, back in America, Motown moved to Los Angeles in 1972, where it continued to produce records, and then to diversify into film and television. The first two films were star vehicles for Diana Ross (formerly a Supreme), *Lady Sings the Blues* (1972) and *Mahogany* (1975). It was in 1981 when Henry Krieger and Tom Eyen wrote a fictional story based on Diana Ross, The Supremes, and the history of Motown Records, writing original music characteristic of that history: *Dreamgirls*.

CASE STUDY: *Dreamgirls* (1981)

Music: Henry Krieger. Lyrics and book: Tom Eyen.

Beginning in 1962, a three-girl close harmony group (Effie, Deena and Lorrell) enters a competition at the famous Apollo Theatre, Harlem. Although they do not win, they meet Curtis Taylor, a car salesman, who wants to be their manager. He takes them on, and the girls, now known as the Dreams, become backing singers for Jimmy Early (a successful R&B singer) for his tour. As Curtis persuades Jimmy to enter the commercial pop market, CC, Effie's brother and an aspiring songwriter, writes 'Cadillac Car' for the new group. The song, however, is quickly recorded – or stolen – by a white group who are more successful with it. As a result, Curtis (illegally) bribes radio disc jockeys (DJs) into playing their next recording, 'Steppin' to the Bad Side', which becomes a hit. Personal entanglements start to complicate the situation as Curtis and Effie begin a relationship and Jimmy (although married) has an affair with Lorrell. Curtis's attention quickly turns to the girls, rather than Jimmy, and Curtis increasingly encourages pretty, slim Deena to take the lead vocal, replacing the more full-figured Effie. Effie, now known for her tantrums and inconsistency, suspects Curtis of having an affair with Deena and is replaced by Michelle in 1967. The act closes with Effie singing 'And I Am Telling You I'm Not Going', a song that gave Jennifer Holliday, the original Effie, a number one hit on the US Hot R&B/Hip-Hop Songs *Billboard* chart in 1982.

Act 2 is set in the 1970s when the group is the most successful female group in the country, Curtis and Deena are married, and Effie is at home raising the child she had with Curtis. Meanwhile, CC tries to reconcile with Effie and persuades her to record the original version of 'One Night Only'. Annoyed at the competition, Curtis uses bribery again to promote the Dreams' disco version of the song but is confronted by CC and Marty (Jimmy Early's former manager). Deena and Effie reunite and, when she discovers that Effie's daughter is Curtis's, Deena finally finds the courage to leave him. As Effie pursues a solo career, and Deena works in Hollywood, the four Dreams (including Effie) reunite for a final concert performance.

Dreamgirls was nominated for thirteen Tony Awards in 1982, winning six, and has had a series of subsequent national tours and concert performances. The 2006 film adaptation, starring Beyoncé and Jennifer Hudson, won two Academy Awards, and the musical was first produced in the West End in 2016.

Caribbean and South Asian influences

Meanwhile, although Britain had a long history of non-white performers going back to at least 1738, and a complete act of *Virginia* (1928) was performed by African American British actors in the West End, an unofficial kind of racial separation in performance and the politics of otherness continued. This was evidence of a pushback in the early twentieth century against the appearance of so many African American and South Asian performers in London (Macpherson, 2016, pp. 674–5). Even in the 1960s it was difficult for African American British performers to find mainstream work. However, regional and community-based companies were established, such as Black Theatre Co-operative (Nitro), Rifco, Talawa and Tamasha that eventually led to greater representation, though it would be the twenty-first century before this affected the West End, and the musical influences would arise from the Caribbean and from South Asia rather than from America. Musicals such as *Bend It Like Beckham* (Chadha, Mayeda Burges, Goodall and Hart, 2015), *The Harder They Come* (Henzell, 2006) and *Britain's Got Bhangra* (Kumar, Chopra and Irvine, 2011) began to alter the sound of music in mainstream British musicals – though that is still a work in progress especially given the overwhelming presence of American popular music.

Rap, hip-hop and *Hamilton*

Hip-hop culture, incorporating DJing/scratching, MCing/rapping, breakdancing, beatboxing and graffiti, emerged as an urban youth culture in the 1970s in the Bronx. Like the other styles discussed in this chapter, though, it derived from existing cultural practices, making it impossible to identify a single moment or place of inauguration (Alridge and Stewart, 2005, p. 190). Rapping, for example, may have arisen from a number of sources, including playful and creative uses of language in the African American community, like 'Pattin' Juba' from the nineteenth century. In this form, created by two people, the first laid down a 'patter' of dance music, while the second person accompanied that music by making up verses on the spot (Southern, 1997, p. 602). 'Playing the Dozens' is a modern competitive ritual in which two men exchange clever insults in improvised verses, whereas 'Toasting Rites' is a blend of rap and reggae, plus some rhythm and blues, in which singers practise reciting lyrics over a backing track. In each of these forms, the emphasis on rhythm encourages dance, while the musicians embrace rhythmic complexity through the incorporation of all kinds of diverse content within a steady, but complex, drum track.

However, there was an important person in the development of rap culture in the Bronx, New York. Afrika Bambaataa is a Bronx DJ, a former gang member who read the philosophy of activist Malcolm X and regarded the arts as a potential way for youngsters to escape street violence. He founded a youth organization in 1973, which was later known as Zulu Nation, whose activities included all the arts of hip-hop culture. By the mid-1970s, it 'encompassed not just a musical genre, but also a style of dress, dialect and language, way of looking at the world, and an aesthetic that reflects the sensibilities of a large population of youth born between 1965 and 1984' (Alridge, 2005, p. 190). Before the digital revolution that made sampling much more straightforward, DJs used two turntables so that they could mix fragments of two records together. Likewise, 'scratching' is the practice of moving a record backwards and forwards under the needle to produce a percussive rhythm while mixing between two records. The DJ might recite improvised verses over such a rhythm, but it soon became apparent that it required concentration to do either of these things, so the two skills were split, meaning DJs mixed records and MCs rapped improvised rhyming lyrics.

As illustrated in films like *8 Mile* (2002), street corner competitions have been popular for several decades among young people in inner city America. Through rap and hip-hop, youngsters found a means to comment on the violence and gang culture surrounding them and the often-impoverished conditions in which they lived. By the 1980s, hip-hop culture had spread to many countries, including Britain, where separate traditions emerged. British culture has spawned numerous music and dance groups, including Katie Prince's ZooNation Dance Company, which creates original hip-hop dance musicals (like *Into the Hoods* [2008]) to a score compiled of samples of various types of popular music, with a voice-over narration. Meanwhile, in America during the 1990s, Gangsta Rap, and other regional styles, emerged (as depicted in the film *Straight Outta Compton* [2015]), with some forms of rap becoming extremely complex, layering sounds and incorporating samples from all kinds of popular music, especially jazz.

As a result, hip-hop has become a reflection of a way of life and represents the disempowerment and alienation felt by young people in urban ghettos. At the same time it unites the world through its incorporation of all kinds of musical samples and textual quotations, as well as its reference to contemporary events. Black music history thus becomes the source and reference point in rap music at the same time that popular culture more widely has become increasingly reflexive. Hip-hop has been important for promoting Black nationalism and empowerment, and this is what rap and hip-hop dance bring to the musical megahit *Hamilton* (2015): a document of the struggle for empowerment and national identity, and an equivalent sense that this is still necessary for Black equality.

Lin-Manuel Miranda's *Hamilton* is famous for its inclusion of rap and hip-hop styles, yet it was not the first American musical to feature these musical genres. Unlike in *Bring in da Noise, Bring in da Funk*, a tap/rap musical from 1995 (tap dance informed by funk and rap rhythms), Miranda's *In the Heights* (2008) or *Bring It On* (2012) (a collaboration with Tom Kitt and Amanda Green), rap is performed in *Hamilton* to create a character type rooted in the form's urban sub-cultural associations, rather than as a signifier of time and place. Whereas *In the Heights* is set in a contemporary America, in which some of the characters might well use rap to signify their urban background and musical tastes, *Hamilton* is set in and after 1776 – during the American War of Independence. In this case, rap represents the disempowerment, drive and urgency of the characters, many of whom are ambitious politicians who debate in cabinet/rap battles. Likewise, the rhythmic and verbal dexterity, plus the competitive nature, of rap means that certain characters reflect the rappers of the ghetto from which rap emerged – those who, as Hamilton repeats, are 'young, scrappy and hungry' – according to author Miranda, who is himself of Puerto Rican descent. By contrast, the British King, one of the few caucasian cast members, sings a number reminiscent of The Beatles (a British band that 'invaded' America in the 1960s), while Eliza, who comes from a different socio-cultural background to her husband, Hamilton, sings in a contemporary musical theatre style. Interestingly, The Beatles pop songs derive from a blues history, while, as documented above, contemporary musical theatre derives partly from a history of jazz and soul.

CASE STUDY: *Hamilton* (2015)

Music, lyrics and book: Lin-Manuel Miranda.

Based on Ron Chernow's 2004 biography, the musical depicts the American War of Independence told from the perspective of founding father Alexander Hamilton, himself a recent immigrant from the Caribbean. It concerns the competitive relationship between Hamilton and Aaron Burr, who eventually kills Hamilton in a duel, and the love triangle between Hamilton and two of the Schuyler sisters – his wife, Eliza, and her sister, Angelica. Hamilton also has an affair with Maria Reynolds, whose husband later bribes Hamilton. Upon discovering this, Eliza destroys many of her husband's letters and, in doing so, 'erases herself from the narrative' because the record of their relationship is gone. After Hamilton's death, Eliza looks to return herself to 'the narrative', calling into question how history is documented and whose stories are told. She spends the rest of her life becoming a noted philanthropist by co-founding an orphanage alongside preserving her husband's legacy.

The musical opened on Broadway in 2015, winning eleven Tony Awards and the coveted Pulitzer Prize for Drama, followed by multiple national tours and a West End transfer in 2017.

Like other historical musicals, including *Evita* (1978) and *Ragtime*, *Hamilton* is performed by a self-aware cast that knowingly constructs a story. The casting is specified in recent calls as 'non-white' for most characters (with the noted exception of the 'caucasian' King George), unlike the historical figures most of the performers play, and the musical has been celebrated for this fact. That said, scholars have also challenged the musical's diversity, given the lack of African American characters and narratives in the show. Of particular note is the absence of any consideration of slavery and slave ownership (see, for example, Galella, 2018a).

Conclusion

To return to *Ragtime* and the discussion at the start of this chapter, as well as our title and its references, it would seem that the history of musical theatre and the history of Black music are completely entwined. Just as Alexander Hamilton's musical style says something about his character, history and culture, so does the music of Coalhouse Walker. The important linking factor in all these musicals is that African American music offers the creative teams the opportunity to revisit some of the power imbalances and injustices that tarnish world history. In recent years, there has been a dramatic increase in the number of musicals that document the history of Black culture and Black music, including *Sarafina!* (Ngema, 1988) and *Fela!* (Kuti and Jones, 2009).

These shows all offer opportunities to performers of colour playing a full range of dramatic roles, led by racially diverse creative teams. This history is embedded in the bodies of the performers, the characters, the representations and the performances they enact. It is also embedded in the music and the stories of musical theatre. Racial discrimination and the incorporation of Black music are both part of the history of musical theatre as it has spread around the world, and this cannot be ignored. As we record how music is produced through the interactions of people from many races, and via the transatlantic exchanges both to and from America, the history of inequality is inescapable.

As the company sings 'who lives, who dies, who tells your story' at the end of *Hamilton,* a comment is revealed both on the fallibility and incompleteness of history and on who has the power to ensure a story is told. This applies in all the musicals we have identified in this chapter where the content is equally political in commenting on power, equality and oppression. In *Ragtime,* a story told by white American writers, the African American characters die leaving their music to influence popular culture, while they are excluded. Although Tateh, the European immigrant, assimilates himself into American life, the musical comments on the failure of the American Dream to effect the inclusion of all. In the 2016 version of *Shuffle Along,* the history of the original 1921 musical is told by an influential African American creative team that reminds audiences of some of the recent history of segregation, plus the importance of creatives and performers of colour in the history of musical theatre. The stories of *The Scottsboro Boys* were turned into a musical by white American writers using a controversial minstrel format to draw attention to the power imbalances that are still present in society. *Dreamgirls* documents how power is predominantly in the hands of men, especially the white men who controlled the recording industry, though curiously the development of the 2016 London production in South Korea by an American team added yet another layer of racial complexity to this popular piece.

Finally, *Hamilton* allows the story of the War of Independence to be seen performed by non-white bodies, using a musical style that arose in Black culture as a form of resistance and empowerment, in a show developed by a writer of Puerto Rican descent. All these shows thus demonstrate the power imbalances in musical theatre, history and in documentation, but also illustrate the rich cultural heritage arising from the mixing of traditional, classical and ethnically diverse musical styles and genres.

As we have seen, African American music derived from a combination of European and Afro-Caribbean influences, developed in an American slave context before spreading across America, where it interacted and combined with other musical forms. All these forms subsequently travelled back across the Atlantic, as a result of touring, publishing and later recording. Interactions and exchanges are therefore continuous and nebulous – almost impossible to document – and so this chapter has inevitably painted this history in broad brush strokes. However, this history allows the music and stories to be recognizable and applicable in a larger global context, where they may also apply to other instances of disempowerment or inequality. This is not the end of the story, though, since wealth and opportunity are still not equally shared, and new music will continue to arise from interactions within and between cultures of unequal power and to filter into and regenerate musical theatre around the world.

Tasks

Research an African American, or non-white, musical theatre composer, performer or creative that has been 'lost' from musical theatre history. What did they contribute to the development of the form? How did they interact with any of the developments outlined in this chapter? What contextual factors might have impacted their contribution being lost from musical theatre history?

Explore the history and reviews of *Porgy and Bess* (1935). How has the musical's reception altered over time? What are the issues raised since George Gershwin, a white Jewish American, wrote the music? Does his research allow him to understand African American music and how it relates to history and context? Should composers only write music from their own cultural history and/or lived experience?

Discussion topics

Why do you think hip-hop and rap might be an appropriate language to tell the story of *Hamilton* (2015) and the American Revolution? What might this musical style suggest or say about the characters and the narrative?

What kinds of musical languages are used in *Hairspray* (2002) and *The Color Purple* (2005)? How do they reflect African American history and what does this association contribute to your understanding of the narrative? How do they differ from the styles used in musicals by African American writers, like *Passing Strange* (2008) and *A Strange Loop* (2020)?

Further reading – conceptual

Gilbert, D. (2015) *The Product of Our Souls: Ragtime, Race and the Birth of the Manhattan Musical Marketplace*. New York: University of North Carolina Press.

Hoffman, W. (2020) *The Great White Way: Race and the Broadway Musical*. 2nd Edition. New Brunswick: Rutgers University Press.

Young, H. (2013) *Theatre & Race*. Houndmills: Palgrave Macmillan.

Further reading – case study

Edney, K. (2014) 'Tapping the Ivories: Jazz and Tap Dance in *Jelly's Last Jam* (1992)'. In: D. Symonds and M. Taylor (eds) *Gestures of Music Theater: The Performativity of Song and Dance*. Oxford University Press, 113–27.

Hodges Persley, N. (2021) *Sampling and Remixing Blackness in Hip-Hop Theater and Performance*. Ann Arbor, MI: University of Michigan Press.

Linton, D. (2021) *Nation and Race in West End Revue 1910–30*. Cham, Switzerland: Palgrave Macmillan.

Rumsey, P. (2019) 'Reparation and Reanimation in Musical Theatre: Savion Glover's Choreography of *Shuffle Along – or the Making of the Musical Sensation of 1921 and All That Followed*'. In: S. Whitfield (ed.) *Reframing the Musical: Race, Culture and Identity*. London: Red Globe Press, 129–48.

3

'Waving through a window': From intertext to Instagram

Officer Lockstock welcomes the audience to *Urinetown: The Musical* (2001) by saying: 'Well, hello there. And welcome – to *Urinetown!* Not the place, of course. The musical. Urinetown "the place", is ... well, it's a place you'll hear people referring to a lot throughout the show.' Elsewhere, the Narrator in *Into the Woods* (1987) welcomes the audience with 'Once upon a time' ... 'in a far-off kingdom' ... 'lived a young maiden' ... 'a sad young lad' ... 'and a childless baker' ... 'with his wife'. In *Cabaret* (1966), the Emcee welcomes the audience to the Kit Kat Klub with the words 'Willkommen, Bienvenue, Welcome'. In all of these, and many other, musicals, clues are given to the audience at the start of the show that the musical is neither realistic nor integrated and that a narrator figure sits outside (or sometimes both outside and inside) the world of the show. These characters speak directly to the audience about musicals and performances (known as reflexivity); they reference well-known stories and use language that is familiar from other texts. Not only is such language familiar from literature, but also from other musicals, television shows, films and elsewhere.

Another example, *[Title of Show]* (2006), opens with the words 'A D D D D Fsharp A will be the first notes of our show'. The song refers to song creation and the creation of a 'show' that is entirely reflexive as the characters set about the process of writing a musical. This was also extended in the casting of the original production with the writers of *[Title of Show]*, Jeff Bowen and Hunter Bell, playing fictionalized versions of themselves.

We have argued in the previous chapters that musical theatre is a product of diverse influences and opportunities among its creative teams. In this chapter we are pushing this idea further and exploring the ways in which musicals refer to other musicals, to performances on stage or in other media.

In short, rather than thinking of a musical as having a single chronological narrative from which a single meaning emerges, what Roland Barthes describes as a '"message" from the author/god' (1977, p. 146), many musicals construct their story by consciously referencing a number of different sources and texts (in which 'a variety of writings, none of them original, blend and clash' [ibid.]). The result is that audiences are aware of the fact that they are constructed works, being performed on a stage by performers, as in the examples above. Rather than sitting in isolation, musicals are cultural artefacts that adapt to local contexts and popular culture, often referencing that culture deliberately and provocatively within the text.

As implied in the quotations from Roland Barthes, as argued in his essay 'The Death of the Author', such works generate multiple ideas about interpretation or stimulate new texts and conversations. From this we argue that the idea of a musical as having a single discoverable meaning starts to splinter. Instead, the focus shifts from analysis of a single production or work whose meaning (the meaning imposed by its author) is to be discovered, to texts that can be interpreted by diverse audiences, in different contexts, who may or may not recognize all the references. This concept is called intertextuality, and it can be produced in many ways, one of which is by referencing other musicals or other well-known texts. Because of its multiplicity of signs (in music, lyrics, dialogue, dance, design and action, that might reference songs, films, novels, plays, television shows and even online tweets or hashtags) musical theatre is an important vehicle for understanding how interpretation and the role of the audience in constructing meaning began to change.

Alongside film to stage and stage to film 'intermedial' adaptations that have existed since the early years of film, in recent years new media has made more musicals available in more ways. Not only have audiences become valued for their work in the construction of meaning within contemporary texts, but those texts have become more available in more forms to larger and more diverse global audiences who ultimately become co-creators of original content.

Consequently, rather than thinking of a musical theatre work simply in relation to the written source material or even a production of that work in one or several physical locations, we start to understand that a musical expands to include its ephemera, its offshoots, the social media, digital discussions and performances as well as cast albums, programmes and performer blogs. Rather than a text being interpreted just by directors and producers, audiences or 'readers' can take ownership of their experience.

A musical becomes not just an expensive performance in a fixed form but exists as a catalyst for a network of new and diverse, globally available, digital texts way beyond our original transatlantic axis. This chapter, then, traces the musical from its physical location in one of the centres of musical theatre, to its globally available democratized (or seemingly democratized) iterations among fans.

KEY CONCEPT: Intertextuality

The term 'intertextuality' refers to a connection between two (or more) texts. It was coined by theorist Julia Kristeva in the 1960s to describe how all language is recycled. For instance, we used the word 'recycled' in the previous sentence because this word has been used in similar ways before, perhaps in similar sentences, and so seemed an appropriate choice. It also has connections with environmental concerns that are not directly relevant here but might inform the currency and context of the word. For Kristeva, then, all language comes with a kind of 'cultural baggage' – what she describes as being dialogic – where a word's current use is laden with memories of other usages. More recently, the term has been used to refer to intertextual references: the direct acknowledgment or quoting of another text. All adaptations are intertextual, of course, where one whole text becomes another whole text, and if the adaptation has crossed between media (say from screen to stage) they are referred to as intermedial. Therefore, even the phrase 'Once upon a time' is not an isolated phrase but understood in the context of other works of literature, film and more.

Musical theatre has always been an adaptive and highly intertextual art form. Since Claudio Monteverdi's *L'Orfeo* in 1607, an opera based on the Greek myth of Orpheus (over four hundred years before *Hadestown* [2019] recycled the same story), various forms of musical theatre have borrowed from literature, film, popular music and classical mythology, while also featuring satire, pastiche and various cultural references. Literary adaptations – in our case we refer to musicals derived from plays, novels or poems – are the first and most pervasive form of borrowing. There have also been numerous film musicals turned into stage shows, and stage musicals turned into films, as well as jukebox musicals that craft a story around a collection of popular songs. Musicals have also been created online, on television, or as specific episodes in non-musical television series. Moreover, musicals are understood alongside other artefacts and paratexts such as programmes, posters, cast recordings, printed music, award shows, social media posts and reviews. Such texts sometimes even replace the theatrical experience, to the extent that the definition of what a musical is, and how far its network of texts extends, is rather expansive.

This web of connections and exchanges is also transatlantic and, beyond that, transnational. Professional productions in their Broadway and West End productions now reach across media, as well as across countries and continents, and productions can be accessed and interacted with in locations far removed from London and New York. The Internet empowers audiences potentially to be more involved and know more about the works they choose to see, meaning they can be fans of musicals they have never seen live. The ubiquity and availability of all forms of popular culture has reached new levels online, and that has resulted in musicals that consciously respond to cultural trends by recycling books, films, popular songs and more, from across the globe. This chapter, then, tells another story about the development of musical theatre, as a multifaceted form that both borrows from, and is borrowed by, numerous texts and media. It not only tracks musical theatre and film backwards and forwards across the Atlantic, but it also traces the idea that the role of audiences as 'readers' and interpreters of texts became increasingly important and empowering as the opportunities provided by new media transformed and internationalized fan culture.

Literary adaptations

From *Show Boat* (1927) and *Pickwick* (1965) to *Aspects of Love* (1989) and *Wicked* (2003), on both sides of the Atlantic, there exists a long-standing tradition of musicals being based on novels and literary sources. Moreover, American musicals like *My Fair Lady* (1956) and *Sweeney Todd* (1979) are adapted from British plays, while *Cats* (1981) and both versions of *The Wild Party* (LaChiusa, 2000; Lippa, 2000) are based on poetry. This reliance on literary sources, particularly novels, stems from such works featuring 'carefully developed storylines, usually with copious forward momentum, and well-rounded protagonists' (Jubin, 2016, p. 120). In taking what was once written prose and communicating it as musical theatre, however, the creative team must reduce long and complex narratives into a mimetic (action-based) medium, as well as into a theatrical experience that alternates between song, dance and dialogue (each of which conveys information at a different speed). Charles Dickens's novel *Oliver Twist* (1839), for example, is typically printed at around 300 pages, which would take approximately ten hours to read, yet Lionel Bart's musical version, *Oliver!* (1960), plays for only two and a half hours. Although several passages of text can be illustrated visually (for instance, by staging a description of London using scenery and lighting), multiple characters and events were removed from the novel to produce a more concise theatrical experience that has been globally popular (see Napolitano, 2014). At the same time individuals on seeing the show might also connect it with the film version of the musical (Reed, 1968), or any of the eight earlier films of *Oliver Twist*, or the 1988 Disney animated film version *Oliver & Company* (Scribner) with animals as the main characters. Each interpretation becomes distinctive with different themes foregrounded.

Literary texts are adapted to fulfil the structural requirements of musical theatre (two acts, in less than three hours, with music, dance and spectacle), but they are also adapted to speak to changing cultural contexts. For example, *West Side Story* (1957) relocates Shakespeare's *Romeo and Juliet* from Verona to examine teenage gang-warfare in 1950s New York. It derives the key plot events from Shakespeare (who had himself adapted an earlier text) but substantially alters the context, character names, and more, to reflect the context in which the musical was written and performed. Contemporary audiences might also relate this musical now to other adaptations on both sides of the Atlantic. Such works include many productions of the Shakespeare text, operatic and balletic performances, any number of film versions including the Baz Luhrmann film (1996), the Bollywood blockbuster, *Ram Leela* (Bhansali, 2013), Tom Stoppard's *Shakespeare in Love* (Madden, 1998), or indeed, Lin-Manuel Miranda's musical *In the Heights* (2008), of which there is also a film version (2021). Individual audience members draw their own connections as they interpret and enjoy the narrative.

Steven Sater and Duncan Sheik's 2006 musical, *Spring Awakening*, based on Frank Wedekind's play of 1891, makes a feature of the clash between two opposing onstage worlds to reflect the gap between the story's setting and the context of the performance, as well as the worlds of adults and teenagers. The cover image of the libretto (Figure 3.1) demonstrates

Figure 3.1 Cover of the libretto of *Spring Awakening* (2007) demonstrating anachronistic costume and sexual content.

this ambiguity as well as the sexual content. In the 2006 production, the characters wore anachronistic costumes, they reacted in accordance with the historical setting, but the expressionism of the play text is reflected in the Brechtian production concept. This includes a 'sung' world of the adolescent students, in which they use contemporary hand-held microphones to sing alternative folk and punk rock songs, with modern lyrics (dating the contemporary period as 1980s or 1990s). The songs are expressions of confession, denial and admission, which may resonate with contemporary teenagers experiencing issues similar to the fictional characters (Sater and Sheik, 2007, p. ix). In 'Totally Fucked', for example, the male protagonist, Melchior, is blamed for writing an explicit essay describing sexual intercourse (despite the work being written by his late friend, Moritz, who had killed himself). As Melchior is pressured by his teachers for a confession, their demands are interrupted by increasingly violent electric guitar riffs. The 'spoken' action stops as Melchior pulls a microphone from his jacket and begins a contemporary song of teenage angst: 'There's a moment you know ... you're fucked', watched by the other young characters who later participate in the song.

CASE STUDY: *Spring Awakening* (2006)

Music: Duncan Sheik. Book and lyrics: Steven Sater.

Spring Awakening depicts a group of teenagers who feel isolated and distanced from adult life by their parents and surrounding authority figures. One girl, Wendla, is denied any knowledge of sex and reproduction by her mother and soon becomes pregnant by her boyfriend, Melchior. Later, however, the shame of unwed, teenage pregnancy leads Wendla's mother to enforce an illegal, backstreet abortion that causes Wendla's death. Overall, the musical explores education and youth, the isolation felt when communication breaks down or is denied between generations, and the often very different treatment of girls/women and boys/men.

Based on Frank Wedekind's play of the same name, which was written in 1890/91, *Spring Awakening* was not performed until 1907. The play was subject to bans and/or censorship in some countries. The musical, however, ran for over two years on Broadway, though only for two months in the West End in 2009, and remains a popular selection for amateur groups and colleges. In 2014, the multiple divisions within the narrative were exaggerated in Deaf West Theatre's revival production (which transferred to Broadway in 2015), since it featured both deaf and hearing performers. The musical was presented in simultaneous English and American sign language, often with two actors playing each role (one speaking/singing and one signing). In this case, the production explored a different kind of isolation in within minority groups.

The dialogue is set in the world of the source material, 1890s Germany, whereas the songs are set in the contemporary (and notably American) world that is experienced by the actors and the audience. On stage, these two transatlantic 'worlds' are juxtaposed aesthetically, aurally, nationally and more, meaning attention is drawn to the themes rather than audiences being immersed only in the plot. The songs and the anachronistic elements not only embody the repression of young people, but also allow audiences to understand the contemporary relevance of the politics. This is a central element of the show's dramaturgy, which adapts the source material for a twenty-first-century audience and whose anachronisms allow audiences to interpret the work in diverse ways.

Stage and screen interactions

So far, we have seen a how literary texts are refashioned for the musical stage but might have intertextual references to or connections with other performances on film or stage. There is a more obvious connection, though, as films are adapted directly into musicals (and vice versa), some of which demonstrate transatlantic journeys.

In the 1930s, for example, many vaudeville stars filmed their routines and songs, while many of the vaudeville venues were transformed into movie theatres, ultimately sounding the death knell for a whole branch of popular performance. In Hollywood, Broadway writers were hired to provide songs for film musicals, with Irving Berlin, George Gershwin, Nacio Herb Brown, Eubie Blake and Cole Porter among the many composers gathering film credits for scores or inserted songs. Such writers were also involved in the stage-to-screen transfer of existing works, which were often difficult for the creative artists since studio bosses would insist on plot changes, new material and different songs for the film version. Meanwhile, studios employed performers on long-term contracts so that they could only perform for that studio. Judy Garland and Mickey Rooney were stars of Metro-Goldwyn-Mayer (MGM), for example, while Fred Astaire and Ginger Rogers were signed to RKO where they made several films, including *Top Hat* (1935) and *Shall We Dance* (1937); thus, there are multiple intertextual connections between films with the same stars.

In Britain, many of the film musicals shown in the 1930s were American, but equally some British stars and writers were involved in the British film industry and, for film musicals, some of the leading theatre performers led the way. Gracie Fields, for example, became the highest-paid star of British film musicals in the 1930s, while *Evergreen* (1934), a film starring Jessie Matthews and based on a West End hit, largely included songs by American writers Rodgers and Hart. The interaction between theatre and film was assisted by the fact that the West End was only a few miles away from the British National Studios (now Elstree Studios) in North London with other studios based around London in Cricklewood, Ealing and Islington, rather than the 2700+ miles that separate New York and Los Angeles in America. So it was not only stories, but performers, songs, writers and composers who were significant in the network of intertextual connections between stage and screen.

The Wonderful World of Oz

Meanwhile, back in Hollywood, *The Wizard of Oz* became a landmark musical film in 1939 that has resounded in adaptations and appropriations. The film was an adaptation of L. Frank Baum's 1900 novel, *The Wonderful Wizard of Oz*, which is regularly cited as an American fairy tale: America's answer to the popular quest narratives of the Brothers Grimm and other European writers. The 1939 film, produced by MGM and starring a young Judy Garland, featured songs by Harold Arlen and lyrics by E. Y. (Yip) Harburg, with the rest of the score and incidental music composed by Herbert Stothart. The adaptation of the fantasy novel into a film script was completed by several writers hired by Arthur Freed, who produced the film, though only three were later credited. This was one of the issues many Broadway writers had with the transition to Hollywood, where they were no longer in control of their own productions. In any case, *The Wizard of Oz* was not the international success and popular cultural icon it is today. It was only after its rerelease in 1949 and its televised broadcast in 1956 that it became an annual televised treat.

MGM's *The Wizard of Oz* was not the first musical version of this story, with Baum himself adapting it as a stage musical extravaganza that toured America in 1902 – meaning this story began right at the start of the twentieth century. The production was structured in three acts and, unlike the 1939 film, acted as a star vehicle for vaudeville double act Montgomery and Stone (who played the Tin Woodman and Scarecrow), rather than the actress playing Dorothy. Jonas Westover describes this adaptation as the 'birth of a [musical] brand' that only later became synonymous with ruby slippers, a green-faced witch and the song 'Over the Rainbow' (all elements introduced in the 1939 film) (2019). That is not the end of the story, of course.

In 1945, a stage version was created using the novel and the songs from the film for a production in St. Louis. Later, in 1987, the Royal Shakespeare Company in Britain developed a stage version of the film, with a book adapted by John Kane, which incorporated most of the songs from the film. This production, directed by Ian Judge, was an exceptional production for the company, since it employed an American orchestrator to recreate the sound of the film score that would be played live by twenty-three musicians at the Barbican Centre in London. Both these adaptations were commercially successful, but the next British adaptation of this American classic would be even bigger. In 2011, Andrew Lloyd Webber, working with director Jeremy Sams, adapted the 1939 film for a West End production. Alongside songs from the film, this version contained additional songs by Lloyd Webber and Tim Rice and, in a novel twist, the role of Dorothy was cast through a reality television competition called *Over the Rainbow* on primetime national television (more below). The production later toured to Canada, the United States and Australia. Again, that is not the end of the *Oz* story.

While the British were creating new theatrical adaptations of this successful and much-loved film musical, American creative teams were appropriating elements of the story to develop new works that had intertextual connections with the film or novel (see Birkett and McHugh, 2019). *The Wiz* (1975), for example, is a reimagining of Baum's novel for a contemporary African American context and cast of performers of colour. It had a book by William F. Brown and original music and lyrics from Charlie Smalls, Luther Vandross and others. Supported by Twentieth Century Fox, the production opened in Baltimore and had a Broadway try-out in Philadelphia in 1974, before arriving on Broadway in 1975. This was followed by tours and revivals in Europe, Australia and Britain. A film version was made in 1978, starring Diana Ross and Michael Jackson; plus NBC developed *The Wiz Live!* for television in 2015. And then came the megahit *Wicked* in 2003.

CASE STUDY: *Wicked* (2003)

Music and lyrics: Stephen Schwartz. Book: Winnie Holzman.

This musical is based on Gregory Maguire's 1995 novel *Wicked: The Life and Times of the Wicked Witch of the West*, which is a revision of Baum's original novel. Rather than focusing on Dorothy and her journey through Oz, however, *Wicked* explores the backstory of the two witches, especially Elphaba, the Wicked Witch of the West.

Glinda (formerly Galinda – the good witch) tells the story (in flashback) of how she and Elphaba became friends. Both were pupils at Shiz University, where, at first, they are enemies; Elphaba is different, reclusive and green, while Galinda is blonde, pretty and popular. They disagree over many things and are rivals for the love of Fiyero, a popular new arrival, but they quickly start to respect each other and later become friends. Elphaba's magical power is immense, and she is invited to meet the Wizard. Elphaba takes Glinda with her to ask for help in saving the anthropomorphic Animals who are losing power of speech. At the meeting, it becomes obvious not only that the Wizard is a fraud, but that he is behind the policy of removing speech from Animals and caging them. Elphaba swears revenge on the Wizard, runs away and takes to the skies on a broomstick to escape. Gradually, more and more offences are falsely blamed on Elphaba, and the Wizard tries to capture her using her sister, Nessarose, as bait. Elphaba returns to discover that her sister has been killed when Dorothy's house fell on her, and Glinda has given her ruby slippers to Dorothy as she heads down the yellow brick road (or so the familiar story goes). Elphaba and Fiyero are united but both are being pursued, so they fabricate Elphaba's death; she melts when water is thrown on her, while Fiyero is turned into the scarecrow for protection. The two leave Oz together in secret, sorry that Glinda, who vows from now on to earn the title of good witch, is left to mourn them alone.

Opening on Broadway in 2003, in London in 2006, and having played internationally ever since, *Wicked* is both an adaptation of Gregory Maguire's novel and an intertextual appropriation of *The Wizard of Oz*. The result is a musical that revises how various characters in the earlier film are viewed, which ultimately encourages audiences to consider how appearances can be deceptive. Elphaba's green skin, Nessarose's disability and the caging of the speaking animals can all be viewed as political comments about difference, about minorities and about discrimination. Moreover, to amplify the intertextual relationships, the musical 'self-consciously poaches lines from the movie: for instance, when Nessa asks, "What's in the punch?" Boq answers, "Lemons and melons and pears," and Nessa replies, "Oh my!"' (Wolf, 2008, p. 4), thus parodying lines from the earlier film.

Finally, the importance of female friendship is at the centre of this work, with the representation of Elphaba and Glinda operating in dialogue 'with a contemporary lexicon of "girl power" images such as strong, independent, supernaturally powerful television action heroines like Xena or Buffy, or girls' friendship films like *Heathers, Mean Girls*, or even *High School Musical*' (Wolf, 2008, p. 5). In fact, Stacy Wolf argues further that it is possible not just to see the two girls as friends, co-conspirators and competitors, but 'if one sees them through the conventions of musical theatre upon which *Wicked* is built, they look like a queer couple' (2008, p. 20). While this is a very particular argument that we need not pursue here, the presence of two women as the protagonists of this work is important in relation to girl power and the interactions of feminism within musical theatre texts (see Chapter 5). This work, as an adaptation of one text, appropriation of another, and containing intertextual references to many, is also important for its politics, that are revealed by considering its intertexts and its contexts. Given these complexities and overlaps, *The Wizard of Oz* continues to be told through song on both sides of the Atlantic, though in different versions and adaptations, and remains a key example of how musical theatre recycles and revamps across media and across the world.

The Hollywood film musical

In the 1940s and early 1950s, MGM began to create original film musicals such as *Meet Me in St. Louis* (1944), *Anchors Aweigh* (1945) – in which Gene Kelly famously danced with an animated mouse – and *Seven Brides for Seven*

Brothers (1954). These films expanded the celebrity status of Hollywood stars like Judy Garland, Frank Sinatra, Bing Crosby and Howard Keel. In the decades that followed, the film musical became a central part of popular cinema and culture.

The film *Singin' in the Rain* (1952), for example, documents the development of the film industry in a comedy classic that is also notable for its intertextuality and reflexivity; the film takes every opportunity to refer to the creation and performance of film and theatre. It includes images of the early development of film, from the silent film studios to the later sound recording efforts of several pioneers, and the efforts of actors to transition between silent and sound film. With music by Nacio Herb Brown, lyrics by Arthur Freed, and book by Betty Comden and Adolph Green, the film also incorporates scenes from *The Jazz Singer* (1927), the very first film of the 'sound era' or the first 'talkie'. *The Jazz Singer* is considered problematic today due to the depiction of Al Jolson in blackface make-up for a performance in a stage musical (*April Follies*), but it is also a musical in which Jolson performs six numbers, including 'My Mammy', that has been remade twice on film (in 1952 and 1980) and once on television (1959) in America. *The Jazz Singer* is not only the first sound film, however, but the first Hollywood film musical. Accordingly, *Singin' in the Rain* is a reflexive record of its own history, particularly as most of Brown and Freed's songs had already appeared in earlier MGM musicals (making the film somewhat of an early jukebox musical). The film won an Academy Award for Donald O'Connor, a Writer's Guild of America Award for Comden and Green and is often regarded as the greatest film ever made by the 'Freed Unit' (headed by Arthur Freed) at MGM.

As with *The Wizard of Oz*, the enormous success of this film was followed, years later, by a theatrical adaptation that mirrored the film version very closely. *Singin' in the Rain*, the stage musical, was developed in Britain in 1983 during a period of interest in American popular culture and was directed by Tommy Steele (who also starred as Don Lockwood), with choreography by Peter Gennaro (the American co-choreographer of *West Side Story* with Jerome Robbins). Gennaro also worked with Bob Fosse on the original production of *The Pajama Game* (1954), meaning he brought distinctly American choreography and physicality to this adaptation. The book was a particularly faithful adaptation of the film's script, with all the same writing team on board, and the additional songs were also classic songs of the era. The show transferred to Broadway for a season in 1985 but otherwise has been almost entirely a British favourite with repeated revivals and tours. One of the most notable features of the production is the use of onstage rain during the recreation of the famous 'Singin' in the Rain' sequence, which demonstrates the extent to which the show aims to offer audiences a recreation of the famous movie from which it has been adapted. It is in productions like this that questions emerge about the nature of originality in works that reference, adapt or appropriate earlier successes. And, of course, the argument has long been made that such works are popular because of audience familiarity, not just with the works and their titles, but with music and stars as well. Musicals like *Singin' in the Rain* thus remain globally popular – or at least recognized – because of the recreation of iconic images and songs that originated in 1950s Hollywood.

Several important film adaptations in the 1950s and 1960s followed, including *West Side Story* (1961 [1957]), *My Fair Lady* (1964 [1956]), *The Sound of Music* (1965 [1959]) and *Oliver!* (1968 [1960]) each of which won the Academy Award (Oscar) for Best Picture in their respective years – meaning four of the decade's most acclaimed films were musicals. Later, Richard O'Brien's cult hit *The Rocky Horror Show* (1973) and *The Rocky Horror Picture Show* (1975) achieved transatlantic success, having been written and performed in Britain but set in America (though arguably the world inside the castle/spaceship is a parody of British culture). Its star, Tim Curry, can be seen in the costume worn in the original production in Figure 3.2. This last theatre/film translation is also intertextual in populating an original narrative with countless references to horror and science fiction 'B' movies, gothic literature, rock 'n' roll music and even nods to the popular bodybuilder, Charles Atlas.

Other innovations were film-to-stage musicals like *The Producers* (2005 [2001/1967]) and *Hairspray* (2007 [2002/1988]) that were adapted, once again, as musical films, making them film-to-stage-to-film musicals.

Numerous film adaptations of stage musicals followed through to the twenty-first century, where Rob Marshall reinvented the genre with *Chicago* (2002 [1975]). Since the turn of the century, the film-to-stage musical has also become more significant again, led by Baz Luhrmann's *Moulin Rouge!* (2001) that is now a stage musical adapted by John Logan (2019). In 2005, *Billy Elliot: The Musical* inaugurated the recent spate of adaptations in Britain, as one of the most celebrated and critically lauded musicals in recent decades. Following this, films like *Made in Dagenham* (2014 [2010]) and *Calendar Girls* (2017 [2003]) have been transformed into stage musicals with rather less success.

Figure 3.2 Tim Curry in the stage version of *The Rocky Horror Show* (1973), a role he recreated in *The Rocky Horror Picture Show* (1975), and a performance that has become iconic. Photo: © Johnny Dewe Matthews.

The next innovation in America was that film studios like MGM, DreamWorks and Warner Bros. each developed stage divisions to convert their popular hits into stage shows. *Legally Blonde: The Musical* (2007 [2001]), *Shrek: The Musical* (2010 [2001]) and *Elf: The Musical* (2010 [2003]) have found varying success on Broadway, in the West End and around the world. *Legally Blonde*, for example, played for nearly double the number of performances in London than it managed in New York and is a touring and amateur hit, despite (or perhaps because of) being the adaptation of a quintessentially American film. Meanwhile, the British-born *Charlie and the Chocolate Factory* (2013), based on the 1964 book by Roald Dahl, played for less than a year in New York, despite the Broadway version adding songs from the 1971 film, *Willy Wonka & the Chocolate Factory*, to boost the show's familiarity and American appeal. In other words, there is no single formula for producing a successful film-to-stage musical on either side of the Atlantic. The levels of critical and popular acclaim can vary on each side of the Atlantic. More interesting, though, are the different kinds of adaptation in respect of how songs are framed in the more realistic performance of film, and the level of mirroring of the film's visual world as well as the content of the plot. For audiences it is interesting the extent to which the work seen first is regarded as the originator in an individual's conception of the text – so those people who saw the stage version of *Sweeney Todd* or *Into the Woods* first tend to prefer them to the film versions and vice versa.

Disney and the animated musical feature film

One corporation illustrates the development of cross-media interactions to the greatest extent. Founded during the silent film era by brothers Walt and Roy Disney in 1923, Disney has produced numerous successful full-length animated musicals since *Snow White and the Seven Dwarfs* in 1937. From *Cinderella* (1950) and *Peter Pan* (1953) to *The Rescuers* (1977) and *Tangled* (2010), Disney has produced over fifty animated feature films to global success, many of which are musical adaptations of literary texts, often fairy tales. However, in the 1990s, following the Broadway adaptation of several classic live-action film musicals in the 1980s, including *42nd Street* (1980 [1933]), Disney Theatrical Productions (now a subsidiary of the Disney Theatrical Group [DTG]) was formed (1993) to produce stage versions of their existing animated musicals, with related merchandise, tie-in products and even a new theatre to house these shows (as addressed in Chapter 7). Starting with *Beauty and the Beast* in 1994, an adaptation of Disney's 1991 animated film, these stage works typically retain the songs from the original film ('Belle' and 'Be Our Guest', for example), plus add new material to lengthen the score, expand dramatic moments and allow for further character development ('If I Can't Love Her' and 'Home'). This has continued since the mid-1990s, with Disney Theatrical Productions having adapted several of their films on Broadway and in the West End, plus several for the amateur market and as regional productions.

From a transatlantic perspective, one of Disney's most notable stage productions is *Mary Poppins* (2005) – a collaboration with British producer Cameron Mackintosh based on the 1964 part-animated, part-live action film musical. To expand the film's score for the stage, British writers George Stiles and Anthony Drewe were hired to provide new arrangements for existing songs by the Sherman Brothers (including 'Supercalifragilisticexpialidocious'), plus add their own songs (such as 'Practically Perfect') to merge these different musical impressions of P. L. Travers's original novel. An entirely British creative team was hired, including writer Julian Fellowes (now known as the creator of TV drama *Downton Abbey*), to bring a 'clear understanding of the social niceties of the English class system that prevailed in the Edwardian era' to this classic American film set in London (Sibley and Lassell, 2007, pp. 348–9). The musical opened first in London (the first Disney production to do so), then New York in 2006, and has played internationally ever since. Disney's strategy has brought family audiences to experience the fairy tales (and other stories) that are now better known in Disney's adaptations, rather than in earlier versions gathered by authors like Perrault, Grimm or Anderson.

Disney has not always found commercial success when adapting their films for the stage, however. For every megahit like *The Lion King* (1997 [1994]), there are assumed 'flops' (playing for over a year on Broadway is now insufficient to recoup costs) like *The Little Mermaid* (2008 [1989]) and *Tarzan* (2006 [1999]). However, the latter musical had a successful second life in a translated adaptation in Europe, where it is still playing, produced by Stage Entertainment.

Beauty and the Beast was dismissed for how similar it was to the animated film and for relying too heavily on visual spectacle. In response, Thomas

CASE STUDY: The Disney Renaissance

Since 1937, the Walt Disney Company has produced nearly sixty animated films, including *Dumbo* (1941) and *The Jungle Book* (1967), most of which are musicals. In the late 1980s, however, Disney Animation had all but died; non-musical films like *The Black Cauldron* (1985) had proved financial disasters and the department needed reenergizing. A new direction emerged when theatrical lyricist, Howard Ashman, was employed to work on *Oliver & Company* (1987) and then suggested developing *The Little Mermaid* (1989) with his theatrical collaborator, Alan Menken (the pair are remembered for their film-to-stage-to-film musical *Little Shop of Horrors* [1960 non-musical film, 1982 stage musical, 1986 film musical]). *The Little Mermaid* was a major hit, bringing musical theatre-style storytelling to animation. The pair then developed *Beauty and the Beast* (1991) and *Aladdin* (1992), though Ashman died in early 1991 before *Beauty and the Beast* had been completed. Nonetheless, his influence remains strong at Disney Animation, which produced a series of highly successful animated musicals known as the Disney Renaissance across the 1990s. Many of these animations had music composed by Menken with stage lyricists Tim Rice, Stephen Schwartz and David Zippel, while pop stars Elton John and Phil Collins also wrote songs for Disney musicals during this period. Both Fox and DreamWorks sought to compete with Disney during this time by producing *Anastasia* (1997) and *The Prince of Egypt* (1998), respectively (both of which have since been adapted for the stage). Disney Animation later turned to computer-generated, non-musical films for several years but returned to musicals with their traditionally animated (hand-drawn) film *The Princess and the Frog* in 2009 and has since produced several computer-generated musicals, including *Frozen* (2013) and *Moana* (2016).

Schumacher, the president of DTG, hired acclaimed opera director Julie Taymor to inject Disney's next stage adaptation, *The Lion King*, with her unique theatrical flair. Through a blend of Japanese Bunraku puppetry, South African music, Indonesian shadow theatre and more, Taymor developed *The Lion King* as a uniquely theatrical experience. The audience was required to suspend disbelief as puppet-laden performers roamed the auditorium and stage as though on the Serengeti plains. The show has since travelled the world, having played in London since 1999, and was turned back into film using a photo-realistic computer animated format in 2018. This process not only confirmed Disney as a corporation with an enormous impact in global musical theatre, but one whose stage productions, films, popular music, television, theme parks and merchandising are intertextually related.

Cast recordings and popular music

The stage performance is not the only means of accessing the work of musical theatre creators. At the start of the twentieth century, audiences could buy individual songs or songbooks of music that had been sung by star performers in concerts and theatre performances to play and sing around their pianos at home. It was theatre composers who provided the music industry – or the pop music charts – with songs that became popular on radio and phonograph recordings. By the 1930s, musical theatre performers were the celebrities of the day, while composers like Noel Coward, Ivor Novello, Eubie Blake, Irving Berlin and George Gershwin were household names.

Early British cast recordings came in the late 1910s with *The Mikado* being recorded and released by His Master's Voice (HMV), the first Gilbert and Sullivan operetta to be recorded in full. This was followed by the release of British recordings of American musicals like *The Desert Song* (1926) and *Show Boat* (1927) in the 1920s. These recordings were printed on vinyl and designed to be played on a home gramophone (by the privileged few that owned one).

In America, most musical theatre songs that were recorded in the 1920s and 1930s were either individual songs or short collections of songs, often in new arrangements, without a supporting ensemble, and sung by a studio cast (rather than the original cast). In 1943, however, *Oklahoma!* became the first American musical to record what would today be considered an 'original cast recording'. Much of the score was recorded with the original stage cast and orchestra, using the original orchestrations, and was led by the musical's original conductor, Jay Blackton. The recording (consisting of six 78 RPM 10-inch double-sided discs) sold over a million copies, both to the show's audience and those who could not get to New York. In this way cast recordings, or cover versions of songs performed in variety, and later on radio and then television, became important means of disseminating the music of a musical to wider audiences. It is due to this that songs are often the signifiers of a musical, known more widely than its plot.

In the decades to come, following the creation of the single (long playing) LP in the late 1940s, cast recordings frequently topped the billboard charts (alongside popular music artists). Indeed, the original Broadway cast recordings of hit musicals like *The Music Man* (1957), *Funny Girl* (1964) and *Hello Dolly!* (1964) all reached the top of the Billboard best-sellers chart. Likewise, the original Broadway cast recording of *My Fair Lady* (1956), at the time of writing, has appeared on the Billboard 200 charts for over 480 weeks (the fifth longest run for any album of any genre). Cast albums successfully reminded audiences of what they had seen, advertised what they had not seen and generated their own sales and those of sheet music providers. The music of musical theatre has thus become a separate element in this story of intertextuality.

During the 1970s and 1980s, Andrew Lloyd Webber achieved commercial success with pop albums in Britain that were only later turned into musicals, such as *Jesus Christ Superstar* (1971) and *Evita* (1978), a strategy followed by Tim Rice, Benny Andersson and Björn Ulvaeus with *Chess* (1986). In both countries, cover versions sometimes attracted attention to a musical, such as Boyzone's pop version of 'No Matter What' from Lloyd Webber's *Whistle Down the Wind* (1998), though the musical was never as successful as that song. More recently, the cast recordings of pop-influenced American shows like *RENT* (1996), *If/Then* (2014) and *Dear Evan Hansen* (2016) have become chart successes. In 2015, the Broadway cast recording of *Hamilton* (which itself references many successful rap songs) became the first cast album ever to reach number one on the fringe 2017 Billboard rap charts. Likewise, the cast recording of British musical *Six* (2018) had been streamed over 100 million times on Spotify by early 2020; it was a global phenomenon before the show had even played outside of Britain in Sydney, New York and other cities. Cast recordings remain a popular way of distilling a musical for a wider audience and are perhaps the 'most lasting documentation of performances', especially when cast recordings of revivals preserve new performances and, sometimes, revisions to the text (Reddick, 2011, p. 190).

However, the effect of cast albums on sound design is another aspect of this story that we do not have time to pursue here. Briefly, having heard albums first, audiences expected a similar sound quality in the theatre, which was much more difficult to achieve and led to significant innovations in sound technologies.

You already know you're gonna love it …

The relationship between pop music and musical theatre runs both ways, just like that between theatre and film. The reverse journey, however, has provided musical theatre with numerous jukebox musicals: a similarly transatlantic, even global, phenomenon.

CASE STUDY: The jukebox musical

Jukebox musicals are productions that feature scores constructed of existing pop songs. Such interjections have been prevalent through popular theatre history in ballad opera, burlesque, pantomime and revues, where both familiarity and intertextual reimaginings stimulated audiences to enjoy songs in new settings. However, starting with British-born *Buddy: The Buddy Holly Story* in 1989, a new wave emerged of musicals that interact with the pop music industry by recycling the music of a specific artist, group or time period/genre as part of a narrative. Not all jukebox musicals are structurally and stylistically similar, however. *We Will Rock You* (2002), for instance, threads the music of Queen through a futuristic fictional story in which rock music has been banned and needs to be recovered by a troupe of British bohemians. *On Your Feet!* (2015), on the other hand, uses the music of Gloria and Emilio Estefan, whose Latin-influenced music crossed over into the mainstream music charts in the 1980s, to depict their biography. *The Bodyguard* (2012) is an adaptation of the 1992 film of the same name, laced with the music of the film's star, Whitney Houston. There are also different approaches to diegetic performance, as the majority of *Jersey Boys* (2005), for example, depicts Frankie Valli and the Four Seasons performing in recording studios or at concerts. *Sunshine on Leith* (2007), on the other hand, mostly consists of fictional characters communicating their emotions through the music of The Proclaimers. Many of these shows end with an opportunity for audiences to sing and dance to a compilation of songs from the show in a mini-concert version (see Taylor, 2009, pp. 149–65).

Many jukebox musicals are promoted by producers eager to capitalize on an assumption that audiences will be attracted by a catalogue of songs they are already familiar with. However, in some cases the songs are revoiced in quite interesting ways. Willy Russell's *John, Paul, George, Ringo … and Bert* (1974), for example, a story about the early years of The Beatles, contained some of their famous songs revoiced by female folk singer Barbara Dickson (who went on to star in Russell's *Blood Brothers*). The songs took on a completely different intertextual potential, and new meanings emerged from the lyrics when sung by a woman. This strategy also accentuated the absence at the centre of the work, particularly as The Beatles had disbanded in 1970.

CASE STUDY: *Mamma Mia!* (1999)

Music and lyrics: Benny Andersson and Björn Ulvaeus. Book: Catherine Johnson.

Set on a Greek Island, *Mamma Mia!* depicts a young girl, Sophie Sheridan, trying to discover which of her mother's past boyfriends is her father: Sam, Bill or Harry. Sophie secretly invites all three men to her wedding (to fiancé, Sky), much to her mother, Donna's, disbelief. Confusion reigns, and the identity of Sophie's father is not discovered, but ultimately Sky and Sophie decide not to marry but to travel, while Donna and Sam rekindle the flames of their old romance and marry.

The musical opened in London in 1999 and in New York immediately after the 9/11 terrorist attacks in 2001. The Broadway transfer is cited by actress Meryl Streep, who later played Donna in the 2008 film version, as acting as a form of medicine for the city's grief. *Mamma Mia!* has since been performed in twenty languages, in over forty countries, to over 60 million people, and has regenerated a cultural interest in the music of ABBA.

Arguably, the most significant and successful example of the jukebox musical trend is British-born *Mamma Mia!* (1999). Structurally, Catherine Johnson threads twenty-one existing ABBA songs across the musical. For scholar Olaf Jubin, each song is used in one of four ways: as a classic book number, an acknowledged performance, background music or an impromptu performance where the characters sing along to famous pop hits such as

'Dancing Queen' (Gordon et al., 2016, p. 200). These different song types generate a variety of musical storytelling moments across the score, meaning that ABBA's songs are threaded through these characters' lives in intricate ways (just as they may be threaded through the lives of the audience members). Perhaps more importantly, the strategy taken by Johnson to regender the singers, and place certain ABBA songs in a narrative context that results in the rejection of husbands and fathers, subverts each song's original meaning and context to ultimately provide a feminist message (Womack, 2009, p. 201). That the work was developed by a female led production team (including producer Judy Craymer), as well as a female book writer, may to some extent account for the way the appropriation and revoicing of the songs offered a political commentary. What is important here, though, is the opportunity the show provides for diverse meanings to emerge depending on audience awareness of the ABBA songs in their own lives and in earlier incarnations.

Television musicals

With black-and-white television sets becoming standard home appliances in the 1950s (and in colour from the late 1960s), in both Britain and America, television soon became a popular platform for distributing song and dance. Many early television musicals struggled to generate their own characteristics or style, however, and instead relied on imitating live theatre (Stilwell, 2011, p. 153). Mary Martin starred in *Peter Pan* in 1955, for instance, an adaptation of the 1954 American stage musical, in which the camera moved through a series of end-on positions (as if replicating the view of various seated audience members). That said, as technology developed, television musicals adopted a more fluid, often three-dimensional, style that distinguished them from their stage counterparts. In turn, this generated a series of original television musicals that capitalized on the unique features of this growing genre. *The Boys from Boise* (1944), *High Tor* (1956) and *Cinderella* (1957), for example, were each developed exclusively for American television and were thus structured differently from stage musicals. It was also at this time when film musicals began to be distributed on American television where they reached new, younger and more diverse audiences (as with *The Wizard of Oz*).

As with the film musicals discussed so far, the television musical seemed to fade in the 1970s, 1980s and 1990s (though film screenings on television continued). Although there are some exceptions, including Victoria Wood's one-off British musical drama *That Day We Sang* (2014), the feature-length television musical was seen to be a thing of the past. The start of its (rather fragmented) resurgence began, however, when existing non-musical television series. American series *Ally McBeal* and *Buffy the Vampire Slayer*, for example, each broadcast 'musical episodes' in the late 1990s and early 2000s, which, in turn, generated a trend that has been followed by more recent television shows like *Grey's Anatomy* and *Riverdale*. The 2007 musical episode of *Scrubs*, for example, titled 'My Musical', was framed as if a hospital patient, Patti Miller, after falling unconscious, suddenly starts to hear those around her communicating through song. As with film musicals, it is instructive to explore how songs are framed in these episodes: whether or when characters sing within the plot of a television drama, as well as to analyse intertextual revisions from earlier iterations of songs.

Following a string of single musical episodes, several entirely musical television series found popular success in the late 2000s. Fox's *Glee*, for instance, ran for six seasons from 2009 to 2015 and depicted the friendships and romances of a fictional high school glee club. Rachel Bloom's *Crazy Ex-Girlfriend* (2015–19) ran for four seasons, whereas NBC's *Smash* (2012–13) was axed after only two. In Britain, important series were Dennis Potter's *Pennies From Heaven* (1978) in which a sheet music salesman mimes to original recordings of the music he is selling, and *The Singing Detective* (1986) that uses songs in the medicated inner world of the hospital patient as well as in the story he is writing about a detective who, in his free time, sings at a dance hall. Televised versions of Victoria Wood's variety show sketches, and the musical *Acorn Antiques* (2005) followed, but otherwise there have been few recent television musicals produced in Britain. The relative scarcity of television musicals may be because of the perceived difficulty of breaking into song in the more realistic style of television drama.

Elsewhere, NBC's *The Sound of Music Live!* regenerated the feature-length television musical in 2013. Rather than a filmed stage performance, this production was created solely for television – a live television 'event'. The musical was rehearsed over several weeks, led by singer Carrie Underwood as Maria, and was performed and televised live on a single evening. Despite mixed critical reviews, this led to other American television networks creating their own 'live musicals', including Fox's *Grease: Live* (2016), plus further offerings like *The Wiz Live!* (2015) and *Hairspray Live!* (2016) on NBC. In Britain ITV copied the trend with its own live production of *The Sound of Music* (2015). This is an interesting phenomenon because it appears to try to replicate the liveness of theatre in a technologically mediated form, but always using very well-known shows/films from another era that create an intermedial and nostalgic connection.

As noted in the discussion of *The Wizard of Oz* above, another interaction developed between stage musicals and television in Britain – a fashion for casting a leading character for a stage production through a reality television show. This structure gave audiences a new kind of empowerment in relation to popular television and an investment in seeing the live show at a later date. Starting with *How Do You Solve a Problem like Maria?* to cast the 2006 London revival of *The Sound of Music*, Andrew Lloyd Webber devised a series of BBC television shows in which the lead roles of West End revivals would be cast by a panel of judges with the final vote being taken by a television audience. Following the model of reality shows like *The X Factor* (2004–21), television audiences could select *their* Maria, Joseph, Nancy or Dorothy in stage productions he would then produce (only two of which included Lloyd Webber's music).

Many of the shows' contestants (the majority of whom were already trained performers) have since continued their professional careers, including Rachel Tucker and Samantha Barks – neither of whom won their series. These shows provided an expanded audience for musical theatre through the pre-sold familiarity of the leading actor, though there were also complaints that the format was only available to one production company. This trend was also replicated, however briefly, in America, casting Broadway productions of *Grease* in 2007 and *Legally Blonde* in 2008.

Despite their initial popularity, both trends seem to have faded. A stage musical has not been cast on television, on either side of the Atlantic, since BBC's *Let It Shine* found a replica boy band for Take That's *The Band* in 2017. Similarly, the presumed failure of Fox's *RENT: Live* (2019), in which pre-recorded rehearsal footage stood in for an injured performer, led to NBC cancelling *Hair Live!* (planned for later that year). All is not lost, however, since as each medium grows and shifts, so too will the ways in which the musical finds itself circulated across media.

Social media and the worldwide web (of show tunes)

As with every chapter in this book, there are multiple further histories that could be added to what has been a fragmented history of musical theatre's interaction with other media. Missing from the above, for example, is any acknowledgement of West End and Broadway casts performing on television chat shows and at televised special events (such as award ceremonies). This transatlantic history receives its final layer, however, when we consider the rise of the Internet, a global communication space that transcends national boundaries and permits multifaceted interactions across texts and media.

Since the mid-1990s, the Internet has transformed the musical theatre industry and the possible interactions between production, performer, creator and audience (see MacDonald, 2017). Audiences are no longer required to phone the theatre's box office, or go there in person, since tickets can now be booked months in advance via multiple online ticket sellers (and, more recently, digital apps like TodayTix – currently used in cities in Britain, America and Australia). Similarly, it is possible to buy West End or Broadway merchandise from anywhere in the world, thanks to websites like Playbill or Dress Circle. Fans can become 'walking advertisements' for a musical, by donning a *Mamma Mia!* T-shirt, for instance, without ever having set foot in the theatre, city or continent in which the musical is playing (Rebellato, 2009b, p. 47). Likewise, cast recordings, YouTube clips and video adverts provide moments of visual, as well as aural, performance that can be downloaded as digital files, or streamed via subscription services like Spotify, thus rendering physical CDs somewhat redundant.

In addition to expanding the availability of musical theatre-related paratexts, the Internet has also enabled the construction of various online fan communities. Since the mid-1990s, distinct fan communities have collectively been generated in relation to specific musicals, often with identifiable group names. *RENT* (1996) fans, for example, were collectively termed 'RENT-heads', a title fans bestowed upon themselves, to create a group identity as they queued outside the theatre for rush tickets (day seats in Britain) or discussed the musical on early online message boards (MacDonald, 2017, pp. 23–4). More recently, bootleg recordings of live performances have become one of the key interaction points for fans online. With most smart phones now facilitating HD filming, fans regularly help to generate and prolong a production's fan following by capturing and sharing it online. Websites like YouTube are littered with full-length videos of Broadway and West End productions, often hidden under obscure titles, which fans actively watch and comment on. Fans not only watch musicals they may never get to see live, however, but edit together compilation and comparison videos that merge several recorded performances for further discussion. The vocal riffing of Elphaba in *Wicked*, for example, is a conversation topic in multiple fan-created videos that compare various actresses singing certain phrases in songs such as 'Defying Gravity'. Furthermore, bootlegs can also provide 'power and status' within fan communities. If a fan has secured a particularly rare bootleg, for instance, especially when the producers of shows like *Hamilton* (2015) attempt to remove these recordings online, they often have the cultural caché to accept payment to share their findings or 'work'. Fans therefore 'choose either to perform the role of beneficent gift giver or hardened capitalist' when interacting with other fans, who may not have access to such desirable material (Hillman-McCord, 2017, p. 135). Here, we arrive at the audience or reader having transformed themselves into creators of content that references the musical source text that may already be an adaptation.

The Internet has also enabled increased interaction with, or access to information about, certain performers and shows on social media. Twitter accounts like @WestEndCovers, for example, announce which London musicals will have understudies or alternate performers that day, enabling fans from across the globe to follow the working patterns of any specific performer (thus generating a culture where fans can follow certain swings or standbys, not the main star). Many productions also use social media to generate further 'performances' online; these can be enjoyed in addition to the live stage musical or even as a replacement. Broadway.com, for example, created their first vlog series (a video blog) for *Spring Awakening* in 2006 and has since generated over 1,000 different 'Backstage at' videos for different shows. Actress Lesli Margherita, for instance, who played Mrs Wormwood in *Matilda: The Musical* (2011), created twenty-four episodes of her vlog, 'Looks Not Books', across her two Broadway stints in this role from 2013. Most of Margherita's videos are between ten and twenty minutes long and document a variety of backstage antics, including Margherita warming up, responding to fan mail, teasing other cast members and more. These videos, along with those created by performers like Laura Osnes and Billy Porter for other musicals, reflect a recent trend in allowing fans backstage at a professional production. In Britain, stage actress Carrie Hope Fletcher has also developed a career as an author and YouTube vlogger. Her vlog, which started as a series of cover versions of popular songs, now features short vlogs documenting Fletcher's preparation for musicals (like 'Veronica Vlogs' for the British premiere of *Heathers: The Musical* [2014]). No longer are musicals 'ticket only' events, then, reserved for those who can afford to visit the theatre in person, but for fans around the world looking to discover more about live theatre. Fans are allowed backstage, albeit digitally, into an environment that was previously the exclusive domain of professional theatre makers, and performers have a social media presence and 'brand' identity. The musical source has become a catalyst for a host of new creative offerings by PR companies, but also, crucially, by fans.

Other social media sites have, in turn, continued this interactivity, though often in much more fragmented ways. The official Instagram accounts of various musicals, plus fan-led accounts like 'West End Wilma' in Britain, have created platforms for 'Instagram Takeovers'. These videos are broadcast unedited, usually around a minute in length, and typically provide backstage access for a single day or even a week. These interactions – and others like them – illustrate Patrick Lonergan's argument that, like theatre, 'social media is a performance space'. Social media 'forces new ways of thinking about authenticity, creative proprietorship, authorial intention, and the relationship between artist and audience', with commercial musical theatre acting as a key illustration of these various crossovers (2015, p. 5). Broadway and the West End therefore regularly appear in the hands of fans, many of whom will never see the show they adore, since social media has splintered the form (rather successfully) into one that is accessible across media and, more recently, across devices.

Social media is a central element of popular culture. It has impacted how humans interact with one another, explore their physical surroundings and, for us, access musical theatre away from live performances. Television shows like *Black Mirror* (2011–) have documented (and problematized) this global dependence on digital technologies, yet very few musicals feature characters who are 'defined by and dependent upon the content and context of their high-tech habitations' (Stiehl, 2017, p. 44). Benj Pasek, Justin Paul and Steven Levenson's *Dear Evan Hansen* (2016), however, brings this discussion full circle. It is that rare beast: an original musical. It is not based on a film, television show, set of popular songs, and so on but provides a story of real-world teenagers affected by their use of social media and digital technologies. Having fabricated a friendship with his recently deceased classmate, Evan finds popularity and acceptance online, which promotes positive change in his human interactions. This does not last, however, since social media only promotes temporary improvement.

In addition to exploring the impact of social media in its narrative, the marketing and online interaction framing *Dear Evan Hansen* keeps musical theatre in the contemporary cultural mainstream. Ever since the musical first played in Washington, DC, in 2015, fans have been invited to provide photos of themselves, videos, and other content, that will then be used in the production's marketing campaigns. For example, fans are invited to upload photos of themselves for inclusion on the musical's poster. These are then selected and included as part of a mosaic of faces that appears behind the show's main logo and text. This relates to the text of one of the musical's key songs, 'You Will Be Found', in which isolated individuals are advised that there is a community out there for them (that will, in turn, find them). The production therefore capitalizes on the isolation felt by many teenagers, like those depicted onstage, and repurposes their generosity as marketing material (see Rush, 2021a). This example alone illustrates the now highly interactive environment in which musical theatre operates. Fans are not restricted to singing along to a cast recording at home, but, often, actively invited to share their fandom around the world and be a part of a much broader (though digital) conversation.

Conclusion

This story is almost at an end, but the ways musical theatre will continue to interact with other media and forms are not. As we have stressed from the start, musical theatre is a cultural artefact, one that has flourished in both Britain and America, that interacts with the culture and society in which it is created. It is a transatlantic hybrid of theatrical traditions, but, also, an art form that intersects with the history of multiple other media; it is undeniably intertextual and intermedial to its core. *Les Misérables* (1985) was adapted from Victor Hugo's 1862 novel, for example, but it now exists in a web of different productions and paratexts, which includes various cast recordings, film versions, song covers, social media accounts, merchandise and more. In this way, musicals take on a new life that transcends nationalities, languages, cultures and, as we have seen, media, in a web that is more commonly known as popular culture, and which is (arguably) increasingly democratized. Interpretation and, more recently, creation of content have become the domain not only of writers and producers but of audiences and fans. The expansion of social media, interactivity and the digital domain into musical theatre is likely to continue with the potential to generate further evolutions in the form.

Tasks

Take one musical from the following list and analyse it to discover some of the intertextual links and references: *Into the Woods* (1987), *Moulin Rouge!* (2001/2019), *Priscilla, Queen of the Desert* (2006), *In the Heights* (2008), *The Book of Mormon* (2011). What texts are being referenced? What do these references offer the narrative? What do they say about the characters?

Devise your own jukebox musical. Would it contain an original story, be an adaptation of an existing work or tell the biography of the original artist(s)? What music would suit this story? Would it be that of a solo artist, group or from a certain era/in a certain style? Would the music be performed as acknowledged performances (diegetic) or with characters singing their emotions (non-diegetic)? What is the intended impact of each choice/selection?

Discussion topics

Why do audiences pay West End prices to attend a live performance of a film that is already well known and available at home? What is it about the experience of seeing a familiar text recycled on stage that makes film-to-stage musicals so popular?

Take one musical theatre example and examine all the paratexts associated with it (programme, poster, songs, advertising, reviews, social media posts etc.). What impression of the musical do you get from those materials? To what extent do you think they represent or even replace the live theatre experience?

Further reading – conceptual

Barthes, R. (1977) *Image, Music, Text.* Trans. Stephen Heath. London: Fontana Press.
Hillman-McCord, J. (ed.) (2017) *iBroadway: Musical Theatre in the Digital Age.* Basingstoke: Palgrave Macmillan.

Kessler, K. (2020) *Broadway in the Box: Television's Lasting Love Affair with the Musical*. New York: Oxford University Press.

Lonergan, P. (2015) *Theatre & Social Media*. Basingstoke: Palgrave Macmillan.

Further reading – case study

Rodosthenous, G. (ed.) (2017) *The Disney Musical on Stage and Screen: Critical Approaches from 'Snow White' to 'Frozen'*. London: Bloomsbury Methuen.

Rush, A. (2021a) '#YouWillBeFound: Participatory Fandom, Social Media Marketing, and *Dear Evan Hansen*'. *Studies in Musical Theatre* 15/2: 119–32.

Sternfeld, J. (2013) 'Everything's Coming Up Kurt: The Broadway Song in Glee'. In: D. Symonds and M. Taylor (eds) *Gestures of Music Theatre: The Performativity of Song and Dance*. London and New York: Oxford University Press, 128–45.

4

'Easy to be hard': From censorship to sex

During the first act of *Avenue Q* (2004), the satirical puppet musical by Robert Lopez, Jeff Marx and Jeff Whitty, several of the characters, all of whom stem from different racial, ethnic, social and cultural backgrounds, discuss what it means to be 'racist'. Gary Coleman, the once popular child star, dictates that only he can tell 'Black jokes', as the superintendent and only African American resident of the block. Similarly, white American Brian cannot refer to his Asian wife, Christmas Eve, as 'oriental', just as Kate Monster, the puppet protagonist, declares that not all 'monsters' are related or look the same. The song, 'Everyone's A Little Bit Racist', is an illustration of the covert censorship of political correctness, where both the puppet and human characters inform each other what is 'right' or 'wrong' and what is accepted terminology in the new millennium. The musical overall, however, which includes frequent swearing, racial slurs, songs about pornography and puppet sex, was in no way censored or altered. Its potentially offensive content, like that of Lopez's later musical, *The Book of Mormon* (2011), played to a liberal New York (and then international) audience, where it won the Tony Award for Best Musical. Although the show's use of puppets somewhat softens the crude humour, as a parody of the educational TV show *Sesame Street*, *Avenue Q* identifies the contemporary musical stage as a site of artistic freedom and liberty.

This was not always the case, however, especially in Britain. From 1737, until as recently as 1968, there had been official censorship of the British stage by the Lord Chamberlain's Office. This meant that the script of any play scheduled to be performed on stage had to be sent to the official censor, with a fee. The play would then be read by one of the team and, either permission would be given for the performance of that script (with no ad libs, improvisation or other adjustments), or the censors might require adjustments to the text, without which the play could not be performed. The Theatres Act of 1843 also outlawed the use of profanity, nudity, reference to royalty and any sexual acts in licensed British theatres. By the twentieth century, there was a marked contrast between the openness and liberalism of New York theatre and the strict regulations of the West End of London, meaning that revues containing glamorous and scantily clad dancers, such as George White's *Scandals*, the *Ziegfeld Follies* and the Shuberts' *Passing Shows*, developed on Broadway (not in London). There were no federal censorship laws in America, but individual states, towns and cities were responsible for licensing and funding theatres (using those controls to limit what could be performed) and applying obscenity laws at a local level, resulting in less uniformity in how such laws were applied. In New York, which was particularly liberal, nudity gradually became a feature of off and off-off Broadway shows, a move that led to both *Oh! Calcutta!* and *Hair* being developed in small-scale productions and experimental venues in the late 1960s. However, following the removal of stage censorship in Britain in 1968 that allowed these American productions to transfer, there was a backlash in America against the freedoms that had been fought for by these and other productions.

In both countries censorship has arisen as the result of public protests, political correctness or societal taboos, often in relation to the depiction of sexuality, race and religion. Such protests and taboos raise strong questions regarding the right to free speech within a theatre that supposedly reflects contemporary society. This chapter therefore focuses on two kinds of censorship: that arising from legal censorship and that where other laws are used, effectively, to censor productions – both of which may have unknowable consequences on self-censorship. Ultimately, this chapter provokes questions about whether it is a legitimate function of theatre to provoke debate by expressing controversial ideas and whether the state/ government could ever be entirely removed from questions of art, morality and some form of censorship.

This history is explored through five case studies drawn from British or American musical theatre, starting with the most recent. *Mrs Henderson Presents* (2015) dramatizes the experience of legal censorship as it was enforced in 1940s Britain by the Theatres Act of 1843. That history encompasses the Licensing Act of 1737, a legal statute designed to abolish criticism of politics and politicians, that was itself a response to the popularity of burlesques such as *The Beggar's Opera* (1728). By contrast, *The Cradle Will Rock* (1937) demonstrates how, in America, funding was one of the tools used to try to block performances. Later, the producers of *Hair* (1967) were taken to court several times before a Supreme Court decision confirmed the First Amendment Right to free speech within American theatre. Coincidentally, *Hair* was also the first musical to open in the West End after the end of legal censorship in Britain (1968). The situation remained problematic in the United States as the country's legislature moved to the right, and the debate continued over whether theatre funding through the National Endowment for the Arts (NEA) should support family entertainment or progressive depictions of race, sex and gender. Finally, we consider the different responses to *Jerry Springer: The Opera* (2003) as both a theatrical production and a television broadcast to explore the competing values of freedom of expression and the rights of individuals within a society.

KEY CONCEPT: Censorship

Censorship is a complex term to define because it operates in different legal and political contexts. The continuum extends from overt legal censorship, through covert censorship such as controlling funding and programming, or prosecuting other laws (obscenity, for example), to unconscious self-censorship that results from taboos and cultural norms.

Legal censorship is put in place by governments and is designed to enforce conformity to the ethical, moral or religious values of the state. It operates in the mistaken belief that if 'the theatre can be cleansed of obscenity, immorality, indecency and vulgarity, then the pretence that these do not exist in society can also be upheld' (O'Leary, 2016, p. 8). As such, it is generally considered to be an entirely negative concept, limiting the creative freedom of writers and performers, and producing self-censorship of individuals. However, as Michel Foucault argues, it also gives a structure that allows individuals to speak in ways that are acceptable within their community (in O'Leary, 2016). In liberal democracies, where legal forms of censorship are not in place political correctness and discussions about free speech tend to focus on the issue of competing rights, attempting to balance freedom of expression with respect for cultural differences. However, participants need to remain aware of power structures, minority beliefs and viewpoints, and as such, questions of censorship need to be discussed in relation to specific contexts.

In theatre, editors, curators, translators, producers, theatre managers, directors and writers all have a role in the choice and production of works and therefore operate, indirectly, as censors. Funders and sponsors then add further requirements and assessment criteria that similarly limit what is performed through the financial strangulation of some themes.

The first of these shows, *Mrs Henderson Presents*, is a fictional adaptation of a true story about the introduction of nudity to the London stage during the Second World War to entertain the troops on leave. Mrs Henderson, having begun her *Revudeville* (a kind of continuous revue) in 1937, began to lose money after competitors followed her lead. She decided therefore, that, like the Windmill Theatre in Paris, she would introduce female nudity. Her emotional claim was that her son was killed in the Great War having probably never seen a naked woman except in the picture postcard that was found on him when he died. Later, when the theatre was threatened with closure because of the nuisance of crowds queuing outside to see the show, Henderson argued that not only was her show artistic, but that it was only fair that all servicemen should have the opportunity to see beautiful naked women if they were going to serve, and possibly die for, their country. Whatever the truth of her motivations, and however the details of the story are adapted, Mrs Henderson, who had social connections with the second Earl of Cromer (Lord Chamberlain at the time), applied for a licence for the new show and it was granted. Alongside the comic turns, singing and dancing, the show included nude tableaux of women, a fact permitted by the censor only if the naked women did not move.

CASE STUDY: *Mrs Henderson Presents* (2015)

Music: George Fenton and Simon Chamberlain. Lyrics: Don Black. Book: Terry Johnson.

Based on Martin Sherman's 2005 film that stars Judi Dench in the title role, the musical tells the true story of a recently widowed wealthy woman, Laura Henderson, who decides to revitalize her life by buying the Windmill Theatre, Soho, in 1937. Mrs Henderson employs theatre impresario Vivian Van Damm to run the Windmill for her, though she continually interferes. The show focuses on the relationships that are forged within the company of performers and with the management, who famously 'never closed' the theatre or the show during the London Blitz of the Second World War. It also documents the relationship between Mrs Henderson and the Lord Chamberlain's office – the official censors protecting public decency.

For the stage production additional songs by Simon Chamberlain and Don Black were added to the incidental music and diegetic songs that George Fenton had composed for the film. The musical played at the Theatre Royal, Bath, before moving to the West End in 2016, and starred Tracie Bennett as Mrs Henderson.

Legal censorship in Britain, 1485–1843

Censorship in the United Kingdom had begun in 1485, when an officer of the King's court was appointed Master of the Revels under the Lord Chamberlain. It was his job to arrange and oversee performances, supervising players, singers and jugglers who would perform for the King. By 1552, this role had been extended so that a licence of the Privy Council was required before any dramatic work could be performed at court, and, by 1559, the Privy Council would not allow plays with religious or political themes to be performed. From 1581, the Master of the Revels, Edmund Tilney, was paid a fee for approving manuscripts – a process of 'prior censorship' that allowed the censor to request alterations to the manuscript before issuing a licence. The requirement had also spread beyond the court to the main theatres in the city of London. William Shakespeare, for example, became a partner of the Lord Chamberlain's Men's acting company, for whom he wrote. The censor (Lord Chamberlain) decided if the play had the correct moral tone and, if so, gave it a licence to be performed only by that company. Other companies might well complain about a conflict of interests here, since the Lord Chamberlain had a vested interest in securing the success of his own company.

Later, in the seventeenth century, censorship became the subject of an Act of Parliament under King James 1, thus further formalizing what King and government wanted the population to see. King James wanted 'to restrain the abuses of players [...] for preventing and avoiding of the great abuse of the Holy Name of God in Stage Plays, Enterludes, May-Games, Shews, and such like' (Johnston, 1990, p. 25). However, after the Civil War and throughout the period of the Commonwealth (from 1648), all patents and licences were abolished, and the playhouses closed until the Restoration of the Monarchy in 1660. It was then that Charles II issued patents to two London theatre companies who were the only companies allowed to perform plays within the city walls: Thomas Killigrew of the Theatre Royal, Drury Lane (and his company, the King's Men) and William D'Avenant of the Haymarket Theatre. These two venues became known as the patent theatres. Despite this new structure, however, it was not clear whether the patent theatres had been granted the right to perform their own plays or whether they still needed to obtain a licence from the Master of the Revels. Following this confusion, the title of Master of the Revels virtually passed to Killigrew, who became responsible for licensing and censorship.

KEY CONCEPT: Licensing

A licence is an agreement between two parties. Someone who wants something or wants to do something (A) and the owner or controller of that thing (B) agree that, for a certain price, person A can use/do the thing belonging to/controlled by person B. Licences are used in various circumstances and within different legal frameworks. To perform a stage play or musical, for example, one that is protected by copyright, a licence is required. You cannot legally drive a car without passing a test and obtaining a licence, and the licence can be removed if you infringe laws. Similarly, you cannot open/run a bar, a pub or any location serving alcohol, without a licence. Licences were also required at different times to build and operate theatres, as well as to control what was shown within them. In all these cases, fees were paid either to a licensing authority (such as the local council) and/or royalties to the generator of the cultural material (authors and composers). Perhaps more importantly, such regulations, and the uncertainties about what may be licensed, allow the state to intervene in what can be performed or done in order to promote certain moral values.

By 1696, under King William III, all plays were still required to be sent for licensing and, in 1699, notice was given to the Master of the Revels 'not to licence any Play containing expressions contrary to Good Manners and should the comedians presume to act anything he has struck out, notice is to be given to the Lord Chamberlain' (Johnston, 1990, p. 26). At this time, politicians and the monarch were thus primarily concerned with the kinds of behaviours and morality depicted in theatre, perhaps as a way of influencing the behaviour and morality of citizens. However, these powers only controlled the patent theatres, meaning there was no effective method of regulating the many unlicensed playhouses that had recently appeared in and around London.

By the 1720s, the political and theatrical landscape was changing. Robert Walpole had risen to considerable power and influence in the British parliament, despite having been briefly imprisoned for corruption in 1712. Political theatre was also becoming increasingly prevalent, most notably in the works of John Gay and Henry Fielding. Gay's *The Beggar's Opera* (1728), for instance, included a thief named Bob Booty – a nickname given to Walpole. The story satirizes the state of British political life, social inequity and injustice, in a manner that was considered unfavourable by Walpole and his party. Figure 4.1 pictures the wealthy (and therefore rotund) Peachum who acts with the same self-interest as Walpole.

Due to the popularity of *The Beggar's Opera*, its successor *Polly* (1729), and several other satirical works, Walpole decided to restrict the freedom to criticize politicians on stage. This resulted in the Licensing Act of 1737 that did far more damage than anyone could have foreseen. It controlled the spread of new theatres (since operating them was now subject to licensing) and effectively stopped the development of new playwriting by placing large fines and penalties on managers who presented drama at unlicensed venues. Only the two patent theatres could continue to produce plays, and the power of the Lord Chamberlain as censor was increased with heavy fines imposed for offending. There was no appeal or redress and, since the decisions were made by the Lord Chamberlain, they came under the royal prerogative (meaning they could not even be challenged by Members of Parliament).

New writing suffered immeasurably as the managers of the patent theatres preferred to programme tried-and-tested work of earlier periods. However, unlicensed theatres gradually reappeared in the provinces, as local magistrates issued licences for short seasons and eventually for the erection of new theatre buildings. As a result of the unenforceability of the law, then,

Figure 4.1 Front cover of the score of *The Beggar's Opera* published following its 1920 production at the Lyric Theatre, Hammersmith.

CASE STUDY: *The Beggar's Opera* (1728)

Lyrics and book: John Gay. Arrangements: Johann Christian Pepusch.

The Beggar's Opera is a ballad opera, an early British musical that featured a score built out of popular tunes of the day, with new lyrics written to fit the fictional characters and plot (as such, it is also often cited as an early jukebox musical). In it, Gay 'burlesqued' Italian opera conventions, as well as poverty, injustice and corruption (at all levels of society). Introduced by the Beggar and the Player, who directly address the audience, the story concerns corruption in a society where the rich have all the power yet manipulate the poor in order to get richer.

Peachum employs gangs of thieves (in the style of Fagin in *Oliver!* [1960]), one of whom is Macheath. Macheath, a notorious womanizer, is having an affair with Peachum's daughter, Polly, her mother, several prostitutes and Lucy Lockit. Macheath marries Polly to gain control of her entitlement to Peachum's wealth. When Peachum discovers this, he decides to betray Macheath to the authorities, so that Macheath will be hanged and Polly will inherit his money. Despite Polly helping him escape from the house, Macheath is arrested and taken to jail to be guarded by Lockit, a business associate of Peachum, whose daughter Lucy was jilted by Macheath when he married Polly. In order to escape, Macheath lies and assures Lucy he is not married, is released and immediately reverts to his old ways and is promptly recaptured. Lucy and Polly put aside their enmity to plead with their fathers for his release, before four more women enter, all of whom claim to be Macheath's wives. As Macheath asks for the hangman to be brought, the Beggar and the Player re-enter to discuss whether the play should end happily or not. Deciding it should, they encourage a reprieve for Macheath, who declares Polly his wife and the show ends happily.

The piece has been revived and adapted many times, including as Elisabeth Hauptmann, Bertolt Brecht and Kurt Weill's *Die Dreigroschenoper [The Threepenny Opera]* in 1928.

parliament was forced to make changes that gave magistrates power over the building of theatres, in many of which (even in London) light entertainment forms, with music, were permitted. It was still the case, though, that only the patent houses were allowed to perform comedy and tragedy, which were still subject to censorship. This is likely to have limited the kinds of works promoted, especially those with music and variety. In 1843, the Act for Regulating Theatres repealed the part of the 1737 Act relating to theatre buildings and licensing of theatres, but not the part relating to censorship of plays.

A changing landscape, 1843–1968

As a result of the earlier Licensing Act and the 1843 Theatres Act, but also because of Victorian sensibilities, moral propriety on stage was by now considered normal; it had become a kind of invisible self-censorship such that very little actual censorship or adjustment to submitted plays was needed. The 1843 Act confirmed the Lord Chamberlain's powers over Great Britain (but not Northern Ireland); it required one copy of every new stage play, or any alterations to an old play, to be presented seven days before a professional performance. It only applied to works with consistent plot or continuity of action; however, meaning ballet, jugglers, patter acts and circuses were excluded, along with music hall, which means Mrs Henderson's theatre might have escaped scrutiny using this loophole. However, there was no opportunity to appeal against the decisions of the censor, and, until 1909, little guidance as to what might be prohibited, except for the statement that plays should be 'fitting for the preservation of good manners, decorum or of the public peace' (Johnston, 1990, p. 30).

There were some interesting objections raised. The Prince of Wales, for instance, objected to the character of the parson (or priest) in *A Gaiety Girl* (1893). The character was changed and the show ran for 413 performances, later revived in 1899. This example reveals a landscape in which there were several other objections to the representation of the church or churchmen, or to satirical burlesques, that brought ministers of state into disrepute. Henrik Ibsen's play *Ghosts* was refused a licence in 1891, while *The Mikado* (1885) had its licence removed in 1907 during a visit of Prince Fushima of Japan. Librettist W. S. Gilbert, upon being asked to rewrite the plot, allegedly replied that to rewrite the popular operetta was a tacit admission that the 'play has gravely sinned against good taste' (Johnston, 1990, p. 44). The Lord Chamberlain finally relented, but the royal visit was over by this time.

Meanwhile, there were many objections to the continuation of censorship. In 1909, following a report that merely concluded that no legal changes should be made, a number of alterations were made in practice. The presumption to licence was introduced, and an Advisory Board replaced the single male decision-maker. The list of reasons on which decisions were made now comprised avoidance of indecency offensiveness, representation of living persons, religious irreverence or anything likely to incite crime or a breach of the peace. But, of course, there is always a question of how, for example, indecency might be interpreted, or what might constitute an offensive personality, and so on, which would always remain subjective and responsive to a conservative understanding of the social context. Similarly, it would be very limiting for playwrights to craft all their characters within this moralistic framework, even those whose voice does not reflect that of the author or the intended point of view of the play.

By the late 1930s, as depicted in *Mrs Henderson Presents*, the law stated that 'no indecency of dress, dance or gesture to be permitted on the stage'. In order to ensure this, a script was to be submitted to the board – with photographs of the poses concerned – about which the Lord Chamberlain and his (male) staff would make judgements. Members of the Chamberlain's office also attended performances to check that the rules were being complied with. The changes and clarifications that were instated at this time were that 'actresses in movement must not wear less than briefs and an opaque controlling brassiere', 'actresses may pose completely nude provided the pose is motionless and expressionless; the pose is artistic and something rather more than a mere display of nakedness; and the lighting must be subdued' and 'striptease as such is not allowed in a stage play' (Johnston, 1990, p. 127).

The last statement contains a key phrase – these productions were being licensed as *stage plays*. Private clubs and performances without a narrative plot escaped the censor's gaze. Ultimately, it was the exceptions that undermined the law, since censorship might be applied in one building and not in the building next door, making nonsense of the attempt to preserve a particular set of morals. However, during the 1940s, there were some prosecutions for breaking censorship laws, most of which were against revues, and almost all of which were successful, but none was ever taken out against the Windmill Theatre. Occasionally, prosecutions were made when actors improvised beyond or around the script that had been licensed, a particular problem with improvising comics, which led to a pantomime, *Aladdin*, being threatened with closure in Salford in 1948.

In the 1960s, publicly funded theatres were staging more controversial plays, such that there was a 'waiting box' of plays that needed alterations but whose authors or managements did not accept the changes. *Alfie* (1963) had cuts made in its dialogue, especially in an abortion scene, and *Passion Flower Hotel* (1965) was also licensed only after cuts. In response, a debate was held in parliament in February 1966 that set up a joint committee to consider obscenity, blasphemy and violence. Following its recommendations, the government decided that from 26 September 1968 the Theatres Act would be withdrawn, and plays would no longer require a licence. American transfer, *Hair*, was the first musical containing nudity to be performed in the West End. We will return to this story later, since *Hair* is also important in the history of American censorship. First, though, we need to consider what had been happening in America during these earlier centuries.

Censorship in America, 1620–1967

In 1620, the first English Puritans travelled to America aboard the Mayflower and, by 1630, the Massachusetts Bay Company was established in Boston under puritan control. Although there was one attempt at censorship in these early years (1660s), theatre was not yet a popular pastime. It was not until the mid-eighteenth century that theatres began to appear; developing at different times and places with no overarching laws governing them. Each state had its own legislature, which relegated control of theatre to local officials in towns and cities, and so diverse practices emerged.

Boston quickly became an important site for hearing secular music and for dancing, which led to the building of the Faneuil Hall (1742) and a Concert Hall (1754). Despite this new found interest in music, however, legislation was enacted in 1750 to prevent stage plays and other theatricals. Punishment was meted out for allowing performers to use space for 'acting or carrying on any stage-plays, interludes or other theatrical entertainments whosoever' (Houchin, 2003, p. 10). The ban, which lasted until 1790, was the catalyst for theatre companies to move to New York, though variety shows were still performed in Exhibition Rooms in Boston.

In Philadelphia, likewise, the Quakers saw no benefit in theatre. William Penn famously asked, 'How many plays did Jesus Christ and his apostles recreate themselves at? What poets, romances, comedies and the like did the apostles and saints make or use to pass away their time withal?' (Houchin, 2003, p. 9). Theatre was therefore banned from 1682, followed by a battle between the state and the crown, but as thousands of immigrants and increasing prosperity arrived from Europe, the cultural environment developed too. The first company of professional actors to arrive was led by Walter Murray and Thomas Kean, who produced plays at the Warehouse outside the city walls, before moving to New York in 1750 (due to Philadelphia's difficult political climate).

William Hallam closed the New Wells Theatre in London and travelled to the colonies in 1751 with a company led by his brother, Lewis. Lewis Hallam's New York Company of Comedians first played Williamsburg, VA, in 1752, opening with *The Merchant of Venice*. Discovering that the small population's interest in theatre was insufficient, they moved to New York but continued to play wherever it was congenial, including in Philadelphia in 1754 and 1759. On each occasion they had to petition the city fathers for permission in advance, unlike in New York where the situation was more straightforward. The company also toured to the colonies where, in Jamaica, Hallam died. His widow married a West Indian-based theatre manager, David Douglass, who continued the company. Unfortunately, from 1752 to 1774, censorship in the developing states was largely aimed at this company. Theatre was considered a corrupting influence by those who promoted the idea of a link between the church and the state, whereas those with Enlightenment ideals (who promoted the rights of the individual and freedom of speech) fought against such limitations. This debate continues into the present. Following the American War of Independence (1775–83), during which all theatres were closed, the company began to build its own theatres.

Not surprisingly given the freedoms noted above, it was in New York that theatre really took off after the War of Independence. The Bowery Theatre was built in 1826, where melodramatic and equestrian spectacles were performed, and this became the centre for masculine culture and rowdy behaviour as urbanization transformed the city in the mid-century. This area and theatre were considered working class, while the middle classes attended the Astor Place Opera House (opened 1840) further uptown. The Astor Place riots, in which twenty-two people were killed, resulted from a battle between audiences attending performances of *Macbeth* at the two theatres, each claiming that their star actor was better than the other (British William Charles Macready and American Edwin Forrest, respectively). This was also, essentially, a dispute about whether British or American stars were superior performers, at a time when anti-British sentiment was reaching a peak. As a result of the riot, laws to restrict audiences were introduced and a ticket was regarded as a temporary licence for the audience member to attend the theatre, which could be revoked for bad behaviour. At the same time, theatre buildings also needed a licence so that some control over what could be performed was maintained through licensing buildings. Even after the Civil War (1861–6), though, the licensing of theatres was still delegated to towns and cities. Such licences were discretionary and gave cities the opportunity to institute criminal prosecutions for violations. By around 1890, then, auditoriums had been transformed into genteel places, where anything other than polite applause could lead to eviction.

A third type of performance event was instigated by P. T. Barnum, whose career has been documented in the musical *Barnum* (1980) and the film musical *The Greatest Showman* (2017). Barnum purchased Scudder's Museum in 1841, renaming it the American Museum, in which he combined a zoo, museum, lecture hall, wax museum, theatre and freak show. In the theatre and lecture room, he banned prostitutes from touting for trade, as well as banning alcohol and boisterous behaviour, in order to attract a middle-class audience to see biblical dramas and melodramatic performances. This was the start of the promotion of theatrical respectability that was mirrored in Britain at the Gallery of Illustrations and later at the Savoy Theatre. This represents a rather more nebulous form of censorship or 'content control', instituted by theatre managers as a means of attracting a particular demographic, while promoting a socially acceptable type of behaviour and greater economic benefit.

In contrast to the gentrification of theatres, burlesque was developing, at first based on the British model introduced by Lydia Thompson and her British Blondes, among others. Thompson's company arrived in New York in 1868 to perform *Ixion* at Banvard's Museum. Thompson had appeared in London and toured Europe with extravaganzas and burlesques, before responding to George Wood's invitation to New York. Her show lampooned classical culture using rhymed pentameter, puns and topical allusions to divorce cases and political scandals, as well as songs (with topical lyrics set to known tunes) and dances (Houchin, 2003, pp. 32–3). Thompson's show was considered scandalous to some, since the women played male roles and wore Greek tunics that revealed their knees, with tights and ankle boots (similar to those in Figure 1.1). Although these costumes were no more revealing than those of ballet dancers, they were regarded as indecent. Despite their initial success hostility grew around the company when they moved to a new venue, Niblo's Garden (that had been the venue for *The Black Crook* in 1866, the 'first musical', as discussed in Chapter 1). Perhaps more controversially,

Thompson established eye contact with audience members and was regarded as verbally brazen in her use of language.

By the early twentieth century, the desire to maintain purity and morality on the stage led to complaints about performer Olga Nethersole's appearance in *Sapho* and a series of obscenity trials ensued. Whereas vaudeville transcended its working-class roots to attract a broader middle-class patronage in the late 1800s, burlesque devolved from a plotted entertainment, which celebrated the female figure with a degree of respectability, to a low-class form associated with the striptease (as depicted in the musical *Gypsy* [1959]). Ziegfeld's *Follies* (as discussed in Chapter 5), Shubert's *The Passing Show* (1912–24) and Earl Carroll's *Vanities* (1920s/30s), which contained burlesques of Broadway hits, all featured choruses of women in increasingly revealing and spectacular costumes. The *Vanities* featured virtual nudity with girls wearing just G-strings, feathers and beads but were not prosecuted despite complaints to the police. However, a charge was brought for allowing a woman to bathe in champagne at a post-performance party. Rather than any claim of obscenity, she was charged for breaking the Volstead Act, which prohibited the sale or transportation of alcohol.

As at the Windmill Theatre in London, these women were objects of heterosexual desire and were mostly silent, but it is clear that the social context and behaviour outside the theatre were affecting what was permitted within it. While there was no written statute in America that censored any particular type of performance, a host of other laws were used to restrain how nudity was represented in order to limit 'obscenity' or anything deemed immoral or corrupting. Interestingly, US obscenity law was based on an English decision from 1868, *Regina v Hicklin*, that deemed an entire work obscene if any part of the work might corrupt a sensitive mind.

These restrictions relate to the arrest of actress Mae West in 1927. While producing, directing and performing in *Sex*, a play about prostitution, West and her castmates were arrested for performing a work considered dangerous to moral standards. West alone served eight days in prison and the case received significant media attention. Elsewhere, the New York Legislature passed the Wales Padlock Law in 1927, which made the depiction or discussion of sexual degeneracy or sexual perversion illegal, with offending theatres at the threat of being closed.

At about the same time, the Motion Picture Production (Hays) Code was introduced (1930–68) that identified specific restrictions in the content of films: miscegenation and sexual relations outside marriage were not allowed, criminal actions must be punished, authority figures treated with respect, and nudity was removed. The code was relaxed in the 1950s, which became necessary when television became so widespread and had no such controls, before being replaced in 1968 with the Motion Picture Association of America (MPAA) rating system (still in use today). Although the code applied only to film, it demonstrates a similar concern with morality and the fear that theatrical and filmic representations might corrupt audience members.

Politics meets finance

The Great Depression in America followed an economic crash in 1929, which left the country reeling with high unemployment, poverty, deflation and misery for millions. The Federal Theatre Project (FTP, 1935–39) was founded during the Depression, as part of the Works Progress Administration (WPA) whose aim was to get people back to work. The FTP was a national scheme to offer creative employment to artists, writers, directors and other theatre employees using their existing skills, rather than just placing them in any employment. Its national director, Hallie Flanagan, met with Harry Hopkins (head of the WPA) and was tasked with developing a national strategy. She instituted a federation of regional theatres, encouraged experimentation and took live theatre to millions of people across the country, as well as mounting revivals and stock productions. Although she was promised the theatre would be free, adult and uncensored, about ten percent of the productions within the project were criticized by members of congress though not all those criticized were original FTP productions. Congressional displeasure mounted though, as a series of productions, including *It Can't Happen Here* (1937) and works by the Living Newspaper, seemed to criticize the capitalist system. Having lost Congressional support, President Roosevelt agreed to cut spending, and the target identified by conservative Congressmen was the WPA. Strikes and violent labour unrest provided the backdrop for the difficulties experienced by *The Cradle Will Rock* – a work that focused on unionization and the corruption of officials.

As a result of this combination of events and amid considerable unrest, just before the opening of *The Cradle Will Rock* in June 1937, the FTP was instructed not to open any new projects. According to John Houchin, WPA officials feared that its pro-labour message following the strikes would prejudice lawmakers against future projects (2003, p. 142).

CASE STUDY: *The Cradle Will Rock* (1937)

Music, lyrics and book: Marc Blitzstein.

This through-composed, and somewhat operatic, work was commissioned by the Federal Theatre Project, directed by Orson Welles and produced by John Houseman. It is an allegorical tale about the battle between corrupt capitalists and trade unionists. Moll, a prostitute, is thrown into prison when she refuses to bribe a policeman. There she meets Harry Druggist, whose wife and son were killed in an anti-union bombing. Harry tells her the history of the town and about the rise of the corrupt Mister Mister and his Liberty Committee. That night, most of the anti-union Liberty Committee are arrested and arrive at the jail, having been mistaken for the pro-union activists that the police are supposed to arrest. Larry Foreman, the union leader, is also arrested, for distributing leaflets to promote the union. He is beaten and, in response, encourages individuals to rise up with the union against corruption, promising that 'the cradle will rock'. The committee members are all bailed by Mister Mister, who offers money to Foreman to stop his activities. Foreman refuses and promises that the power of Mister Mister, and his committee, will be ended. Despite few major revivals of this work, its Brechtian, political style can be found in musicals like *Cabaret* (1966) and, more overtly, in *Urinetown: The Musical* (2001).

An unproduced screenplay of the story of the making of *The Cradle Will Rock* written by Orson Welles was published in 1994, while in 1999 Tim Robbins wrote another version telling the story of the making of *The Cradle Will Rock* that was filmed and released in 1999 starring Hank Azaria as Blitzstein. It depicts, in a fictionalized account, what happened when the government used economic means to censor the FTP and to close the production.

Consequently, a few days before *The Cradle Will Rock* was due to open, the WPA announced that, following funding cuts, it was closing all theatre productions temporarily, while the arts projects were reorganized. *The New York Times* suggested that the plot that was supportive of unionization was just too radical (1937). The Maxine Elliott Theatre, where the show was due to begin previews, was padlocked with all the sets and costumes inside. There seemed to be no possibility of the production continuing, but the writer, producer and director managed to hire the Venice Theatre further uptown. The actors were banned by their union (Equity) from performing onstage without the approval of the FTP, and the musician's union refused to allow the musicians to perform unless they were paid union rates. On opening night, therefore, with a huge audience that had followed the production, the actors sang from seats in the auditorium, accompanied only by Blitzstein at an onstage piano. Since they were not allowed to go onstage each actor stood in the audience and performed their role, and in this way the work received its first performance. Following this, a new backer was found and the performers were released from their FTP contracts so that the show could continue, where it would be performed in exactly the same format. This was an effective way of communicating the applicability and significance of the issues in the show's plot to audience members.

The importance of *The Cradle will Rock* in the history of censorship is the demonstration of the many levers of power the government has at its disposal to censor works, tools such as funding, and control of funded organizations. The battle between the liberal left and the conservative right over what should be permissible in theatre was continuing here, but this event also demonstrates that it is impossible to censor works without the co-operation, or at least the acquiescence, of the people.

KEY CONCEPT: House Un-American Activities Committee

In 1938 Flanagan was called to appear before the House Un-American Activities Committee (HUAC) because the committee was concerned that the entire project was left wing, too political and overrun by communists.

Developed in 1938, the HUAC initially investigated government officials regarding disloyal and untrustworthy activities. Preceded by the Overman Committee in 1918, with investigations by a committee of senators into pro-German and later pro-Japanese sentiments, an early investigation into the Bolshevik revolution in Russia created the first anti-communist feeling and generated the fear that was to underpin later investigations. From 1930, the Fish Committee investigated people who were perceived to have communist sympathies or leanings, while its successor committee investigated potential Nazi sympathizers. In 1938, Martin Dies took over as chair, concentrating on pursuing people and organizations that were perceived to have communist connections. It was this committee that investigated Hallie Flanagan and the FTP.

The HUAC became permanent in 1945 to investigate real and perceived threats (mostly from 'communists') against the United States. The film *Trumbo* (2015) tells the story of the ten Hollywood film writers who were blacklisted in the late 1940s, despite the lack of evidence against them, and the hundreds of artists who were boycotted by film studios. Some, like Charlie Chaplin and Paul Robeson, fled America to find work elsewhere, while others, including Dalton Trumbo, wrote under pseudonyms. Crucially, those summoned to appear were asked to identify the names of anyone they believed to be communists or face contempt of court charges and jail. Through the work of this committee, the Federal government effectively censored left wing, communist or socialist cultural product, by making it impossible for anyone with those political leanings to find work. This resulted in the creation of propaganda films during and after the Second World War, plus the production of satirical comedies about the committee towards the end of its term. The committee declined in the 1960s, when witnesses were openly hostile, defiant or satirical, while demonstrations were increasingly led against the activities of the committee. In 1969, its name was changed before it was finally disbanded in 1975.

Hair (and all that followed)

As noted above, American obscenity law was based on an English legal decision that would deem an entire work obscene, if any part of the work 'might have a "tendency" to "deprave or corrupt" a sensitive or susceptible mind' (Houchin, 2003, p. 201). By 1957, the district courts were unravelling this, arguing that the whole work must be taken into account to determine its effect and that the jury must consider the effect on the average citizen rather than a child or a susceptible person. In the Supreme Court, the Judge in *Roth v United States* agreed, and determined that the test should relate to the 'average person', that it should relate to 'the dominant theme of the work' and be applied in relation to 'community standards'.

During the 1960s, New York was viewed as a permissive and liberal environment, following experimental works by performance companies like the Living Theatre (Judith Malina and Julian Beck), the Open Theatre (Joseph Chaikin) and the Performance Group (Richard Schechner). Productions such as *Dionysus in 69* and *Paradise Now* (1968) both incorporated nudity, sexually explicit content and, in the case of *Dionysus in 69*, involved the audience in the action. Displays of nudity and sexuality were used to enhance the sense of an anarchic, anti-establishment position and were deemed both provocative and political. These productions were not considered a problem while they remained in downtown New York, but as they moved uptown, and especially to regional theatres, more issues arose.

Meanwhile, when some anti-war activists, including David Paul O'Brien, burnt their draft cards outside the South Boston Courthouse in 1968, the district court ruled that actions could be treated in the same way as speech and thus restrained. Following appeals the Supreme Court ruled that when speech and non-speech elements are combined there may be limitations on First Amendment freedoms (Houchin, 2016, p. 237). The government need only prove that its interests were at stake for actions to be restrained. The consequence was that symbolic actions on stage would also not be protected by the First Amendment Right of Free Speech, meaning actors, producers and directors might be prosecuted for acts on stage, as well as words, whether or not they were actually representing a different point of view. As John Houchin suggests, the central issue 'was the right of theatre artists to use transgressive sexual and political representations to critique contemporary society' (2016, p. 234).

They did not have the legal protection of a production like *Hair* (1967), whose lawyers created a safety net funded by its Broadway success and financial backing.

CASE STUDY: *Hair: The American Tribal Love-Rock Musical* (1967)

Music: Galt MacDermot. Lyrics and book: Gerome Ragni and James Rado.

The musical largely focuses on the individuals and relationships that form a 'tribe' of hippies in 1960s New York. The loose overarching story concerns two men, Berger and Claude, who, like the other male members of the tribe, are of an age to be drafted into the army to fight in the Vietnam War. Most of the men in the group have burned their draft cards, but Claude has not. He passes his physical examination and attends his army induction during the show, while considering whether he should follow his family's wishes and fight for his country, or resist because of his own pacifist principles. Most of Act 2 depicts Claude's hallucinations after smoking a laced joint, which reveal the horrors of war. When he wakes up, Claude slips away and goes to Vietnam; he is seen only as a spirit and as a dead body in the final scenes.

Hair was developed off-Broadway in 1967 and significant changes were made to the work before it arrived on Broadway in 1968 with the narrative outlined above. Many of the show's songs have entered the cultural zeitgeist, including 'Aquarius' and 'Good Morning Starshine', and a film adaptation was released in 1979. A major Broadway revival opened in 2009, which transferred to London in 2010 (retaining its American cast).

Hair began as an anti-Vietnam protest musical, presented first by Joseph Papp at the Public Theatre in New York in 1967, where it was directed by Gerald Freedman. After a series of conflicts and difficulties on the production even before its eight-week run, Papp decided not to take it any further. During that time, the show had been seen by Michael Butler and his partner Bertrand Castelli, who saw political potential in the show as a vehicle to oppose the Vietnam War and champion the counter-cultural lifestyle. Butler invested in the work and moved it to the Cheetah Discotheque for forty-five performances, where it had a mixed response. Nonetheless, he believed in the project enough to hire Tom O'Horgan as director, in place of Freedman, and move the show to the Biltmore Theatre on Broadway. O'Horgan altered the show substantially. Working with the writers, he added thirteen songs and only cut three so needed to reduce the book and character development substantially. O'Horgan thus focused on presenting images of young people living communally outside the norms of mainstream society and openly engaging with drugs and free love/casual sex. The markers of the cultural revolution can be clearly seen in the hairstyling and costumes in Figure 4.2. While still opposing the Vietnam War and racism, *Hair* was presented in an anti-illusionistic format using techniques derived from innovative theatre practitioner Jerzy Grotowski.

Figure 4.2 A scene from the Broadway production of the musical *Hair*. 1970. Photo: Swope, Martha. © NYPL.

Although there were vicious reviews of the show and the Broadway establishment objected to it, *Hair* soon played in New York, London and around the world (often adding local references in each new country/city). In many American cities, however, there were problems. Some theatres/cities refused to book the show, threats were made to take the show to court for obscenity, and a bomb was even thrown outside a theatre in Cleveland. In Boston, a case went to the Supreme Court which ruled that a restraining order should not be issued because the musical was not lewd with the exception of a (now infamous) nude scene and one display of simulated intercourse. Nevertheless, the court required the performers to be clothed 'to a reasonable extent' and that the simulated sex should be removed (Houchin, 2016, p. 239). Rather than comply with what was seen as censorship, Butler closed the show and appealed the decision. In 1970, the Massachusetts District Court decided that theatre was protected under the First Amendment. Audiences who bought tickets for a show did not need the same protection against nudity and sexual obscenity as those on the street, and, in any case, the universal application of a law against lewd and lascivious behaviour would be detrimental to the freedom of theatre makers. There was a further appeal but, in a very close decision, *Hair* could continue its run.

Elsewhere, other cities brought obscenity charges, such as Little Rock, Atlanta, Mobile, Charlotte and Birmingham, but all upheld that theatre was entitled to free speech. However, there was a final stage to this story that arose in Chattanooga, where the authorities decided the show was too indecent and refused to programme it. The producers went to the Federal Court without success, but, finally, in 1975, the case arrived at the Supreme Court of the United States as an issue of 'prior restraint'. It was decided that to deny the production access to the theatre 'in anticipation that the production would violate the law' was unconstitutional. Rather, the board of the theatres concerned should allow law enforcement to deal with any infringements, after they took place. There was a more important point, however. Within the judgement, the justices asserted that live drama was subject to First Amendment rights across the entire country, which meant that no district court could deny that right. This story, documented by scholar John Houchin (2003/2016), demonstrates the importance of *Hair*'s producers in setting legal precedents and securing constitutional protection for theatre productions. Because of its wealthy financial backer, Michael Butler, and the show's commercial success, lawyers could fight the battles, and it was *Hair* that was cited in cases that affected theatre across the United States. By 1975 it had been decided that performances could include offensive or even obscene material in productions, if the production as a whole was not obscene, but simply controversial. Nor could controversial, unpopular or transgressive productions be prevented from being performed in public theatres without due process. Most importantly, theatre productions were a form of speech, and free speech was guaranteed under the First Amendment of the Constitution.

Oh! Calcutta! followed *Hair* in New York in 1969 – before the legal challenges and changes had taken place – and created a storm only equalled by *Che!* (also in 1969). *Oh! Calcutta!* was a nude musical revue containing sketches, songs and dances, developed by British theatre critic Kenneth Tynan. Although it contained sketches by well-established playwrights, Tynan suggested that the work was 'expressly designed to titillate' (quoted in Houchin, 2003, p. 219). The show ran in both America and, after the end of censorship, in Britain, despite critics regarding it very poorly.

Hair was the first musical to open in the West End after the end of legal censorship in Britain. Following this there were occasional prosecutions, notably when Mary Whitehouse took out a private prosecution against the National Theatre over Howard Brenton's play, *The Romans in Britain* (1982), under the Sexual Offences Act of 1956. The Attorney General was tasked to consider whether the show broke obscenity rules but decided not to prosecute, leaving the earlier excitement over nudity to recede.

Meanwhile, in America, President Nixon was elected, and his administration campaigned against the 'indecency' of shows like *Oh Calcutta!*. Nixon appointed Charles Keating to the Presidential Commission on Obscenity and Pornography that published a minority report representing the conservative viewpoint. In 1973 the definition of obscenity was changed and by then Nixon had appointed four conservative judges to the Supreme Court, who were now in the majority, led by Chief Justice Warren Burger. Burger watered down all the gains that had been made as the 'Culture Wars' were waged in subsequent years.

In the 1980s and 1990s, an ongoing battle ensued between the Christian Right and the National Endowment of the Arts (NEA) that often seemed to focus on politics, sex and especially homosexuality as AIDS emerged. Nonetheless, civil rights were improving for women and gay men, but the question remained whether taxpayers' dollars should be used to fund 'difficult' and controversial work. One side wanted arts funding to pay for work that appealed to the majority; that promoted mainstream heteronormative values. The other side supported work that championed equality and represented minority lifestyles. The right-wing Republicans, then in power, attempted to censor theatre by forcing the NEA to withdraw funding from theatres or companies that programmed work that was challenging or provocative (a tactic that, as we have seen with *The Cradle Will Rock*, is not always successful). Especially at the peak of the AIDS crisis, there were court cases over plays like Larry Kramer's *The Normal Heart* (1985) and Tony Kushner's epic *Angels in America* (1991/1993), which both included openly homosexual characters, in functioning relationships, who were dying of AIDS. The result was that Congress, in the Helms Amendment, limited the art that the NEA could fund and obligated it to become the censors of obscenity (Houchin, 2003, p. 239). By the turn of the century, and as a result of a ruling by Justice Sandra Day O'Connor, a compromise had been reached that allowed the NEA to interpret indecency and respect. The musicals that depicted the acceptance of diverse sexualities and of AIDS, however, including *Falsettos* (1992) and *RENT* (1996), were somehow not subject to quite the same vilification.

So far, this chapter has considered how different laws were used in Britain and America, at different times, as the political contexts and socio-cultural frameworks changed. Thus, the comparative histories of the two theatre districts, Broadway and the West End, serve to illustrate the importance of context to the content of theatre works and continuing discussions over censorship, whether implicit or legally enforced. The final case study therefore considers the role of censorship in a, supposedly, liberal and uncensored world where musicals continue to be rendered problematic should they verge too broadly from conservative values.

Self-censorship and political correctness

In 1971, Andrew Lloyd Webber and Tim Rice's rock opera *Jesus Christ Superstar*, quite literally, rocked Broadway before opening in the West End in 1972. The hit concept album, which had topped the Billboard 200 chart in 1970, was staged to both the embracement and rejection of various religious groups. Like Stephen Schwartz's musical *Godspell*, which also opened in New York in 1971, some criticized the musical as blasphemous, with antagonist Judas being considered too sympathetic, and much of the depiction was deemed anti-Semitic (Bradley, 2004, pp. 123–7).

Three decades later, *Jerry Springer: The Opera* would go on to receive a similar backlash from religious organizations. The piece began life as a one-man show by Richard Thomas, titled *How to Write an Opera about Jerry Springer*, which he performed at London's Battersea Arts Centre in 2001. Thomas then expanded the show for four singers and, following that version, joined with comedian Stewart Lee to augment the show further for a cast of twelve, now named *Jerry Springer: The Opera*. Each version of the show was well-received, whether at the Battersea Arts Centre or the Edinburgh Fringe Festival in 2002. Jerry Springer himself saw the production in Edinburgh, and approved, while director Nicholas Hytner offered to include the show in his inaugural season at the National Theatre. Following its National Theatre run, the show was transferred to the West End, where it played to packed houses, received good reviews and won the Olivier Award for Best Musical.

CASE STUDY: *Jerry Springer: The Opera* (2003)

Music: Richard Thomas. Lyrics and book: Richard Thomas and Stewart Lee.

Act 1 is a satire of the long-running talk show, *The Jerry Springer Show* (1991–2018), hosted by Jerry, in which guests discuss their personal problems and relationships. Dwight is having affairs with two people, as well as his fiancée: Tremont, a transvestite, and Zandra, his fiancée's best friend. Montel enjoys dressing in a nappy/diaper and using it for its intended purpose, whereas Shawntel just wants to dance (as a pole dancer). Her husband, Chucky, disapproves, despite regularly frequenting strip joints himself. Chucky is also a member of the Ku Klux Klan and, at the highpoint of the act, the Klan appears to perform a tap dance routine in front of a burning crucifix. Montel, played by a Black actor, is given a gun by the (recently fired) warm-up man, Jonathan, who assists Montel in accidentally shooting Jerry as the curtain falls.

Acts 2 and 3 take place as Jerry lingers between life and death in a kind of limbo/hallucination. All of the characters reappear in an amalgam of Christian themes when Jerry is forced to descend to Hell to host a show, which creates a kind of intertextual connection between the fictional characters of Act 1 and the other characters each performer plays. Chucky and Shawntel become Adam and Eve, Montel becomes Jesus, Dwight becomes God, and the warm-up man becomes Satan. All sorts of chaos ensues before God and the Angels arrive and ask Jerry to help God judge humanity (though God and the Angels continue to fight over him). In the end, Jerry, after speaking platitudes for most of the evening, finally expresses a truthful statement and the scene reverts to the television studio of Act 1. Jerry gives a final speech before dying in Steve's (head of security) arms.

Despite being lauded on stage, the BBC's 2005 airing of the production on national television reportedly received up to 60,000 complaints. The Christian Voice led protests at BBC studios, several theatres that were scheduled to host the show on a forthcoming tour pulled out, while the Arts Council refused funding (though citing the commercial nature of the production, rather than its content, as the reason). No prosecution was ever made, since no evidence of illegality was found, and, more importantly, when the protests were debated in the Houses of Parliament, freedom of speech in theatre and television was reinforced. Many reacted to the show's Christian themes in that the story moves to Hell, where Jerry is supposed to help Satan extract an apology from God, and Heaven, where God wants Jerry to judge humanity. Actress Alison Jiear even added an extra gesture for the filmed version, much to the dismay of the creative team, where she, as Eve, reaches into Jesus's diaper and begins to masturbate him. The language is also extremely colourful, even highly offensive – with the most amount of swear words of any stage work to date – but no worse than is heard on such television programmes. What causes a more shocking effect, though, is the juxtaposition of swearing and crude language with operatic singing, and the clashing of high and low culture in the incorporation of styles from opera to gospel to musical theatre. The show was scheduled to open on Broadway in 2005, but it did not transpire, instead playing two concert performances in 2008, which were picketed by Christian Right protesters. *Jerry Springer: The Opera* has since been performed in several states and regional venues in America, finally arriving at an off-Broadway theatre in 2018.

Trigger warnings and cancel culture

As addressed in other chapters, the Internet and social media drastically altered means of communication and community building in the early twenty-first century. Individuals from anywhere in the world (with an Internet connection and device) were provided with a global platform, one that was somewhat anonymous, to express their views and condemn those of others. By the mid- to late-2010s, the notion of providing a 'trigger warning' and that of building a 'cancel culture' had become cultural conversation topics that pushed discussions around free speech and censorship into the digital age.

A trigger warning, for instance, advises audiences of the content of a performance, often acknowledging problematic themes such as violent or sexual content. While written warnings have long been used in theatre lobbies to acknowledge sudden loud noises, strobe lighting and other physical elements that may be harmful to someone's physical and/or mental health, this was expanded during the early decades of the twenty-first century to include the depiction or discussion of socially and politically troubling content. This has received much critical attention with some suggesting that trigger warnings around topics such as sexual abuse pander to a 'snowflake' generation of sensitive teens, while others, like Rebecca Hodge, argue that they 'keep everyone safe and engaged' in a theatre (2018). Elsewhere, and in other media, the subscription service Disney+, which launched in November 2019, includes trigger warnings at the start of several animated film musicals due to their culturally insensitive (and outdated) content. When viewers stream Disney classics such as *Dumbo* (1941) and *Lady and the Tramp* (1955) they are provided with a message that acknowledges that such films contain 'negative depictions and/or mistreatment of people or cultures. These stereotypes were wrong then and are wrong now. Rather than remove this content, we want to acknowledge its harmful impact, learn from it and spark conversations to create a more inclusive future together' (The Walt Disney Company, 2022). Disney is therefore active in acknowledging and contextualizing potentially harmful material, rather than eradicating it. This serves to maintain the archive while acknowledging the changed cultural context.

Cancel culture, on the other hand, is the process of removing harmful opinions by cancelling speakers, whether live or on social media, and even removing public acknowledgement of those individuals who might now be considered problematic. For instance, a statue of Edward Colston, a Bristol city benefactor of the nineteenth century whose wealth derived from trading enslaved peoples, was torn down and dumped in the harbour during a Black Lives Matter protest in 2020. This may cause no harm to long dead 'heroes', though it may cause distress to their descendants, and reflects a changing cultural landscape in which problematic individuals and actions are 'called out'. This becomes more problematic, however, when cancel culture intersects with free speech and hate speech – as it often does in theatre. For example, British actress Oluwaseyi Omooba had posted her religious views against homosexuality on Facebook five years before being cast in a 2019 UK regional production of *The Color Purple* (2005). Omooba received much social media backlash for her comments, which ultimately led to the producers recasting the role and Omooba losing agent representation. Omooba subsequently lost a legal battle for discrimination towards her in 2021. Elsewhere, American actress Sierra Boggess withdrew from playing Maria in a BBC Proms concert production of *West Side Story* (1957) in 2018. The actress and production received much public backlash for having a white woman in a Latinx role, an accused example of 'whitewashing', that led to Canadian actress Mikaela Bennett eventually played Maria.

Examples like these have been abundant since the 2010s and span far beyond musical theatre. Globally significant figures including author J. K. Rowling have received backlash on social media due to opinions or actions that have been considered controversial by some. Twitter, in particular, has become a site for frequent conversations regarding the appropriateness of certain ideas and thus a contemporary site of censorship. Free speech has almost become an irrelevance in the twenty first century given the consequences of expressing diverse points of view without attracting hate speech. In this way self-censorship and the absence of genuine debate are now increasingly problematic.

Conclusion

Janelle Reinelt remarks that censorship is not just the intentional removal of something that might be deemed offensive, but that it is also choosing not to do something as a form of self-protection. In this light, what plays and musicals have not been written because writers feared they could not be performed? How many have not been performed because directors and producers feared for the safety of participants? On the other hand, some censored material might, in fact, be indefensible. It is clear that cultural context affects these issues, since what might be acceptable in one place and community may not be acceptable in another, and so theatre must always be created within a framework that the communities it hopes to target can engage with. Art may be designed to provoke debate, and perhaps to express controversial ideas, yet this will always be limited, even controlled, by cultural contexts.

As Helen Freshwater claims in *Theatre Censorship in Britain*, 'questions of interpretation and moral relativism dogged the Lord Chamberlain's examiners, as they struggled to negotiate the radical social transformations of the twentieth century' (2009, p. 166). Negotiating a gap between the written and spoken word, and considering the actions of performers and the possible resonances of words and actions for audiences, makes it impossible for the interpretation of a text to be fixed, which was required by the early legal censors. Moreover, the negotiations over whether the arts should have free speech or have such freedom constrained, and, if so, who is to police such constraints and how, are always divisive and controversial issues since they touch on societal conventions and taboos. Overall, then, censorship remains an important, but impossibly fluid issue.

Tasks

Compare the reviews of a provocative or controversial musical that played in Britain and America. How was the production received in each country? Were the same issues problematic in each production? What might these similarities or differences tell us about each cultural context?

Design a marketing scheme for a production of *Jerry Springer: The Opera* (or a similar example of a musical that breaks taboos). How do taboos function in society and how would you market the production in response? Would you identify or conceal the musical's provocative content?

Discussion topics

What are the values we hold as a society? How are they imposed/maintained? To what extent do they, or should they, apply to theatre?

Can, or should, the state be removed from questions of art, morality and censorship? Is there a place for governing bodies and legal restrictions in the creation and production of art and theatre?

Further reading – conceptual

Freshwater, H. (2009) *Theatre Censorship in Britain: Silencing, Censure and Suppression*. Basingstoke: Palgrave Macmillan.
Shanson, L. (2017) *Theatre & Protest*. Basingstoke: Palgrave Macmillan.

Further reading – case study

Houchin, J. H. (2015) 'Freedom of Speech and *Hair*: The Legal Legacy'. In: Catherine O'Leary, Diego Santos Sánchez and Michael Thompson (eds) *Global Insights on Theatre Censorship*, 234–44. London and New York: Routledge.
Soto-Morettini, D. (2004) '"The Clowns of God": *Jerry Springer the Opera*'. *Contemporary Theatre Review* 14/1, 75–87.
Wollman, E. (2013) *Hard Times: The Adult Musical in 1970s New York City*. New York: Oxford University Press.

5

'Stand up': From gender duality to diversity

In the closing song of David Arnold, Richard Thomas and Richard Bean's musical, *Made in Dagenham* (2014), the protagonist, Rita O'Grady, demands that her male colleagues (and the audience, by extension) stand up for women's rights, because 'if not now, when?'. Rita 'won't run' and 'won't hide' until her voice is heard, and women are given the same opportunities and pay as men. Based on the 2010 British film, itself a fictionalized account of the 1968 Ford sewing machinists strike (which led to the UK Equal Pay Act being passed in 1970), *Made in Dagenham* depicts strong and determined women fighting for equality. In one scene, Rita leads the factory girls to the Employment Secretary, Barbara Castle, who advises (in the song 'Ideal World') that gender equality, like a cure for cancer, the common cold or flu, is not possible in the real world. Instead of simply accepting second best, however, Castle advises at the end of the song that the girls should continue to fight for a 'level playing field' so that 'these happy endings' can, and shall, be real.

Meanwhile, the men in *Made in Dagenham*, the husbands and fathers, the factory workers and most of the government, resist this call for equality, assuming that working women are worth less than working men doing equal work. Not only are they worth less, but women should also run the home and raise the children. This growing awareness of inequality had great currency from the 1970s onwards, as cartoonist Bob Thaves noticed when he remarked of Fred Astaire and Ginger Rogers that '[s]ure he was great, but don't forget that Ginger Rogers did everything he did … backwards and in high heels' (1982). While Rita's husband, Eddie, begins by supporting her, and their relationship is a strong loving bond, once her trade union activity means he has to shoulder the burden of childcare, as well as work, things become more difficult. A notable moment occurs when Rita's husband argues that he is unusually supportive because he does not get drunk each night or sleep with other women. When he finally claims that 'I never hit you or the kids', Rita replies, 'You want me to be grateful for that? That, Eddie, is how it should be.' The leading man (perhaps a better epithet than hero) is a kind, loving working-class husband who worries what the other men will think of him but tries his best to accommodate his wife's desire for cultural and political change. Perhaps this was heroic for the 1960s, but the fact that this musical had resonance in the 2000s is a rather sad indictment of the continuing lack of gender equality.

Made in Dagenham ran for less than six months in the West End, yet it has since been performed by schools and amateur groups across Britain and continues to disseminate the work's actively feminist and socialist politics. It is also one of several contemporary shows, like *Wicked* (2003) and *Matilda: The Musical* (2011), that features strong female protagonists who identify and challenge injustice. Meanwhile, the male characters in shows like *Billy Elliot: The Musical* (2005) and *Dear Evan Hansen* (2016) no longer conform to heroic standards; instead they are revealed to be diverse and complex humans. As Charles Mackinnon notes, 'all known societies distinguish between male and female. All known societies also provide their males and females with models of behaviour deemed appropriate to these sexes – in other words, with notions of masculinity and femininity that a culture largely consents to and upholds' (2003, p. 3).

In the musicals discussed in this chapter, we will consider how the representations of masculinity and femininity being performed demonstrate models of behaviour, since popular performances generally conform to expected cultural patterns in mainstream society (typically represented by audience members from white, middle- and upper-class backgrounds). What happens in musical theatre is, to some extent, a reflection of what is happening beyond the theatre. As Susan Cook notes, 'gender is complicated and involves a variety of conscious and unconscious behaviours performed along an unstable continuum of "masculine" and "feminine" norms' (2009, p. 36). The fact that this continuum is unstable can be demonstrated by the changing representations of men and women in musical theatre between the late nineteenth century and the present, and between Britain and America, some of which this chapter will identify.

Late Victorian Britain

As W. S. Gilbert and Arthur Sullivan's operettas played to packed houses in London's West End, the simple argument is that men and women across the country lived in separate spheres. Men commuted to work in offices or factories, having moved to towns and cities as a result of the Industrial Revolution, while middle- and upper-class women were left at home to complete domestic duties, including childcare, cooking, cleaning and so on. The separation of the two sexes rested on patriarchal assumptions that women lacked the physical capacity and intelligence to contribute to the wider workplace, while men should be the leaders, owning the property and making the decisions. Some of this practical separation may be true, though clearly the intellectual differences are not, but the extension of this binary, where men lived in the public sphere and women in the private sphere, has been challenged – it was much more complicated than that (see Macpherson, 2018). For example, some women worked even in the late Victorian period, while others were housewives and mothers who enjoyed leisure time in towns and cities. On the other hand, men worked outside the home but also enjoyed a range of leisure activities within and without the home. This was also the time when the New Woman appeared, trade unionism and proletarian socialism rose to prominence, meaning theatre was adapting not just to a boom in popular entertainment, but also to the increasing respectability of London's West End.

KEY CONCEPT: The New Woman

In the late nineteenth century, a term emerged that influenced feminist thought well into the twentieth century. The term 'New Woman' was used to refer to independent career women in Europe and America, who promoted changes in ideology and politics, but also made a difference to women's material presence in the world. Independence included the freedom to engage in activities such as cycling, walking, shopping and commerce, and moving freely around in cities. Women also became increasingly sexually autonomous in law (they were able to own their own bodies and children, as well as retaining their own property rights). Some were well educated with university degrees, awarded by women's colleges, and many women took a much greater part in artistic and cultural life. These freedoms were almost exclusively available to the white middle classes, however. It would be many years until similar rights were available to other classes and races.

One of the strategies employed by Gilbert, Sullivan and their producer Richard D'Oyly Carte, to attract this increasingly diverse audience, was to reposition their operas to appeal to 'middle-England'. To do this, they represented bourgeois respectable values in works of popular culture, such as the binary separation of men and women, and the patriarchal gender roles that supported it. Their success was also facilitated by the increasingly safe and acceptable accessibility of the West End, including transport, shops and theatre, for unaccompanied women from the London suburbs.

The theory of the separation of the sexes, and the patriarchal assumptions that girls would obey their fathers and then marry 'suitable' men, that played to this more diverse audience, can be seen in one of Gilbert and Sullivan's operas, *The Pirates of Penzance* (1880). This work also demonstrates an early opportunity for male displays of machismo and excessive politesse.

CASE STUDY: *The Pirates of Penzance* (subtitled *The Slave of Duty*, 1880)

Music: Arthur Sullivan. Lyrics and book: W. S. Gilbert.

The story concerns the young pirate, Fredric, who was apprenticed to a pirate, rather than a pilot, because of his nurse mishearing instructions. Fredric has just reached twenty-one and is thus able to leave his apprenticeship. He vows that, morally, now that he is no longer a pirate, he must seek out and kill his former comrades. Meanwhile, having never seen a woman other than his nurse, Ruth, and not being acquainted with commonly accepted notions of beauty, he believes her to be beautiful. On land, however, Fredric meets and instantly falls in love with Mabel, one of a group of beautiful young sisters, daughters of Major General Stanley. The pirates are unsuccessful since, as orphans themselves, they will never harm another orphan. As this is widely known, everyone who is threatened by them claims to be an orphan, so, when the pirate band returns and captures the sisters, the Major General has only to claim they are orphans for the sisters to be released. The local police, led by Fredric, arrive to arrest the pirates, but Fredric is informed by Ruth and the Pirate King that since his birthday is on 29 February, leap year day, he has not had twenty-one birthdays, only five, and must therefore remain indentured until he is in his eighties. As Fredric is once again a pirate, he tells the Pirate King of the Major General's deception. Police and pirates, both somewhat scared, battle over the Major General, who asks them all to desist 'in Queen Victoria's name'. They comply before the patriotic pirates are all revealed to be dispossessed noble men. All are now of sufficient status to marry the Major General's daughters. All is forgiven and all ends happily!

Joseph Papp revised the opera in New York in 1981, a production that was imported to the West End and filmed in 1983.

The men in this late nineteenth-century saga reflect the concerns of the day – militarism and xenophobia, and the girls are naive and inconsequential – both acceptable middle-class values that are gently mocked. As Michael Goron notes, the works were popular with an affluent audience that was interested in maintaining a 'hierarchical and essentially deferential society'. The audience was therefore presented with 'a satirical critique of itself which avoided any kind of true radicalism, and which implicitly celebrated the very values which were being mocked' (2016, p. 3). The uniformed men are far from heroic: the pirates are so gentlemanly that they refrain from all fighting and killing, being portrayed rather as emotionally sympathetic and a bit naive, while the police are portrayed as a band of comical buffoons. The Modern Major General himself is another old buffoon, with a wonderful wordy song and an enormous host of beautiful and very silly daughters (all of surprisingly similar ages!). The point is that the story is facetious, containing several comic reversals of fortune and revelations of farcical coincidences (the world of Gilbert and Sullivan is noted for its Topsy Turvydom). Meanwhile, the characters are merely cyphers playing out the actions and singing wonderful songs. As such, these characters are simple stereotypes.

Mabel, the heroine, is pretty, kind-hearted and bold enough to speak to Fredric and the pirates, silly enough to fall in love instantly with a handsome boy whom she has only just met and never had a conversation with, and has an extremely ornamented song (a parody of the 'Queen of the Night' from Mozart's *The Magic Flute* [1791]) that demonstrates her remarkable attribute – her soprano voice. She attends to, and obeys, her father as her primary duty. Fredric, the hero, demonstrates his moral superiority by remaining loyal to the pirates while apprenticed, but immediately handing them over to the police when released, before switching loyalties again when his age is farcically revealed. His loyalty is therefore paper-thin and based on perceived duties, rather than developed relationships. He is young, handsome and has been a pirate (perhaps a profession that could be perceived as daring and devil-may-care), which brings a raffishness and disregard for authority that is contradicted by his adherence to duty. He is also a tenor. The hero and heroine are thus both fairly simple and are defined by their voices, beauty, good humour, kind nature and regard to duty. Older men are buffoons with comic patter songs, whose every whim is satisfied by their wives or daughters. Older women (like Ruth) are motherly figures, more independent than the girls, but also bound to duty (in Ruth's case to her care of Fredric). Although some of Gilbert and Sullivan's operas feature different characteristics, these sweeping generalizations of broad stereotypes, plus the pattern of action taking precedence, characterize many of their works, as well as those by subsequent writers (many of whom had far less wit).

Music hall, variety and revue

In other areas of theatre, the challenging of misogynist norms was evident in British music hall. This typically working-class entertainment started in pubs and coffee houses, meaning patrons would eat and drink during performances that consisted of a variety of acts. From popular songs and comedy to animal acts and magic, music hall was a popular variety form that dominated British entertainment from the 1830s (with its popularity fading after the First World War). In 1852, Charles Morton opened the first purpose-built music hall, the Canterbury Hall, which housed 700 (typically male) patrons. Believing that men and women should be entertained together, Morton introduced 'Ladies' Thursday' – a day on which men could be accompanied by women. However, instead of taking their wives, prostitutes regularly frequented the hall, walking the aisles of the auditorium touting for business (thus giving the halls a seedy reputation).

On the music hall stage, however, women were increasingly appearing as popular acts, challenging the virginal or motherly representations seen elsewhere. Marie Lloyd (1870–1922), for instance, once considered the 'Queen of the Music Hall', began performing at the Eagle Tavern in Hoxton, London, in 1885 (aged fifteen). Known for her risqué and forthright manner, Lloyd sang seemingly innocent songs that featured much innuendo and double meaning. 'She'd Never Had Her Ticket Punched Before' and 'When You Wink the Other Eye', for example, saw Lloyd challenge class and gender norms as a strong woman who could control a male audience, without having to resort to prostitution. Lloyd was a great success across London, regularly topping the bill at various West End music halls, while also making several transatlantic visits to perform in New York. Lloyd's death in 1922, six years before she was likely to have been able to vote, coincided with the demise of music hall, which transformed into variety.

The male stars of music hall were diverse and included comedians, singers (whether operatic or comic) and acrobats, but most interestingly there were cross-dressed performers of both sexes. Female impersonators played strong, often working or lower middle-class straight-talking matriarchal women in sketch comedy and comic songs. The characters and performers moved into variety (and then pantomime) in Britain, playing everything 'from charwoman to *grande dame*, incorporating elements of the clown' (Baker, 1994, p. 179). In America, such impersonations were perhaps first seen in minstrel shows, though later the performances became more varied, elegant and glamorous as drag performance developed. Male impersonators of music hall (including the popular Vesta Tilley) played aristocratic rakes and dandies (like Burlington Bertie). These stereotypes continued within musical comedy for some time, representing the feminized man or sometimes the aesthete and the masculine (or butch) woman even when played without cross-dressing.

Meanwhile, the American equivalent of British music hall, vaudeville, featured a similar variety of acts and appeared 'in summer gardens, dime museums, on riverboats and trains, in circuses, and as parts of minstrel and burlesque shows through the eighteenth and nineteenth centuries' (Wollman, 2017, p. 25). Since they had become rowdy, male-dominated drinking saloons, attempts were made to clean up vaudeville houses. While vaudeville became more respectable, burlesque houses became the home for sexualized entertainment (as described in Chapter 1). These two types of entertainment combined not only in the later musical comedy, but in the revues of George White, Earl Carroll and the Shubert Brothers.

Most famous, however, was Florenz Ziegfeld and his 'chorus girl factory' (Mizejewski, 1999, p. 65). Through a renowned series of theatrical revues, the *Ziegfeld Follies* (1907–31), Ziegfeld was considered the 'glorifier of the American girl'. His shows were elaborate theatrical revues, with extravagant sets and costumes, and often over 120 girls on stage (in comparison to the

Figure 5.1 Unidentified showgirl in the stage production *Ziegfeld Follies of 1957*. Photo: Friedman-Abeles Collection. © NYPL.

twenty of earlier revue shows). Interestingly, these revues provided some of the first opportunities for African American performers in multi-racial shows. However, the showgirls, the Ziegfeld Girls, were typically tall, white, slender and dressed in revealing outfits, as seen in Figure 5.1, which created an American ideal of womanhood (as exaggerated by the revue's patriotic staging). Men appeared as foils to the 'girls', as singers and comedians, and occasionally, as in Britain, stronger female characters appeared as singers, comedians, dancers and character performers.

A key example is comedian and singer Fanny Brice (1891–1951), famously depicted by Barbra Streisand in the stage and screen versions of *Funny Girl* (1964). Brice first worked for Ziegfeld in 1910, where she capitalized on her difference – her spontaneity, wit, clumsiness, brashness, even Jewishness and lack of (stereotypical) beauty – through her comedy. In 1934, for instance, Brice mocked the all-American female ideal (or at least her own distance from it) in a short comedy film in which the 'Most Beautiful Girl in the *Ziegfeld Follies*' is being selected. As the other girls smile sweetly, Brice performs clownish facial expressions and stands with a fake leg, which she then removes and hands to the host as a punchline. Brice typifies the rise of the female musical comedy star using the comic devices of music hall and vaudeville, while the chorus girls perhaps derive more directly from burlesque. Although we might question the progressiveness of Brice's act, given that her comedic value relies on mocking her appearance, the early twentieth century produced a variety of new opportunities for women on the musical stage.

Early twentieth-century transatlantic transfers

On both sides of the Atlantic, women were increasingly leaving the domestic sphere to pursue leisure activities, such as shopping, dancing or visiting amusement parks (like Coney Island in New York). Even the assumption that women were 'pure, nurturing, homebound, and demure' was now an outdated ideal (Mizejewski, 1999, p. 67). Meanwhile, the 'girls' in many areas of the workplace (though particularly shop girls and actresses) became the heroines of many musicals, when musical comedy began to focus on contemporary modernity, rather than a fantasy time or place.

This was reflected at the start of musical comedy, both in Britain and America, partly through the interactions of impresarios Charles Frohman (US) and George Edwardes (UK), who imported each other's shows to Broadway and the West End (as documented in Chapter 1). In America, Frohmann noted in 1914 that a 'strong *human* play, with good characters (and clean) is the thing over here [in London, whereas] [...] throughout the United States a play really requires a star artist' (quoted in Valencia, 2017, p. 69). Although Frohman carefully adapted British materials for the Broadway audience, many with interpolated songs by Jerome Kern, he claimed that at this time British works 'held greater potential for theatrical integrity than the available American models' (Valencia, 2017, pp. 71–2).

In Britain, George Edwardes produced *In Town* in 1892, which 'became the paradigm for a series of so-called "girl musicals" in which an independent young woman ends up marrying a well-to-do-man' (Everett, 2017, p. 57). *A Gaiety Girl* (1893), whose hero (a military officer) romanced an actress, was followed by a series of shows with 'girl' in the title, including *The Circus Girl* (1896), *The School Girl* (1902), *The Quaker Girl* (1910) and *After the Girl* (1914). As Ben Macpherson remarks, the infantilizing of the heroines as 'girls', rather than 'women', indicates something of the patriarchal and patronizing representation, and yet they were 'simultaneously embodied by means of the coquettish eroticism of the chorus girl' (2018, p. 65). These 'girls' were both virginal and conservative, *and* high-spirited and independent, while the chorus of 'Gaiety Girls' were elegant, sophisticated and always dressed in the latest fashions. While modern, dynamic and with common sense aplenty, these 'girls' contrasted the image of the New Woman as educated and intelligent. Rather than education and intelligence then, in these shows, the 'ideals of Victorian womanhood became increasingly linked to conspicuous consumption, challenging the private and domestic ideals of the separate spheres ideology' (Macpherson, 2018, p. 68). Indeed, Len Platt, in his analysis of *Our Miss Gibbs* (1909), concludes that at this time such performances 'reproduced consumerism in a theatrical extravaganza that transformed the Edwardian stage into a fantastic celebration of fashion, shopping and general excess' (2004, p. 4) and turned these shows into some of the earliest vehicles for product placement.

These became the characteristics represented on stage at this time: women work, lead independent lives and are undoubtedly modern. Although represented as slightly risqué, the female characters are nonetheless a product of a cleaned-up West End in which pretty working-class women are able to ascend to a much higher class by marrying wealthy or aristocratic men (much like Cinderella). As William Everett notes, many of the female performers 'wed into wealthy families or the peerage', a fact that was satirized in one of the earliest of this group of shows, *A Gaiety Girl*, as contemporary art and life overlapped (2017, p. 57).

Meanwhile, the young men, especially in the 1910s, were rebelling against patriarchal structures and were thus represented as wayward, drunken, debauched and profligate, or as young dandies (descended from the aesthetes and fops of Gilbert and Sullivan, and leading on to those of Noel Coward). As Platt remarks, 'masculinity did not perform well in musical comedy', with debilitated men overshadowed by lively heroines (2004, p. 114). Older men remained comic buffoons, and soldiers were always young, handsome and desirable. This trend was then followed in America, when the transatlantic team of Jerome Kern, Guy Bolton and P. G. Wodehouse began writing their 'Princess Theatre' shows. Including *Very Good Eddie* (1915) (an adaptation of *Mr Popple of Ippleton* from London) and *Oh Boy* (1917), these new musical comedies stimulated a flowering of new work by American writers such as Cole Porter, the Gershwin brothers and Rodgers and Hart. They featured modern American settings, farcical plots and independent sharp-witted women, mirroring developments in London. The most enduring musical to open following this period was *Anything Goes* (1934), which perhaps best exemplifies the farcical plots of these musicals and the representations of men and women that were now prevalent.

CASE STUDY: *Anything Goes* (1934)

Music and lyrics: Cole Porter. Book: Guy Bolton and P. G. Wodehouse.

Billy Crocker is a stowaway on a liner bound for London, the SS American, following the woman he fell in love with at first sight, Hope Harcourt. She is engaged to Lord Evelyn Oakleigh, the rather effete dandy of this story – an English aesthete. Nightclub singer Reno Sweeney, who is in love with Billy, attempts to help him win back Hope. The story is complicated by the presence of a familiar gangster, Moonface Martin, who engages in numerous switches of clothes and employs several false identities. The marriage between Hope and Oakleigh, which had been arranged for financial reasons, is called off when Hope discovers she is independently wealthy, so she and Billy can be married, while Reno and Oakleigh also find happiness. The extremely complicated farcical plot contains numerous witty songs, like 'You're the Top', plus several opportunities for dance numbers by the chorus of passengers and sailors, including Reno's show-stopping number 'Blow, Gabriel Blow'.

Although there have been a number of revivals of the show in London or New York (1962, 1987, 1989, 2003 and 2011), as well as tours and productions elsewhere in the world, there are fundamentally four versions of the text itself: 1934, 1962, 1987 and 2011. In 1962, Russel Crouse and Howard Lindsay, the musical's original director, heavily revised the book. This happened again for the 1987 Broadway revival, this time by John Weidman and Timothy Crouse (Russel's son), a text that was revised in minor ways largely in respect of musical arrangements by Bill Elliott in 2011.

The two women in *Anything Goes* are Hope, the heroine, who is young, beautiful and dutiful, aiming to marry Oakleigh, first, to support her family's business and, later, because of that promise. These are the attributes of the kind, beautiful and dutiful heroines we have already seen. Reno Sweeney, however, is a working woman, talented, high-spirited, independent and a woman of the world. The hero, Billy, is handsome, kind, educated, charming and loving, but not wealthy, and he falls instantly in love – the all-American hero. This, again, is a familiar pattern. Oakleigh, on the other hand, derives from British musical comedy. He is somewhat weak and dutiful, often appearing cold and dry, until, in a novel twist, Reno livens his life with her all-American wit and spirit. It is here where national identities start to overlap with gender identities to reveal a perception of the British aristocratic male as being saved by the independent American woman (a pattern that was happening in practice as young wealthy American women were marrying poor, but landed, British aristocrats). Meanwhile, Moonface is a development of the kindly and buffoonish older man, a comedy figure that would appear again with the gangsters in Porter's *Kiss Me, Kate* (1948).

To consider these transatlantic connections further, *Anything Goes* can be compared with the British musical, *Me and My Girl* (1936), to reveal some of the differences in representation that had started to appear. *Me and My Girl* opened in London in 1936 and was revived twice in London during the Second World War. It demonstrates the hierarchy of class and status in its representations of gender (something much less apparent in *Anything Goes*). Written by Douglas Furber and L. Arthur Rose, with music by Noel Gay, *Me and My Girl* tells a male Cinderella story in which a working-class hero, Bill Snibson, inherits the title (and fortune) of the Earl of Hareford, conditional on him learning upper-class etiquette. The Duchess attempts to teach him, encouraging Bill to leave behind his former girlfriend, Sally. Sally, a working-class girl who has impressed the elderly, genial and kindly Sir John with her noble spirit and kind heart is also taught to speak more elegantly. In true musical comedy fashion, some of Bill's good-natured high spirits and common sense rub off on his new relatives so that when Sally reappears with her old spirit and kindness, but with a gentrified voice and accent, all are united and live happily ever after. The issue this musical reveals is a concern with class and hierarchy with both hero and heroine struggling for acceptance from aristocratic relatives. The heteronormative coupling still features a pretty, virginal, though increasingly independent, heroine, while the male protagonist is not the heroic male of the American musical. This hero is a working-class 'cheeky chap', with common sense and 'street-smarts', who is also good natured, high spirited and popular in contrast with the upper-class male who is handsome, well-mannered, educated and charming but rather effete.

The 'Golden Age' – post–Second World War

The Second World War concluded in 1945, with Britain stricken by the blitz and rationing, but buoyed by the socialist introduction of the welfare state (including the NHS). Americans, on the other hand, having participated from December 1941, in a war on foreign soil, had a very different experience and response. It is here that representations of men and women begin to differ, even more fundamentally, on either side of the Atlantic. Despite the differences that will be outlined below, however, both the Broadway and West End stages offered audiences escapism through the reinforcement of conservative values and the concept of the nuclear family. Stacy Wolf notes, for example, that many Golden Age American musicals depict a leading heterosexual couple who 'reconcile their differences, sing together, and marry by the end' (2002, p. 2). This is true, also, of British operettas, including those by Coward, Novello, and later Gay, and American musical comedies and book musicals. Nevertheless, the characters within these entertainments are now quite different and diverse.

KEY CONCEPT: The nuclear family

This 1950s heteronormative ideal suggests that the 'perfect family' consists of a strong father, a loving mother, two children (one of each sex) and, quite often, a pet dog. This model, while considered acceptable for several centuries, grew in prominence in post–Second World War America when families were increasingly splintered by war. It was expanded by the slowly increasing acceptance of diverse identities from the late 1960s onwards (non-white, non-heterosexual etc.). This utopian ideal was promoted throughout popular culture, through television shows like *Father Knows Best* (1954–8), and has since been referenced, or perpetuated, in several musicals. Audrey in *Little Shop of Horrors* (1982), for example, a musical that pastiches 1950s culture, longs for this normative lifestyle in 'Somewhere that's Green'. She sings of settling down with Seymour, the musical's protagonist, in a small-town house (with a white picket fence) to raise children and enjoy pre-prepared meals in front of the television.

The women, particularly in post-war American musicals, developed in complexity, even though traditionally they conformed to heteronormative endings. While *Carousel* (1945) is perhaps best known for its problematic depiction of domestic violence, many of Rodgers and Hammerstein's works feature female leads that advocate equality and have their own voice, while simultaneously looking to form a nuclear family. This paradox is illustrated by Wolf's observation that even the strongest and quirkiest of these female characters are considered problematic. For instance, Nellie in *South Pacific* (1949) and Anna in *The King and I* (1951) are self-determined women who challenge social norms, thus needing to be taught a lesson – typically by a man (Wolf, 2002, p. 1). Anna challenges the King's prejudice and unruly ways throughout the musical yet ultimately falls in love with him as she weeps at his deathbed. Likewise, Maria in *The Sound of Music* (1959) does not conform to either the life of a postulant or the rules enforced by Captain von Trapp. She is sent to the Captain (and his children) as a governess, having been determined a 'demon' and a 'headache' by her fellow nuns. Maria later marries the Captain, fleeing from the Nazis with her newfound family as the show ends. Maria therefore shifts from delinquent nun to loving matriarch, and thus from defiant to conformist, across the musical. She does not embody victimhood like Julie in *Carousel*, written only fourteen years earlier, yet she still fulfils assumed American values by forming a nuclear family in the post-war decades.

Among other Golden Age roles like Sarah in *Guys and Dolls* (1950) and Maria in *West Side Story* (1957), women are all at once conventional and unruly. *Guys and Dolls* (1950) and *The Pajama Game* (1954), for instance, both feature a classic boy-meets-girl narrative, a heterosexual love story (that leads to marriage – or implied marriage), powerful male figures and subservient female roles, mostly in contemporary stories. Most interesting is *Annie Get Your Gun* (1946), in which Annie Oakley is assertive, sings with a forceful belted sound and the syncopations of jazz, while outdoing the hero, even in the range of her voice, in 'Anything You Can Do (I Can Do Better)'. Indeed, Dominic Symonds, like Wolf, reads the female characters of Golden Age musicals as a queer and sexualizing force, whereby they challenge the patriarchal and heterosexual norms of the day (2016).

Meanwhile, the Second World War 'reshaped masculinity' with countless men performing an 'especially heroic, public, [and] gendered citizenship' by going to war and defending their homes and loved ones (Cook, 2009, p. 46). These were represented in Rodgers and Hammerstein's *Oklahoma!* (1943) with cowboys taming the Wild West, and defending their land, offering 'homespun folk-wisdom in common, direct, everyday language' (Knapp, 2005, p. 124). Characters like Curly and Will Parker are young, white and well muscled, and represented 'a new sexualized masculinity embodied by the American GI stationed on British soil' (Symonds, 2016, p. 231). They had dynamic energy in their singing and dancing, which contrasted with the 'English Gentleman', who continued to dominate British representations of a 'hero'. As Symonds notes, 'the Brit was smaller and slimmer, plucky, polite and refined; the American was a product of a popular upbringing that emphasized virility and masculinity' (2016, p. 232). Thus, the American hero and heroine had become more dynamic and sexualized in comparison with their (still) chaste and refined British counterparts.

In another Golden Age musical, *Damn Yankees* (1955), the above roles and stereotypes are expanded even further. Although later musicals, like *How to Succeed in Business Without Really Trying* (1961), returned to outdated ideals, thus complicating a clear trajectory of development, men and woman were being represented in much more diverse ways by the mid-1950s and into the turbulent 1960s.

CASE STUDY: *Damn Yankees* (1955)

Music: Richard Adler. Lyrics: Jerry Ross. Book: George Abbott and Douglass Wallop.

This Faustian story depicts Joe Boyd (a long-time fan of baseball team, the Washington Senators) sell his soul to the devil (the greasy salesman, Mr Applegate) in exchange for the opportunity to lead his team to victory as the young 'long-ball hitter', Joe Hardy. Unusually for such Faustian tales, the wily Joe insists on an escape clause that will allow him to return home to his loving wife, Meg, if he refuses to play in the last game of the season and walks away that evening. Young Joe soon becomes successful but misses his wife. Applegate, meanwhile, sensing defeat, needs to find ways to ensure he wins the deal. He sends a seductress, Lola, to distract Joe, and even involves him in a court case, but ultimately Joe's love for Meg wins the day (meaning Lola and Applegate disappear back to hell).

Originally directed by George Abbott, with choreography by Bob Fosse, and starring Gwen Verdon as Lola, *Damn Yankees* won seven Tony Awards in 1956, including Best Musical, Best Actress and Best Choreography. The musical was adapted for film in 1958, again starring Verdon, and has since been revived in both New York (1994) and London (1997).

The women in *Damn Yankees* include the wife, Meg, who is suddenly left by Joe when he disappears. As Jessica Sternfeld observes, Meg is 'less a passive 1950s housewife and more a World War II-style war widow' (2009, p. 78); she is the archetypal wife, a loving and forgiving homemaker. Her counterpart, and the leading actress in the show, is the dangerous and sexy Lola, as seen in Figure 5.2. These two images, the devoted housewife and the glamorous diva, create a contrasting pair that is found in many films and musicals. In this case, however, both characters move beyond these stereotypes. Meg becomes landlady to the young Joe Hardy and speaks out in his defence, while Lola, having attempted to seduce him, becomes a friend.

Meanwhile, the male characters are Joe Boyd, the aging, soft, suburban 'couch potato' and loving husband, and his alter ego, Joe Hardy, the young, healthy, fit and successful sportsman, while the second male character is the magical villain of the piece (known as Mr Applegate). The pairings of young

Figure 5.2 Posed publicity photo of Gwen Verdon in the stage production *Damn Yankees*. 1955. © Billy Rose Theatre Division, the New York Public Library for the Performing Arts.

and aging Joe, plus that between Meg and Lola, seem to reflect something of the zeitgeist in the post-war years. It warns 'of the dangers of flying too close to the sun and the comforting beauty of the simple things at home', which is a direct representation of the conflicts of its era: 'between soldiers and suburban men; between war and leisure; between men and women; between types of women' (Sternfeld, 2009, p. 82). The show is therefore sexualized, in both female and male representations, through the presentation of the fit, healthy and able male body and the dancing female seductress, even as it finally resolves that home and family – the heteronormative duality – is best.

In Britain, the most popular musical of the (supposedly sexually liberated) 1960s was Lionel Bart's *Oliver!* (1960). Based on Charles Dickens's novel *Oliver Twist* (1839), the musical is set in Victorian London and features one female heroine: the prostitute, Nancy. Although Nancy does not enter until towards the end of the first act, she dominates the proceedings when she does. She is excessive, brash, though motherly and caring, and leads Oliver, the Artful Dodger and Fagin's gang in two consecutive numbers. In those songs, Nancy claims that she 'rough[s] it' and 'love[s] it', without a care for what the world may think of her, since her existence is 'a fine, fine life'. She is a sexually active woman, a liar and a thief, though a motherly and caring one, who must be punished for her 'bad woman' character. Nancy is not left alone and unhappy like Fagin in the same musical, or Charity in *Sweet Charity* (1966), but dead, thus illustrating the cultural 'anxiety about strong, assertive women in the 1960s' (Wolf, 2011, p. 86).

Nancy is the victim of domestic abuse, something of a norm in representations of working-class culture (as noted in the earlier discussion of *Made in Dagenham*). Despite her best efforts to protect herself, and later Oliver, this situation is inevitable for Nancy, which leads to her death at the hands of her lover, Bill Sykes. As the musical's villain, Sykes is feared for his violent temper. The kind, dutiful and loving child, Oliver, however, is the closest to a hero in this show, while Fagin is perhaps an example of the anti-hero. Fagin is the adult protagonist of the story, a father figure to the gang of young boys, but one who lacks the heroic qualities of goodness, morality and courage. Although Sykes dies for his crimes, Fagin closes the musical alone with the promise of a fresh start (unlike in Dicken's novel where he is executed).

Diversity and difference – after the 1960s

Alongside the gender representations explored above, many of which were created, developed and produced by educated white men, there exists a series of contributions that demonstrate the greater appreciation and understanding of diversity that began around the time of the counter-cultural and civil rights movements of the late 1960s. The diversity of representations snowballed after these movements won greater freedom to overtly perform multiple sexualities and equality between races. In some works, this increased diversity was reflected in much more complex characters. Stephen Sondheim and his collaborators, for example, wrote characters that no longer conformed to the tropes of hero or heroine. Sweeney Todd, for example, in the 1979 musical of the same name, is a man who is both victim and villain, with all of the musical's other characters also being represented as damaged or vulnerable in some way. In *Sunday in the Park with George* (1984), George struggles to simultaneously maintain his work as an artist and a romantic relationship with Dot, constantly having to compromise one or the other. In Act 2, similar issues are faced by a second George, another artist (and Act 1 George's great-grandson), thus illustrating such issues as human, rather than context specific. Humanity is ultimately flawed, and Sondheim's great skill is to represent that complexity, in both female and male roles, in works that have been effective as stripped-back chamber pieces, as well as on larger West End and Broadway stages. The same can also be said for the work of contemporary composers like Michael John LaChiusa, Adam Guettel and Jeanine Tesori.

Meanwhile, the megamusicals produced by Cameron Mackintosh and/or Andrew Lloyd Webber's Really Useful Group moved in the other direction. The scale of these works led to a regression of interest in character complexity, which meant a greater reliance on the broad brushstrokes of stereotypical representations. In *Jesus Christ Superstar* (1971), Jesus is the hero and Pilate is the villain, while Judas is conflicted. The only role for a woman is the prostitute Mary Magdalene, a loving suppliant and aide (though she does not die). *Evita* (1978) is the fallen woman at the centre of her story, and once her complexity and her mistakes are revealed, she dies. Although this is historically correct – Eva Peron died of cancer at the age of 33 – the stereotype is reinforced by yet another fallen woman in a commercial and global success. *Les Misérables* (1985) is perhaps the exception with Javert and Valjean – villain and hero – both given complex motivations for their actions, even though audiences are clearly intended to empathize with one (Valjean) over the other (Javert). Meanwhile, Cosette is a virginal heroine and Madame Thénardier is an unscrupulous thief, while Fantine and Eponine, the fallen and jilted women, must die. Perhaps excused, only in part, by the historical settings of these shows, the British megamusical returned musical theatre to its narrow and misogynist past.

Undoubtedly, this has been a narrow, predominantly white history so far. As Lisa M. Anderson (1997) notes, however, racial stereotypes such as the Mammy (a matriarch), the tragic Mulatto (a mixed-race woman) or the Jezebel (a promiscuous woman) have been widespread in representations of black women until very recently. This began to change in the late 1960s and has made little progress since. *Hair: The American Tribal Love-Rock Musical* (1967), for example, as detailed in Chapter 4, has been read as both typically sexist and a site for resistance. In 'Black Boys/White Boys', for instance, a trio of white female singers resemble a girl group (The Andrews Sisters or the Beverley Sisters), while singing about their desire for black men (thus challenging the taboo of interracial sex/relationships). In response, a trio of women of colour (like The Supremes or The Three Degrees) generate conformity and community with the white trio by singing of their own desire for white men. Although this playful number sexualizes these women, it notably depicts both black and white women with equality and sameness (Browne, 2018, p. 294). Moreover, *The Wiz* (1975), created by an African American creative team for a cast of non-white performers, reimagined *The Wizard of Oz*. Unlike Judy Garland's child-like interpretation in the 1939 MGM film, *The Wiz* presents Dorothy as a sophisticated and mature young African American woman. Songs like 'Home' are used to empower Dorothy to understand the world's dangers and the importance of finding home, something that may have been 'influenced by black histories of migration, struggle and faith' (Bunch, 2015, p. 61).

Since then, musicals like *Dreamgirls* (1981), *Bombay Dreams* (2002), *Caroline, Or Change* (2004) and *Hamilton* (2015) are among musicals that have provided opportunities for performers of colour in both performance centres. Audra McDonald, for example, an African American actress, has won more Tony Awards than any other performer in history (with six awards across all four acting categories). Despite frequently playing downtrodden women of colour, like Sarah in *Ragtime* (1998), McDonald represents, alongside actors like Lin-Manuel Miranda, Billy Porter and Norm Lewis, a challenge to musical theatre's 'whitewashed' past. Furthermore, the presentation of non-white bodies on stage has provoked awareness of the diversity of topics, creators, performers and representations in the commercial centres of musical theatre. *Dreamgirls*, in particular, was not just complex in its representation of gender, but of difference, where Effie is not an acceptable size or shape to be considered beautiful but is also problematic in that it was an all-black show with an all-white creative and production team (as with some of the musicals noted above). As Wollman notices, the musical's 'feel-good ending', where all four members of the Dreams are reunited, 'allowed the musical to evade condemnation of structural racism in America and its entertainment systems' (2017, p. 165).

In addition to racial diversity, sexual diversity began to be more openly depicted in representations of both men and women. In the late 1960s and early 1970s, two musicals, one British, one American, dramatically altered the representation of contemporary men and women. *Hair* has been referred to above for its racial diversity, but it also introduced overtly sexualized behaviour and communal living, as well as featuring the pregnancy of an unmarried women. By contrast, most of the male characters are feminized except Claude, the soldier who dies. British-born *The Rocky Horror Show* (1973), meanwhile, introduced both transvestism and bisexuality (even pansexuality) to British and American stages, led by characters from another planet. The central human couple, Brad and Janet, engage in sexual acts with Frank-N-Furter, a self-described 'sweet transvestite', that leave them shocked, even changed. They remain, however, white, Anglo-Saxon, protestant (WASP) and heterosexual characters – the all-American teenage sweethearts. A safe distance is therefore created around queer behaviours, where the excesses of Frank and his entourage, and even the humans among them, are framed and contained.

By the 1980s, however, and throughout the AIDS crisis, there began to appear (typically American) representations of gay men in relationships, leading ordinary lives, and living through difficult situations. *La Cage Aux Folles* (1983) was the first successful Broadway musical to feature such a positive representation of the relationship between two men. Even though the structure and depiction of family stereotypes remained conservative, the show avoided political statements, and perhaps appeased straight audiences, 'rather than attempt to educate, inform, or challenge stereotypes' (Wollman, 2017, p. 167). The strength of its characters and plot mean that it is frequently revived, bringing a different representation of homosexuality to the mainstream commercial stage. Later, *Falsettos* (1992), that was developed as separate one-act musicals in 1979, 1981 and 1990, introduced a nuclear family in which the gay lover (Whizzer) is also the only man with the sporting ability to instruct the child (Jason) on how to play baseball. Then, as with the 'bad women' of earlier musicals, he is the one to contract AIDS and die. On the other hand, love songs and loving relationships are presented here not just between the bi/homosexual men but also between the (self-described) 'lesbians from next door'. Interestingly, the latter couple has often been cast to include at least one Black woman, introducing yet another aspect of diversity.

Sexual and racial diversity are also apparent in *The Color Purple* (2005), the musical adaptation of Alice Walker's 1982 novel (and the 1985 film that followed). While these categories do not always cleanly apply, Sophia (matriarch), Celie (tragic mulatto) and Shug (jezebel) embody many racial stereotypes at the start. Protagonist Celie is beaten, raped and frequently abused by her stepfather and her husband. Paradoxically, however, Celie discovers her identity and freedom as a strong independent woman through a lesbian relationship with the feisty local performer, Shug Avery. In 'Too Beautiful for Words', Shug encourages Celie to embrace her own beauty, a notion that is continued in their later love duet, 'What About Love?'. By the time Shug decides to leave Celie, for a young male musician, Celie has embraced her newfound power and agency and has begun her own business, meaning she stands firm and sings of her newfound self-belief in 'I'm Here'. For James Lovelock, the success of *The Color Purple* does not stem from its position as a 'black musical', a 'feminist musical' or a 'lesbian musical', but the combinative (or intersectional) power of these three identities (2019, p. 195).

We will return to more recent examples of non-conforming gender and sexual identities to close the chapter, yet a production that perhaps best encapsulates the increasingly diverse representations of men and women at the end of the twentieth century is *RENT* (1996).

CASE STUDY: *RENT* (1996)

Music, lyrics and book: Jonathan Larson.

Based on Henri Murger's *Scènes de La Vie Bohème* (1851) which is also the source for Puccini, Illica and Giacosa's opera *La Bohème* (1896) (a more widely known intertext), the sung-through musical concerns a group of starving artists living (and dying) in New York's East Village at the peak of the AIDS crisis. Roger and Mark share a freezing garret apartment, from where they both try to work as artists. Mark leaves to help his former girlfriend Maureen (a performance artist), and her new girlfriend, Joanne, set up her protest performance. She is protesting the threatened closure of a nearby homeless lot. Meanwhile, exotic dancer Mimi knocks on Roger's door to ask for help and begins to establish a relationship with him. It is only later when they discover that they are both

HIV positive, as a result of drug abuse, that the relationship moves forward. In a third story line, Tom Collins (another member of the group) is helped by Angel (a drag performer) when he is attacked and robbed on the street. They soon form a romantic relationship and are both, also, HIV positive. In the course of the musical these relationships develop, are strained and break partly as a result of their economic situations and their career choices. Angel suddenly dies, and the friends meet again at the funeral. Roger discovers that Mimi has been unwell and has sought protection from Benny (Roger and Mark's reviled landlord), and briefly leaves New York for Sante Fe. The musical closes with both Roger and Mark having found artistic inspiration presenting their new artistic offerings to the reunited group. Mimi almost dies, but recovers on hearing Roger's new song, and all move forward together, vowing to enjoy what time they have left.

RENT received the Pulitzer Prize for Drama and the Tony Award for Best Musical, among others, in 1996, and ran for twelve years on Broadway. It opened in the West End in 1998, closing the following year, and was heavily revised as *Rent Remixed* in 2007 with British characters and radical new arrangements. Many of the original Broadway cast starred in the 2005 film adaptation.

These are diverse representations, even though the musical is based on a novel and opera that enacted many of the old stereotypes of strong men and subservient women. Mimi (cis) and Angel (often read as trans) are two sexually active and confident women. While both characters are ultimately victims (Angel dies and Mimi suffers), and Angel's femininity is often read as constructed through drag, *RENT* is notable for its open acceptance of diversity and the engagement of the characters in complex loving relationships of all types. The two lesbian (or bisexual) figures, Joanne and Maureen, fulfil the butch and femme stereotypes of lesbian pairings, with Maureen depicted as feisty and unfaithful and Joanne as a workaholic who demands loyalty and faithfulness. Meanwhile, Roger and Mimi fulfil the stereotype of vulnerable women saved by strong men. Despite the predictability of these patterns, this musical diversifies the former duality of heteronormative characters and relationships.

Into the twenty-first century

Mamma Mia! opened in 1999 and depicted motherhood as an act of independence and strength. While it was not the first British musical to depict single mothers (*Blood Brothers* had dealt with the subject in a much more complex and political narrative in 1983), it echoed the increasing rise of single parent families in Britain (with one in four families including a single parent by 2018). More recently, Margaret in *Everybody's Talking about Jamie* (2017) is depicted as a feisty and supportive mother who relies solely on the support of her female friend, Ray, in raising her son, Jamie (a drag queen). Jamie's father, on the other hand, is presented as a one-dimensional bigot, who rejects Jamie and his life choices. Jamie's drag queen companions, however, all of whom understand the ways toxic masculinity can affect homosexual teenagers, sing of using feminine items, like make-up, as a defence mechanism to go 'over the top' as a way to counter discrimination. It is femininity, here, or objects that represent exaggerated femininity, like heels and handbags, that provide these men with perceived strength.

In a different kind of representation, *Calendar Girls: The Musical* (2017), formerly *The Girls*, depicts a group of middle-aged women who raise money for a hospital sofa by posing nude for a charity calendar (based on a true story, and the earlier film and play). One mother, Cora, resists joining the group in fear that the calendar will only exacerbate the struggles she faces as a single mother 'trying to pull off a hard duet'. Having hidden her involvement from her son, Tommo, the calendar is revealed in the final scene in which Cora worries that she has set a bad example. However, Tommo quickly expresses his pride for his strong and outspoken mother, suggesting that she is the 'best dad a mother could be'. The family unit is thus presented here as led by women, and strong women at that, who rarely require husbands or father figures to set admirable examples for their children.

In America, a country with similar percentages of single mother-led families, this trend is perhaps best illustrated by Sara Bareilles and Jesse Nelson's musical *Waitress* (2016) – a show celebrated for its all-female creative team. Unlike the above British works, however, *Waitress* relies on a narrative of domestic abuse, before celebrating single mothers. Jenna, the pregnant protagonist, spends most of the musical intending to leave her abusive husband by winning a cash prize at a local pie-baking competition. She needs the support not just of her friends but of a sexual relationship with her male gynaecologist to build the courage to achieve independence, later being gifted the pie diner in which she works by its dying owner, Joe, whom she has befriended. She is represented as talented and kind, but her success results from the interventions of men. The politics of this show are therefore complex and rather old-fashioned. On the other hand, it adds a new perspective that reflects the recent trend of 'choice feminism' in which women, discounting the limitations afforded by race, sexuality and other identities, are able to make their own choices. *Waitress* portrays a woman finding strength and courage in perhaps the most stereotypically feminine act, having a baby, supported by her close and diverse group of female friends. Meanwhile, the men in these musicals have become cyphers and stereotypes, rather than fully rounded or complex characters. Instead, it is often the teenage boys of musicals such as *Billy Elliot: The Musical, Dear Evan Hansen* and *Everybody's Talking about Jamie* that demonstrate mature and emotionally intelligent characteristics.

In recent years, this progression has moved beyond male/female or masculine/feminine binaries and identities across the LGBTQ+ (or queer) spectrum have been depicted. In 2015, *Fun Home* became the first Broadway musical to feature a lesbian protagonist, Alison Bechdel, whose autobiographical graphic novel is the source text for the musical. Alison is played by three actresses who represent Alison at age 10, as a college student, and in middle age looking back on these important periods of her life. She recalls her growing awareness and enactment of her own sexuality as she reflects on her father's inability to acknowledge his sexuality. Ultimately, she recalls and becomes reconciled to the pain of her father's suicide that happened just after she came out while still at college. Alison fulfils the butch lesbian trope while Alison's father, Bruce, challenges conventional perceptions of masculinity and fatherhood, since he is known for his passion for interior design and is seen attempting to seduce a young man (see Knapp, 2020). Elsewhere, Broadway musical *If/Then* (2014) featured a bisexual character, while *The Prom* (2019) depicted a lesbian couple fighting to attend their high-school prom together. In 2020, Michael R. Jackson's autobiographical musical, *A Strange Loop*, won the Pulitzer Prize for Drama, among other accolades. The show follows a self-described 'angsty, gay, black man' named Usher, so called because of his day job as a theatre usher, trying to ghost-write a new play for Tyler Perry in a world that is overwhelmingly heteronormative and white.

Hedwig and the Angry Inch (1998), on the other hand, is an early example of transgender representation, though the musical relies on the trauma caused by an individual's failed gender reassignment surgery, rather than its achievement. Despite transgender or non-binary identities being frequently depicted in film or on television today, however, as in FX's series *Pose* (2018–21), transgender and non-binary identities are either rarely or thinly represented in contemporary musical theatre. The limited examples include the non-binary roles of May in the British Max Martin jukebox musical, *& Juliet* (2019) and Pythio in *Head Over Heels* (2018), the American Go-Go's jukebox musical. This latter role was originated by Peppermint, a past contestant on *RuPaul's Drag Race* (2009–), who was the first transgender woman to originate a principal role on Broadway. While these works have been celebrated, the Alanis Morissette jukebox musical, *Jagged Little Pill*, was considered regressive when a non-binary role was removed between the show's pre-Broadway and Broadway productions. In particular, the role of Jo, as played by Lauren Patten (a cisgender woman) in both versions, was no longer a non-binary character negotiating their gender identity when the musical finally opened in New York; 'gender identity' was removed from the list of themes tackled within the show and cast members insisted that the role was always cis in interviews (Lewis, 2021).

Perhaps more frequent is the trend of transgender performers including Laverne Cox playing typically cast cisgender roles, such as Dr Frank-N-Furter in FOX's television version of *The Rocky Horror Picture Show* (2016). The casting of transgender roles with cisgendered performers, however, and so the reverse of this inclusive trend, has caused some controversy. For example, the producers of *Breakfast on Pluto* (2020), a new musical scheduled to tour prior to a London run, though stalled by the Covid-19 pandemic, was criticized for casting a cisgender actor, Fra Fee, in the leading transgender role. His castmate, Kate O'Donnell, a transgender actress cast in a cisgender role, quit the production in response to the controversy and the casting practices, with Fee also later withdrawing. Similarly, the musical adaptations of *Tootsie* (2019 [1982]) and *Mrs Doubtfire* (2020 [1993]), both older films that feature cisgender men living as women, were criticized by some critics and audiences as transphobic (Lewis, 2019). Nevertheless, this was not the case when Julie Andrews and Barbra Streisand (both cisgender actresses) played cisgender women living as men in 1980s film musicals *Victor/Victoria* (1982) and *Yentl* (1983), respectively; time and cultural conversations have clearly moved on.

Although many of the aforementioned examples are playful, lacking depth and sophistication, they signal continuing development in the representation of personal identities in musical theatre, including those outside traditional racial, gender and sexuality binaries. It is clear that women are no longer only expected (or permitted) to pose, half-dressed in silence, though objectification certainly still occurs, just as men are no longer merely macho heterosexual heroes. It is clear, also, that such binary identities are themselves increasingly outdated in a society that continues to diversify the vocabulary that defines various personal identities. As addressed at the start of this chapter, musicals like *Made in Dagenham* suggest that everyone, no matter their gender identity, should 'stand up' for equality and inclusion. This chapter, in turn, has shown that musical theatre has attempted to do just that. The road may have been bumpy, with musicals often valuing conservative representations over contemporary alternatives, yet significant progress has occurred in works that have reached, entertained and perhaps influenced popular, conservative audiences. This story, however, is not yet finished. Misogyny, race crime and hatred of sexual diversity continue to be battled across Britain, America and around the world and will only be resolved when collectively we, as Rita O'Grady suggests, 'make a stand for everyone'.

Tasks

Propose a new contemporary musical that is both diverse and complex in terms of its representation of gender and personal identity. What might a relevant story or topical themes be? Would the production draw upon current or past representations of identity? If so, how and why? How might you cast the production to reflect its content?

Explore the reviews and production history of a musical with typically problematic gender representation, such as *Carousel* (1945) or *My Fair Lady* (1956). How have directors and creative teams tackled these issues in different productions? How have these shows been revived in relation to new cultural contexts?

Discussion topics

The history of the American showgirl (think Ziegfeld's *Follies*) relies on the commodification of the female body. To what extent is this still the case today? How might the New York–based dance company, *The Rockettes* (1925–), be read as a contemporary iteration of the *Follies*? How does this compare with the representation of men in London-born *Magic Mike Live* (2018)? Has any progress been made in light of these examples?

What does the depiction of women in contemporary musicals like *Six* (2017) or *Mean Girls* (2018) say about contemporary culture? How are recent works rewriting or perpetuating existing stereotypes? The same can also be considered regarding masculinity in musicals such as *Dear Evan Hansen* (2016) and *Be More Chill* (2018).

Further reading – conceptual

Knapp, R. (2006) *The American Musical and the Performance of Personal Identity*. Princeton and Oxford: Princeton University Press.

Lovelock, J. (2019) '"What about Love?": Claiming and Re-Claiming LGBTQ+ Spaces in 21st Century Musical Theatre'. In: S. Whitfield (ed.) *Reframing the Musical: Race, Culture and Identity*. London: Red Globe Press, 187–209.

Solga, K. (2016) *Theatre & Feminism*. Basingstoke: Palgrave.

Wolf, S. (2011) *Changed for Good: A Feminist History of the Broadway Musical*. New York: Oxford University Press.

Further reading – case study

Forsgren, L. D. L. (2019) '*The Wiz* Redux; or, Why Queer Black Feminist Spectatorship and Politically Engaged Popular Entertainment Continue to Matter'. *Theatre Survey* 60/3: 325–54.

Lewis, C. (2021) 'One Step Forward, Two Steps Back: Broadway's Jagged Little Journey toward Nonbinary Inclusion.' *The Brooklyn Rail*. Available at: https://brooklynrail.org/2021/04/theater/One-Step-Forward-Two-Steps-Back-Broadways-Jagged-Little-Journey-Toward-Nonbinary-Inclusion. [Accessed: 23 March 2022].

Sternfeld, J. (2009). '*Damn Yankees* and the 1950s Man: You Gotta Have (Loyalty, an Escape Clause, and) Heart'. *Studies in Musical Theatre* 3/1: 77–83.

6

'Another national anthem': From ourselves to the other

In the centre of Times Square in New York, also considered the heart of Broadway, stands a statue of George M. Cohan. Having cut his teeth as a performer and writer, Cohan became famous for his ability to transfer the American vernacular of vaudeville to the musical comedy stage at the turn of the twentieth century. He developed a distinctively patriotic persona, using language, tone, character and wit, through which he could perform enthusiastic statements of nationalism in songs like 'Give My Regards to Broadway'. In *Little Johnny Jones* (1904), which he wrote and in which he played the eponymous role, Cohan sang, 'I'm a Yankee Doodle Dandy / A Yankee Doodle, do or die / A real live nephew of my Uncle Sam / Born on the Fourth of July'. *Little Johnny Jones*, like many other early musical comedies, represented a particular kind of American patriotism. Set at a time when British imperialism was waning, and being replaced by American cultural imperialism, industrial expansion and immigration, the show offers the possibility to understand how American musical theatre characterized itself (and other nations) at the start of the twentieth century. *Little Johnny Jones* does not only represent Americanness, however. It is set in England and includes English characters, as well as an offensive stereotype of a Chinese man. The musical is thus cross-cultural and transatlantic in its depiction of American and British characters by American performers on the Broadway stage (a trope that has continued from *My Fair Lady* [1956] to *Kinky Boots* [2013]).

Even in musicals that contain little within the narrative that seems to have social relevance, understanding what is taken for granted or what is treated as normal can illustrate what was happening in society at a particular time. At which moments in history were American creatives representing, even celebrating, their national heritage, and at which times were they not? By analysing the content of works of popular culture, such as musicals, and the depictions of characters they contain, widely held contemporary messages emerge about what it meant to be American, as well as how Americans created stereotypes of the British. This pattern, of course, is not uniquely American, since the British created their own stereotypes of themselves, of Americans, and others, which were rarely positive and generally reductive. In most cases, there was an absence of diverse people or non-white people, except as stereotypes. Characters were predominantly English in British works, such that the Scottish, Irish and Welsh were minorities who had their own stereotypes within English/British musicals. As Nadine Holdsworth writes in *Theatre & Nation*, '[t]hroughout history people have established group formations to distinguish "us" from "them", whether territorial, linguistic, or around bloodlines or religion, for example. In the contemporary world, nation is one of the most powerful of these markers of identity and belonging' (2010, p. 9). These representations thus provide insight into contemporary themes, concerns and anxieties in the two countries about their own places in the world.

No matter the prevalence of a depiction in a particular era, such representations of the self and the other, and their interpretations by audiences, remain fluid – constantly changing in relation to international political, economic and cultural contexts. Given that musical theatre 'dramatized, mirrored, or challenged our deeply-held cultural attitudes and beliefs' throughout the twentieth century, analysing these representations enables us to discover the issues, the contexts and the absences from mainstream debate, and review these evolving indicators of identity (Bush Jones, 2003, p. 1). Nations and societies understand themselves in relation to others, a notion that has resulted in treaties and wars, as well as a multitude of interesting and complex representations across the musical theatre canon. Importantly, as a result of migration and colonization the people located within a nation might also be diverse with complex histories that latterly have begun to introduce hybrid forms of national identity and diasporic communities. This chapter will therefore explore several representations of 'Britishness' and 'Americanness', in musicals at key points in the twentieth and twenty-first centuries, as well as representations of immigrant, diasporic or hybrid identities, to explore how representation has frequently shifted to reflect changing contexts and current anxieties.

KEY CONCEPT: Nation and nationhood

A nation is a flexible concept, though it might at first appear to be an obvious one. For example, is a nation defined by its borders to create a territory? In which case, is England a separate territory and nation from Wales or Northern Ireland? Likewise, what are the differences among US states from Arizona to Vermont? If a nation is defined by its boundaries and borders then there are consequences for the movement of people, goods and money. Think, for example, of the troubled issue of immigration at the Mexican border or, in Britain, the problematic history of the Irish border, first through the nationalist and unionist 'Troubles' in Northern Ireland (late 1960s–90s) and then in recent negotiations over Brexit. In some cases, nations define themselves in relation to history or religion, as also happened in the Irish 'Troubles' when Catholic Republicans wanted to unite the island of Ireland, while the Protestant Unionists preferred to retain the Union within the United Kingdom. This even affects football (soccer) in Glasgow, where Rangers fans are traditionally Protestant and Celtic fans are often from Catholic communities. Many of the issues that arose over the redrawing of territories in the Middle East and on the India/Pakistan border by colonizers have resulted in the splitting of tribal and religious communities. Consider the situation of the Kurdish people in Northern Iraq and Southern Turkey who have no home territory, but a shared sense of a historical community. Should the 'nation' result from the tribal history, religion, or lines and borders on a map? Plus, in either case, which point in history should we refer to when assessing the borders or the tribal territories?

One of the results of global dispersion in the postcolonial era (see Chapter 7) is the creation of diasporic communities (a scattered population) who may perceive themselves to have both a home (where they live) and a historical homeland (where their ancestors arrived from). Irish Americans, for example, even after many generations, may retain a sense of affinity to an ancient homeland. In the end, Holdsworth suggests that 'the way a nation sees itself and projects itself to others is tied up in the narratives a nation tells itself about itself including both the "what" and the "how" of the telling' (2010, p. 1). Nation is a fluid concept that in many respects is defined more by the people who populate, or associate themselves with certain locations, and the culture produced by them, than any geographical borders.

Before the Great War

Little Johnny Jones is a fast and farcical show, abounding with patriotic themes and songs, and is one of eleven musicals by George M. Cohan that appeared on Broadway between 1901 and 1911 (known as his 'flag plays'). You can see references to the flag in the poster in Figure 6.1. It is archetypal of Cohan who, according to John Bush Jones, drew plots from Greco-Roman comedy and added a 'thoroughly American spin' (2003, p. 19). These works also often contain reverse depictions of sex and wealth from the original narratives so that, instead of wealthy boys loving slave girls, young men from any background can rise to 'wealth, status, fame and happiness' and

Figure 6.1 Poster for *Little Johnny Jones*.

marry girls of fortune (Bush Jones, 2003, p. 20) – a reverse Cinderella story. Given that this was a period of intense immigration from Europe to America, the myth that it was a land of opportunity was important in giving hope to the poor and dispossessed and in promoting a sense of what nationhood represented. In *Little Johnny Jones*, and other Cohan shows, romantic love triumphs over family, money and class, thereby reinforcing the notion that there are no class barriers in the United States.

CASE STUDY: *Little Johnny Jones* (1904)

Music, lyrics and book: George M. Cohan.

Race jockey, Johnny Jones, arrives in London with his friend, the Irish American, Timothy D. McGee, to ride in the Epsom Derby – and is expected to win. His girlfriend, the wealthy heiress, Goldie, has been left at home in San Francisco for many months waiting for him to be able to afford to marry her. Meanwhile, her aunt, Mrs Kenworth, who intends to marry Goldie to the English Earl of Bloomsbury (the exchange of a British title for an American fortune), has also arrived in London with her paramour, the villain of the piece, Anthony Anstey. Already in London is the sports journalist Flo. Heroine Goldie has arrived incognito but recognizes her friend Flo and tells her of her plan to reveal herself to Johnny after he wins the Derby. However, Goldie discovers the plot to marry her to the Earl and first disguises herself as a French mademoiselle, and then as the Earl himself, in a comic farce that (naturally) goes askew. Goldie attempts to fool others by writing a letter to Johnny claiming that she no longer loves him, and instead will marry the Earl, which Johnny unintentionally receives/reads. Johnny is so downcast that he loses the race and is charged with having deliberately thrown the race – which is not just a stain on his honour and reputation, but illegal. He stays in England to clear his name, while everyone else sails back to America. His name is cleared when the fake Chinese man, Sing Song, is revealed to be an undercover investigator who charges Anstey for setting up Jones. Wilson also reveals Anstey to be the owner of the San Francisco Chinese lottery. Everything ends happily, as Goldie marries Johnny, Flo falls for and marries McGee, and Mrs Kenworth is saved from having her fortune stolen by the fraudulent Anstey.

The show was adapted as a film both in 1923 (silent) and 1929 (an early 'talkie'), with James Cagney later depicting scenes from *Little Johnny Jones* in the popular MGM movie musical, *Yankee Doodle Dandy* (1942). A 1982 Broadway revival, adapted by Alfred Uhry and starring Donny Osmond, closed after only one performance.

Interestingly, in this early period of transatlantic travel, many convoluted and farcical comedies were set abroad, as wealthy Americans arrive in London or Paris. British and European parents attempt to secure titles for their daughters in exchange for wealth from the New World but are outwitted by the successful and worldly young American heroes and heroines. The younger generation frequently outsmarts the older generation and blocks the influence of nostalgia and the old world. The 'Others' in these shows, the British and French predominantly, are less intelligent and lacking in 'street smarts', especially those who belong to the aristocracy who are lazy and effete. As Elizabeth Titrington Craft remarks, '[c]ommon wisdom on "international" or "foreign" marriages, the contemporary terms for those marriages between titled Europeans and high society Americans, held that the member of the nobility was seeking wealth and the American (or her parents) jockeying for a title. In this regard, *Little Johnny Jones* reflected contemporary distaste (tinged, perhaps, with admiration or envy) for these unions' (2012). The locations, however, offer an opportunity for exotic colour and novelty numbers, such as ''Op in Me 'Ansom', which is sung by a chorus of taxi (hansom cab) drivers and female reformers (suffragettes) who sing about touring London.

The absurd disguise of the investigator as Sing Song gives the opportunity for a joke about Chinese laundries, and the entire stereotype demonstrates a level of anxiety about 'Others', not just from Europe and Britain, but with more vitriol in relation to those from Asia. Chinese immigrants had arrived in America to work as labourers in the nineteenth century and were excluded in law by the Chinese Exclusion Act of 1892 (the Geary Act). There were also miscegenation laws in many states to prevent naturalization through inter-racial marriage. Despite the US victory in the Spanish-American War (1898), which led to the acquisition of Puerto Rico, the Philippines and Hawaii, isolationism and distrust of foreigners surfaced following a Russian-Japanese peace agreement and the Moroccan crisis of 1905–6. This distrust of foreign Others is more complex in relation to the British, since the separation of Americans from their British former colonial rulers continues to be a source of pride in America (Independence Day). This sense of pride in being different from other countries is represented in one particular exchange in *Little Johnny Jones* (though there are other examples). When asked 'What makes the Americans so proud of their country?', villain Anstey replies: '*Other* countries'. This show, therefore, seems to be creating the sense of a national identity for America that is different from, and unique among, others at a time when concern over immigration was high.

Cohan used song and dance to express his patriotism, a patriotism that articulates America's difference from the Old World, in his use of vernacular language, fashionable dance styles and popular song-writing (ragtime rhythms and vaudeville-style fast-paced comic verbal interactions and contemporary slang). In *Little Johnny Jones*, the songs include what became his 'first big chauvinistic crowd-pleaser' (Bush Jones, 2003, p. 21). 'The Yankee Doodle Boy' was first performed by Cohan (himself an Irish American) and reflected a nationalistic response to the treatment of Irish immigrants in America (Knapp, 2005, p. 106). Other songs in the show refer to the older European heritage, such as the nostalgic waltz, 'Good Old California', while 'Give My Regards to Broadway', perhaps Cohan's most famous song beyond America, demonstrated an understanding not just of America as the centre of the world, but of New York and specifically Broadway's show business as its beating heart (Bush Jones, 2003, p. 22). As Raymond Knapp notes, that song represents 'a musical genre, deriving from the minstrel stage and black spirituals, that was becoming emblematic of America' (2005, p. 107). It was also a genre that moved away from 'European concepts of nationhood and nationalism' to 'a land where "All men were created equal" (however perversely "men" might have been defined at different times in its history)' (Knapp, 2005, p. 20). In the end, and despite the complex somewhat xenophobic representation of English and Chinese 'Others', *Little Johnny Jones* sends a very clear message that although travelling to Europe – where you will meet all your American friends – is great fun, home and upright American husbands are better. This trend continued well into the twentieth century, particularly given the turmoil caused by two world wars, during which American values continued to be mythologized.

The Great War and its aftermath

While the first shots of the First World War (called the Great War, and 'the war to end all wars', until the Second World War made it apparent that it was only the first) were fired in Europe on 28 June 1914, Americans remained insulated on another continent until joining the war in 1917. Nevertheless, patriotism continued throughout this period, especially in revues such as the *Ziegfeld Follies*. This may have been fuelled by further immigration from Europe, a movement that included composers, writers and artists, fleeing war and persecution. At the same time, the war ended a period when European operetta and British musical comedy had been widely transferred to Broadway. In 1914, thirteen of thirty-four shows on Broadway were imports from either Vienna or Germany, two were revivals, eight were revues, and only eleven were American 'book' musicals, with 'a number of them in the style of Old World operetta' (Bush Jones, 2003, p. 47). Now, only partly because of the war, which closed theatres and made Atlantic travel difficult, America entered a period when Broadway developed its own home-grown book musicals. As Bush Jones remarks, 'new American music, in productions that mostly flaunted style over substance, would mirror and express the lifestyle of the postwar 1920s' (2003, p. 51).

Meanwhile, in London, the onset of hostilities led to a rise in patriotic revues and spectacular escapist musicals set in exotic idealized foreign locations, such as *The Maid of the Mountains* (1917). Interestingly, though, several West End shows began to reflect the aristocracy in a better light, after they had been presented as decadent and dissipated before the war. *Theodore & Co* (1916), for example, presents the younger aristocrats as dynamic and inventive, while the young aristocratic hero, rather than marrying a showgirl, marries a nightclub singer who is, in fact, the daughter of a Duke. This served to reinforce and perpetuate the separation of the aristocracy from the rest of the population at a time when they were promoted as the decision-makers and military leaders. As Len Platt records, however, such representations were misjudged, since not only was the wartime death toll among young aristocrats disproportionately high, but the incompetence of the leadership also contributed to the aristocracy's ultimate decline (2004, pp. 102–3).

The aristocracy's decline in representations of Britishness was mirrored by the gradual decline of musical comedy itself, though there were significant numbers of shows throughout the 1920s and 1930s, and some were very big hits with runs of over 300 performances. While *Mr Cinders* (1928) had a run of 529 performances, the biggest hit of this period was *Me and My Girl* (1937) (as discussed in Chapter 5) in which class distinctions are challenged and subverted. At this time, however, revues with topical sketches and up-to-date song and dance styles became increasingly popular. Noel Coward was one of the most influential writers who contributed most of the material to the revue *London Calling* (1923), wrote the revues *On with the Dance* (1925) and *This Year of Grace* (1928), as well as many plays, including *The Vortex* (1924), *Hay Fever* (1925) and *Design For Living* (1932). Coward also wrote somewhat nostalgic musical comedy pastiches, such as *Operette* (1938), plus several operettas, among which the most famous was *Bitter Sweet* (1928). He invented a style of comedy that built on the pace and urgency of Broadway, but his work, persona and humour were characterized by 'a languid pose that reproduced modernist *angst* as sophisticated irony' (Platt, 2004, p. 146). As Platt notes, British musical comedy was not running to catch up with the Americans. Instead, the West End musical 'experienced a temporary resurgence as an arch culture quietly withdrawn from its present and distinctly nostalgic for its past' (2004, p. 146). It was this nostalgic musical comedy history that Coward felt had great significance for the representation of 'Britishness' at this time. Coward was, thus, not only a significant figure in the decline of musical comedy and in the satire of revue, but also in the way the national culture was represented. Additionally, since he performed on stage and on screen in both Britain and America, Coward's pose of the languid, erudite, effete and satirical Englishman created its own model for British upper-class men and society.

CASE STUDY: *Cavalcade* (1931)

Music, lyrics and book: Noel Coward.

Somewhere between a pageant, a revue and a musical play, this episodic work chronicled the lives of a middle-class family, the Maryotts, and their servants. Family life was set against a chronological pageant of historical occasions drawn from British history between 1899 and 1930. Events included the death of Queen Victoria, the relief of Mafeking, and the Great War itself. The work is notable for its metatheatricality where the relief of Mafeking is announced by the stage manager rushing onstage and interrupting the action, for example. Musical comedy was itself used as a signifier of Britishness in the production, with songs being drawn from musical theatre history, including two of Coward's own songs: 'Twentieth Century Blues' and 'Lover of My Dreams'. To depict the decline of British life from the gay fin de siècle to the decadent 1920s, songs were also included from *The Merry Widow* (1905), while *Our Miss Gibbs* (1909) and *Florodora* (1899) are both referenced in the show. Musical comedy thus becomes identified as an embodiment of national identity in this work, often through reference to earlier shows.

The production was produced by Charles B. Cochran at the Theatre Royal Drury Lane, London, in 1931, where it ran for 405 performances and was attended by King George V and Queen Mary. A film adaptation was made in 1933, which won three Academy Awards (including Best Picture).

Cavalcade presented musical comedy as a key reference point in British identity by relating it to history in a grand and spectacular fashion on the enormously important stage of the Theatre Royal Drury Lane. It required the investment of over £30,000 on new technical equipment for the theatre and the employment of forty-three speaking performers and 200 silent extras. The patriotic celebration it engendered was also partially credited with helping the Conservative party win its landslide victory in 1931 (Macpherson, 2018, p. 200). At the same time, its position is paradoxical since Coward had intended the work to offer a critique of Britain and its imperial past. As Ben Macpherson documents, the concluding scene, described as 'chaos', is a dance to a cacophonic noise of rivets, loudspeakers, jazz bands and other noises of modernity that finally descends into silence as the lights fade. It is this paradoxical position that Macpherson identifies as British – simultaneously critical and celebratory. He likens this to the national anxiety about the way Englishness is often taken to represent Britishness (2018, p. 201). *Cavalcade* is thus an exemplar of how, during the interwar years, and against a background of economic depression, mass unemployment, a hierarchical class system, working-class anger and aristocratic anxiety, musical comedy was an embodiment of a complex and chaotic national identity. Paradoxically, musical comedy also became increasingly separated from any sort of real representation of popular culture. Instead, it promoted a nostalgic memory of glamour, pageantry and order.

The Second World War

The British government closed all theatres on 4 September 1939 at the start of the Second World War. Although they were actually only officially closed for three days, several theatres remained closed for the duration of the war, interrupting the development of the West End. As Dominic Symonds records, travel became dangerous and, especially during 1940 and 1941, there were regular night-time bombing raids on London – known as 'The Blitz'. Drury Lane theatre was co-opted by the Entertainments National Service Association (ENSA) to prepare entertainments for British troops abroad (2016, p. 232). In the absence of American imports (except for several Cole Porter shows) and lacking much new material, audiences enjoyed revisiting the musicals of previous generations. In the years immediately following the war, American shows about American life made an enormous impact in London, with *Oklahoma!* (1943) and *Annie Get Your Gun* (1946) both arriving in 1947. Nevertheless, thereafter the imports were more modest and there were plenty of successful British shows that incorporated the musical and dance styles of the American musical comedies (in works such as Ivor Novello's *Gay's the Word* [1951]). What is interesting about these British musicals is that American characters rarely appear, despite the presence of American style and sound. Indeed, even 'the wholeheartedly Broadway-inspired sound of *The Boy Friend* (1953) was such a nostalgic return to the 1920s that it did not exactly ride the tide of the American invasion, creating instead a fond pastiche of a completely different time' (Symonds, 2016, p. 242).

Post-war reconstruction

The cost of the Second World War meant that Britain was bankrupt by 1950 and dismantling its Empire. Despite the jubilation at the victory of defeating the Nazis and their allies, British people faced the rationing of food and luxury goods until 1954, so that, psychologically, with their American allies having gone home, they were confronting the loss of reputation and considerable hardship. This was exacerbated as Britain was replaced by America as the leading superpower and the United States entered a decade of significant economic growth. On the other hand, the new Labour government in Britain founded the National Health Service and the Welfare State, ensuring social welfare for those unable to work and free primary, secondary and higher education. This 'safety net' represented a move towards social democracy in line with many Western European countries. At the same time, men of all classes had fought together, women had taken on all forms of employment, and neither wanted to give up the freedoms (both class and gender) they had gained. The Festival of Britain in 1951, designed to showcase British achievements in science, technology, design, architecture and the arts, was also intended to promote a feeling of successful recovery from the war and to become a beacon for change. Its legacy was the South Bank Centre in London, and its surrounding complex, including the National Theatre (as discussed below).

American soldiers had been stationed in Britain from the end of 1942 and had influenced the population through interactions in pubs, dance halls and cinemas; their style, fashions, music, plus their vigour and friendliness were all admired and paved the way for the success of the new American musicals in which traditional gender behaviours were reconceived (Symonds, 2016, p. 236). Meanwhile, at home in America, the war had unified the American people and rebooted the economy with the creation of millions of jobs, many of which were filled by women. Elizabeth L. Wollman suggests that America 'emerged relatively unscathed, economically strong and newly powerful' after the Second World War, but nevertheless the nation faced cultural anxieties and contradictions of its own, not least from (largely white) women who wanted to remain free to work (2017, p. 121). African Americans also contributed to the war effort, whether at home or at war, and soon after would fight for equality in the American Civil Rights Movement, which would be followed by the Stonewall riots in New York and the development of LGBTQ+ (then gay) rights.

The effect of the Cold War (approximately 1947–91) was to reinforce the anxiety that the country needed to unite against an unknown enemy, and this resulted in a certain homogeneity in popular culture as America now represented the importance of coming together against external threats. As Knapp (2005) demonstrates, some American musicals from the wartime and the post-war years represented such anxiety by focusing on stories about a group threatened by something from within or beyond the group (an 'Other'). Although initially resistant to intergroup community formation, the depicted parties become more inclusive with a heterosexual marriage as signifier of the coming together (the marriage trope), as in *Guys and Dolls* (1950) and *The Music Man* (1957).

A small group of musicals bucked this trend, however. *West Side Story* (1957) focused on the combination of gang culture and juvenile delinquency that arguably resulted, at least partially, from the creation of underclass communities from different waves of immigration. The importance of *West Side Story* is that despite the creators' attempts to represent the music and dance of a Latinx community, and even though the characters are depicted as complex and tragic victims of circumstance, it pitted the more recent immigrants – the Puerto Ricans – against earlier immigrants of Polish and Irish descent. The white gang members are delinquents but tolerated, while the Latino gang members are perceived as threatening, criminal and violent and treated with disdain by the authorities. Recent scholarship demonstrates how its enormous success, on stage and on screen, consequently promoted certain stereotypes about Latinx people that became prevalent in American popular culture – 'defining Puerto Ricans as criminals (men) and victims (women)' (Negrón-Mutaner, 2004, p. 62). These issues will be returned to below; however, the musical was also an important reflection of post-war McCarthyite, and cold war anxieties, about unnamed and unknowable 'Others' who might affect (or infect) American culture, whether from within or without. In this case, the anxieties were represented not only through the invasion of the Puerto Rican 'others, but through a contemporary issue, that of juvenile delinquency in working class populations of all races, as it was reflected in new media, such as comic books, movies, rock "n" roll and on television' (Wollman, 2017, p. 134).

By contrast, several American musicals produced idealized representations of 'Britishness' at this time. Alan Jay Lerner and Fredrick Loewe's musicals *Brigadoon* (1947), *My Fair Lady* (1956) and *Camelot* (1960), for instance, are examples that variously depict Britain as an idyllic landscape. *Brigadoon* depicts two American tourists who find a mysterious Scottish village, the titular Brigadoon, that appears every 100 years for only one day. The characters exist in a light-hearted narrative of romance and comedy in which optimism and escapism are transposed to Britain. Likewise, *My Fair Lady* has a more positive ending than its source material, George Bernard Shaw's play *Pygmalion* (1913), in which Higgins and Eliza are completely incompatible. The musical, however, opens the possibility of a communal future (married or not), thereby challenging traditional class-based patterns and gender roles. As Irene Morra notes, 'the musical offers an idealized, celebratory picture of Edwardian England (and an idea of English culture in general) that neutralizes the play's social commentary and offers an escapist ideal' (2009, p. 26). A historic nostalgic representation of a lost Britain thus became an idealized escapist fantasy for Americans. These representations somewhat lacked interrogation of the other culture and instead relied on widely held stereotypes and traditions.

On the other side of the Atlantic, British representations of Americans were much more unflattering in the 1950s and early 1960s. As noted above, the culture wars of the 1950s left British audiences excited by American style, fashion and music, but also resentful and keen to rebuild an indigenous British culture. Some of the British musicals of this period reveal these tensions with unattractive American characters. These include a bid by Americans to take over a British boys' magazine in *The Buccaneer* (1953), a rich American seductress in *Expresso Bongo* (1958), naive American buyers who are fleeced by sharp British Wedgewood dealers in *Make Me an Offer* (1959) and the American facilitator of illegal activity in *On the Level* (1966). The presence of these American characters in one branch of post-war musicals reflected the tensions and anxieties as British writers struggled for a distinct style and structure and for cultural predominance in British popular culture (Wells, 2016, p. 280).

CASE STUDY: *Expresso Bongo* (1958)

Music and lyrics: David Heneker and Monty Norman (with Julian More). Book: Wolf Mankowitz and Julian More.

This musical presents a cynical view of the pop music industry, and society at large, as a 'greedy sham' (Gordon et al., 2016, p. 30). The story is loosely based on the meteoric rise of (real life) rock 'n' roll star Tommy Steele, who starred in musicals like *Half a Sixpence* (1963) and directed and starred in the stage adaptation of *Singin' in the Rain* (see Chapter 3). Greedy music producer Johnny notices the popularity of untalented singer and bongo player Herbert Rudge, so he signs him to a very lucrative (for Johnny) contract and renames him Bongo Herbert. Other music industry sharks circle the successful young star, including a sexually voracious American actress who tempts Herbert away from his manager. In the end, lazy Herbert attempts to keep the money flowing by setting up his stripper girlfriend as the next star. The anodyne 1959 film version, which starred Cliff Richard, suppressed all political and satirical content.

These British 'Angry Musicals' were built on the playwrighting of several 'Angry Young Men' whose work was focused around the Royal Court Theatre in the late 1950s and 1960s, under the directorship of George Devine. John Osborne's *Look Back in Anger* (1956) and *The Entertainer* (1957), for instance, depicted British men who were disappointed with, and disillusioned by, their mundane lives. Jimmy Porter in *Look Back in Anger* is an educated young man who feels trapped by his working-class upbringing and spends the majority of the play berating his wife, Alison, goading her to leave him. The 'Angry Musicals' (some set in Soho and known as the 'Soho Musicals') were gritty works that, following this revolution, reflected disillusioned youth in Britain in ways very different from those in America. Works such as *Fings Ain't Wot They Used T'be* (1960), *The World of Paul Slickey* (1959), *Make Me an Offer* (1959), *Johnny the Priest* (1960) and *Stop the World – I Want to Get Off* (1961) tend to express a left-wing socialist perspective that is much more class focused than the American version of disillusionment. *The World of Paul Slickey*, for example, John Osborne's only musical, seems 'to attack every part of society and modern media in a rather unsystematic way' (Wells, 2016, p. 282). These shows are dark and entertaining, containing irony and parody alongside new rock 'n' roll music to reflect social trends such as 'the rise of the Soho coffee bar scene, with its excitement-seeking teenagers, ruthless talent scouts, and petty criminals' (Wells, 2016, p. 276). Altogether, this relatively small group of musicals established a completely new direction and understanding of working-class identities that contrasts with the nostalgic escapism that continued alongside. This new depiction is frequently obscured by larger commercial musicals that followed swiftly in the 1970s and 1980s, those by Andrew Lloyd Webber, Tim Rice, Alain Boublil and Claude-Michel Schönberg, among others, which are discussed in other chapters.

1990s British resurgence (as mythologized in American musicals)

Jumping forward several decades, the United Kingdom witnessed a period of turmoil during the premiership of Prime Minister Margaret (Maggie) Thatcher (1979–90), which included the Falklands War of 1982, plus strikes and high unemployment in the first half of the decade as the power of the unions was broken (as depicted in the film and stage musical *Billy Elliot*

[2000 and 2005]). This was followed by the deregulation of banking and unconstrained economic growth in the late 1980s and 1990s, alongside the first Gulf War (1990–1). A labour government headed by Tony Blair took power in 1997 in a wave of optimism that was soon interrupted by the Second Gulf War (2003–11). However, the increased financial security produced by the economic boom of the 1990s meant there was money to spend on socialist causes, and the patriotism engendered by war resulted in feelings of power, authority and optimism that led to significant liberalization within popular culture.

The United Kingdom thus entered an era of so-called Cool Britannia (a reference to 'Rule, Britannia!'), wherein Britain celebrated its popular culture with receptions at the heart of government. Britpop bands including Blur and Oasis 'invaded' America, as The Beatles had in the 1960s, while the Spice Girls spread a third-wave feminist message of 'Girl Power' (with Geri Halliwell sporting her iconic Union Jack dress at the 1997 Brit Awards). The United Kingdom celebrated its heritage and global prominence from the mid-1990s with work by young, sexy and patriotic artists, while other shows continued to reflect concern about the political direction the country was taking.

British musicals reflected this paradox in representations of American mythology. Andrew Lloyd Webber, Don Black and Christopher Hampton's *Sunset Boulevard* (1993), for example, followed the 1950 film upon which it is based by deconstructing the ideals of Hollywood glamour. The musical depicts Norma Desmond, an aging silent film star, descending into madness in a decaying Hollywood mansion. When an attractive young writer, Joe Gillis, stumbles upon her home, Norma envisions Joe as a symbol of hope: a new lover and a way of returning to stardom. In a final melodramatic showdown, however, Norma shoots Joe who then lies dead in her swimming pool (an image that also opens the musical). Perhaps this musical could be interpreted in Britain as a comment on the fading of the British Empire and the emergence of unbridled capitalism. *Sunset Boulevard* transferred to Broadway in 1994, where it was a nostalgic evocation of the studio system, a bygone era, though it could also be perceived as a cynical tale of decline. It was welcomed with the highest advance ticket sales in Broadway history at the time, and won several Tony Awards, but ultimately lost money and ran for only 977 performances. These mixed fortunes perhaps reflect the paradox between the glorification of nostalgia and America's international anxieties following the first Gulf War. Five years later, Lloyd Webber continued his depiction of American mythology with *Whistle Down the*

Wind (1998), which played in London for nearly three years. Unlike *Sunset Boulevard*, this later musical is based on a nostalgic evocation of Lancashire (a county in North West England) in the late 1950s/early 1960s. Although the musical was relocated to 'bible belt' America (with gospel and rock 'n' roll music to match), *Whistle Down the Wind* remained an Americanized version of a British story that did not have the title appeal of the earlier work. Commercially, at least, it only seemed to appeal to British audiences.

Across the river from these West End ventures, the National Theatre (a major, publicly funded organization on the South Bank) also demonstrated a fascination with American culture. Alongside new British plays about sex and violence, that predominated at institutions like the Royal Court Theatre, the National Theatre favoured the optimism of Broadway. Starting with Richard Eyre's production of *Guys and Dolls* (1950) in 1982, a string of American musicals was staged at the National Theatre that were either written by composer Stephen Sondheim (such as *Sunday in the Park with George* in 1990) or revivals from the American Golden Age (including *South Pacific* in 2001). With Eyre (1988–97), Trevor Nunn (1997–2003) and Nicholas Hytner (2003–15) succeeding each other as Artistic Director, all of whom had successfully directed commercial West End hits, the National became a home for big-budget revivals of American shows. As Sarah Browne notes, however, having a musical revived at a major subsidized venue, with directors who had worked across musical theatre, drama and film, meant that these revivals were often innovative and daring in their approach (2017, p. 375). These reimagined stagings often brought a new context and focus to the texts' social and cultural politics, perhaps revealing more about tensions in Britain than about the themes generally associated with these works.

In Hytner's 1993 production of *Carousel* (1945) and Nunn's 1998 revival of *Oklahoma!* (1943), for instance, the leading couples were not presented as gleeful young lovers, but more realistic characters who had seen certain hardships in life. Rather than resembling the princess-like image of Shirley Jones in the 1955 film, Josephina Gabrielle, who played Laurey in Nunn's *Oklahoma!*, was dressed in worn dungarees and boots, clearly worked to support herself and her aunt and understood the hardships of farming. Likewise, the musical's 'Dream Ballet' sequence more explicitly explored Laurey's sexuality and interest in Jud. As a group of burlesque dancers manipulated her like a doll or a puppet, Laurey smiled as if enjoying her newfound sexuality (in a moment far removed from many, previously sanitized, depictions) (Browne, 2017, p. 369). When this production transferred to Broadway in 2002, however, it was considered too bleak and too rooted in its subtext to truly capture the optimism of this American classic. Audiences and critics dismissed the production for deviating from the nostalgic vision of national mythology that was popularized in the 1940s; Britain had distorted an American classic. *Oklahoma!* was not revived in New York for another seventeen years until American director Daniel Fish opened his radical, somewhat immersive 2019 Broadway production to rave reviews.

While the British revival of multiple American musicals demonstrates the paradox of British national identity in the 1990s, this decade marked a moment when British directors were revisiting key works of the American musical canon. Having 'invaded' Broadway with a string of high-profile megamusicals in the 1980s, British creative teams were taking American classics and, in some sense, treating them with the same tenacity and boldness as British theatre more widely. Dan Rebellato notes, for instance, that rape, death, violence, pornography and drug use are as central to the plot of *Oklahoma!* as they are to the work of British 'in-yer-face' playwrights like Sarah Kane (2009a, p. 61). Although these elements are traditionally overlooked in favour of the musical's depiction of community and nationhood, they were explored at this time – or at least explicitly highlighted – by a British director (Nunn). The British musical retained its Britishness in the 1990s, then, by putting a uniquely British stamp on a series of celebrated American musicals – using the mirrored reflection of the other to address its own political concerns. Perhaps, the distance of the other gave sufficient emotional space for British concerns to be addressed, and, interestingly, at this time few British musicals examined Britishness.

KEY CONCEPT: The National Theatre

Although a dramatic venue at heart, the National Theatre has an interesting history of presenting musicals. Founded in 1963, the National Theatre Company was originally a repertory theatre company based at the Old Vic Theatre in London's Waterloo led by Laurence Olivier. When the company moved to its current home on London's South Bank in 1976, to a new venue consisting of three versatile auditoriums, the National's output started to move away from traditional productions of classic texts. In 1982, six years before he took over as artistic director, Richard Eyre directed

Guys and Dolls (1950) and instigated a string of American musical revivals. More recently, however, the National has produced more inventive, even controversial, new musicals under the artistic direction of Nicholas Hytner and Rufus Norris. *Jerry Springer: The Opera* was produced at the National in 2003, for example, and, in 2011, Alecky Blythe and Adam Cork set a series of real-life interviews to music in *London Road*. This verbatim musical depicted the aftermath of the 2006 Ipswich prostitute murders – an unlikely topic and an unusual compositional process. In 2015, the National transferred (and reworked) Damon Albarn and Moira Buffini's *Wonder.Land* from Manchester to London, and then to Paris. It is a modernized *Alice in Wonderland* musical, which involved digital avatars and an online gaming universe as the titular *Wonder.Land*. The National returned to American musicals in 2018, however, with two sold-out runs of *Follies* (1971).

Challenging American mythology

In America, the mythologies presented in musicals like *Oklahoma!* were no longer depicted so overtly. Despite the two Gulf Wars seeming to bring patriotism to America, several musicals provided 'alternative visions of America' in what Knapp terms a counter-mythology (2005, p. 153). Sondheim and John Weidman's off-Broadway musical *Assassins* (1991), for example, depicts approximately a century of American history through the eyes of several notorious outsiders: those who assassinated, or attempted to assassinate, the American President. By accompanying subversive tales of murder and deception with patriotic musical styles, *Assassins* depicts disenfranchised individuals who realize the 'American Dream' is not available to them. In 'Another National Anthem', the various assassins demand to know where their 'prize' is. When are they going to be thanked, celebrated or helped to achieve their goals because of their brave and ambitious acts? In response, the Balladeer (like a bad politician) tells the group of all the wonderful things ordinary people can achieve ('where the mailman won the lottery'), but ignores, as Scott Miller notes, that America is also built on bloodshed, corruption, greed and prejudice (1997, p. 200). Perhaps unsurprisingly, this challenging of American mythology was not

Figure 6.2 Annie Golden (L. Fromme), Jonathan Hadary (C. Guiteau), Debra Monk (S. J. Moore), Terrence Mann (L. Czolgosz), Victor Garber (J. Wilkes Booth), Lee Wilkof (S. Byck), Eddie Korbich (G. Zangara), Greg Germann (J. Hinkley) and William Parry from the off-Broadway musical *Assassins*. 1990. Photo: Swope, Martha. © NYPL.

well received in 1991. The musical was later scheduled for a 2001 Broadway production but was delayed until 2004 in the aftermath of the terrorist attacks of 9/11. *Assassins* thus remains a subversive and problematic musical, whether playing against a backdrop of national patriotism or turmoil, something for which Sondheim remains unapologetic (quoted in Rothstein, 1991).

CASE STUDY: *Assassins* (1991)

Music and lyrics: Stephen Sondheim. Book: John Weidman.

This concept musical deconstructs the 'American Dream' by depicting individuals who feel excluded from or disillusioned by it. Framed as a carnival game, the Balladeer (a personification of the 'American Dream') invites the assassins to join his sinister enterprise, in which their problems will be solved if they kill a US president. The musical then depicts a series of unrelated sequences, as if in a revue, starting with John Wilkes Booth's assassination of Abraham Lincoln in 1865. The musical closes in 1963 as the ghosts of past assassins (including Booth, Leon Czolgosz and Charles Guiteau) persuade Lee Harvey Oswald to assassinate John F. Kennedy, rather than kill himself. Unlike most mythologizing American musicals, then, *Assassins* 'focuses on the shadow of that more hopeful narrative line, projecting a dark and sinister spirit hovering disturbingly close to America's main road' (Knapp, 2005, p. 163). The Balladeer lures the assassins from this so-called main road, by duping them into believing that the death of a president will bring them fame and glory – the equivalent of the American Dream.

Not every American writer followed Sondheim and Weidman's model in the 1990s. Jason Robert Brown's *Songs for a New World* (1995), for instance, is a song cycle about individuals on the verge of a decision that will help them find clarity ('It's about one moment'). Each song depicts an individual at a time of change, in ever shifting circumstances, in which they face a future as 'uncharted as the New World was to [explorer Christopher] Columbus' (Miller, 1999, p. 141). Songs like 'The Flagmaker, 1775' place characters in historical settings, while, in turn, exploring personal turmoil and broader cultural concerns. Underlying these individual stories of love, loss and self-fulfilment is an exploration of national identity. Through a conceptual framework and loosely connected songs, *Songs for a New World* is about discovering a new America – one that may be far removed from the mythologized depiction laid out by Rodgers and Hammerstein.

In 1997, *Bat Boy*, *Side Show* and *Violet* all explored the journey of a disfigured Other trying to locate themselves in American society. Whether by depicting small-town prejudice, violent freak shows or a fraudulent televangelist, these musicals depict disillusioned Americans trying to overcome their non-conformity in a culture obsessed with beauty, fame and celebrity. A year later, historical epics *Ragtime* and *Parade* (1998) opened on Broadway, both depicting the troubling consummation of different racial, ethnic and socio-economic groups in early twentieth-century America. America as a utopian community was, at this time, mythologized in Britain, rather than at home. As British audiences tapped their feet to Hugh Jackman celebrating Oklahoma's transition from territory to state at the National Theatre, American audiences watched Audra McDonald murdered, as

Sarah in *Ragtime*, during a scene in which she (presumably a dangerous African American woman) tries to gain the attention of the US president. Each nation continued to depict the Other, rather than celebrating their own heritage, even if that meant depicting the disenfranchised Others who resided in their own country. Many new shows portrayed individuals hoping to create or join a temporary community – like that of a group of famous assassins – rather than assimilate with the nation's established norms (Knapp, 2005, p. 163).

Hybrid influences in musical theatre

The discussions above have focused almost exclusively on white representations of nationhood, and, with the exception of *West Side Story*, only in the last paragraph have African Americans entered the picture. There are many other minority communities, though, in two countries that both have slave-trading, colonial and migrant histories, and the interactions between cultures during and after colonialism have been both problematic and transformative as noted in Chapter 2 above. One of the features of the recent past is that descendants of enslaved peoples, and of formerly colonized communities, as well as economic migrants and refugees have established new diasporic communities around the world, including in Britain and America. As a result, new hybrid cultural forms have emerged from the interactions of cultural practices. The term 'hybrid' is used by theorist Homi Babha to represent the situation of, for example, a British Asian person who perceives themselves to be in a state of ambivalence between cultures or ethnicities or an American-Latinx with a multi-racial or multi-lingual history or ancestry. Although there are concerns about the term, *hybridity* refers to works that actively draw on a multi-racial heritage and negotiate the experience of having both a home and a homeland.

In the Heights (2008) is an example of an American musical that incorporates the languages and experiences of diasporic Latinx communities. The book writer, Quiara Alegria Hudes, and composer-lyricist, Lin-Manuel Miranda, both identify as descended from/raised by Puerto Ricans (formerly a Spanish colony, Puerto Rico is an unincorporated territory of America). *In the Heights* must be considered a hybrid work not only because of the heritage of its writers, but because it uses multilingual sentences, phrases

KEY CONCEPT: Post-colonialism

Any colonizing process must contain and alter the colonized, whose cultures and beliefs are sidelined by the conquering power. However, the indigenous belief systems and imagery of the conquered subjects also affect the culture of the dominant system in that colony, at least. Although the power relations between colonizer and colonized might be considered oppressive – imposed on the colony by the powerful colonizer – and the institutional histories and processes were fraught with antagonism and oppression, there was an effect on the colonizer too. Moreover, colonizers were never completely successful in their attempts to suppress cultural practices, so that experiences and remembered traditions survived and could later be incorporated into new forms. As Paul Gilroy notes in relation to the history of slavery, 'residual traces of their necessarily painful expression still contribute to historical memories inscribed and incorporated into the volatile core of Afro-Atlantic cultural creation' (2002, p. 73).

After independence or freedom there has often been a burgeoning of activity in retelling the history from the perspective of the 'subaltern peoples' rather than the dominant power, hence offering new voices, philosophies, languages and practices. Traditional cultures and histories are revisited, leading eventually to new hybrid forms. However, as with all these terms, *post-colonialism* is a very slippery term to define, since what it tries to address are the contradictions and difficulties within the space between the colonizer and the subaltern. Post-colonialism thus deals not with a specific time after colonialism, but 'an engagement with, and contestation of, colonialism's discourses, power structures, and social hierarchies' (Gilbert and Tompkins, 2010, p. 657). Post-colonialism is also concerned with avoiding stereotyping or oversimplifying the different identities that are revealed, and yet, at the same time, such stereotypes are sometimes appropriated by the subaltern group described in them, revealing an incredibly complicated and diverse set of practices.

and lyrics in a narrative about an immigrant community in New York, that explores the tensions between the experience of home and homeland for its characters. It also demonstrates the impact of postcolonial history in its music, in that it incorporates a combination of musical genres including hip-hop, Latin American dance rhythms, alongside intertextual references to Broadway musicals.

In the Heights depicts a multicultural neighbourhood, Washington Heights in New York, that is populated by individuals who have immigrated from, or are the children/relatives of those born in, several Hispanic countries; its characters are frequently searching for 'home'. One character, Nina Rosario, feels lost as, what she deems, a faux member of three different communities. She does not feel Puerto Rican (a homeland she idealizes as 'my people!'), nor is she successful at Stanford University, yet she also does not belong in Washington Heights (where she is 'the one who made it out'). More broadly, the theme of 'home' resonates in the musical's depiction of a location under redevelopment, where literal, physical 'homes' are being lost. Elena Machado Saez analyses the representation of 'Others' in this work, who become incorporated into the middle-class through their business ownership and economic stability. She argues that by effectively becoming middle-class the 'inherited stereotype about Latinx criminality' is undermined (2018, p. 185), and by drawing spectators into 'an affective identification with the middle-class US Latinx characters depicted in *In the Heights*' the largely white middle-class Broadway audiences have a means of identification with these internal Others through property ownership. While James McMasters argues that '*In the Heights* is a *critique* of the violence of gentrification – an ongoing urban process of displacing black and brown people from their homes, colonization by another name' (2016), Saez interprets the end of the musical differently. While there is no space for the working-class poor, the work 'nevertheless acknowledges the legacy of class and race stereotype on Broadway' (Saez, 2018, p. 188). Nevertheless, it allows those who 'contribute to the market(ability) of the neighbourhood [to] combat stereotypes and embody hope on the Broadway stage' (Saez, 2018, p. 189). While protagonist Usnavi confirms Washington Heights as his home at the end of the musical, *In the Heights* continues to question the age-old concern of who belongs in America (and who does not). In this case, middle-class business owners who contribute to the economy are seen to belong.

Meanwhile, in Britain, there are diasporic communities from Africa, the Caribbean and the Indian subcontinent who bring different languages and histories to the islands. All these communities have gradually developed theatre that represents the experience of being in Britain using forms that incorporate aspects of their diverse genres and cultures. While it was not easy for immigrant communities to gain a foothold in a country that legislated for equal race relations while maintaining institutional barriers and cultural segregation, many small scale, community and local theatre companies began to appear from the 1960s. The key features of these companies were that they incorporated music and theatrical traditions from their homelands alongside British culture, and that they spoke of the experience of alienation from the homeland, and the experience of living in Britain. Companies such as Talawa, Nitrobeat, Rifco, Tara Arts and Tamasha all have distinctive visions and ambitions for the development of new British multicultural theatre. Tamasha, for example, developed *Fourteen Songs, Two Weddings and a Funeral* (1998) at the Lyric Theatre, Hammersmith using a plot from a Bollywood film (*Hum Aapke Hain Koun*). Elsewhere, Caribbean-inspired theatre companies such as Nitrobeat incorporate music from reggae, salsa, calypso and hip-hop, as well as contemporary opera, in works like *Slamdunk* (2004).

In addition to their annual multicultural pantomimes, the Theatre Royal Stratford East (in outer London) produced *The Big Life* in 2004, which documented the experience of Caribbean migrants arriving on the SS Empire Windrush. *The Harder They Come* (2006) was based on a 1972 Jamaican film whose soundtrack of reggae introduced Caribbean music to a wider British audience. The musical version opened at the Theatre Royal Stratford East and reached London's Barbican Theatre in 2008. The stage musical version of the film *Bend It Like Beckham* (2002) arrived in the West End in 2015. Led by Sonia Friedman Productions, the producers included Deepak Nayar Productions, the team behind the film, and several other companies from the UK, India and elsewhere. This production united experienced white British and British Asian creatives in a story that 'constructs Otherness *at home*, not in Bollywood, or the Caribbean, or Vietnam' (Macpherson, 2016, p. 688).

However, all these signs of increasing plurality in British musical theatre were preceded by *Bombay Dreams* (2002). Like *In the Heights* the score was a hybrid comprised, in this case, of Bollywood and musical theatre traditions. The musical used marketing strategies developed for Tamasha's successful *Fourteen Songs* to attract a new audience to a British musical that specifically targeted British Asians. It also offered performance opportunities and experience to performers and audiences who had not been represented in the West End until this production.

CASE STUDY: *Bombay Dreams* (2002)

Music: A. R. Rahman. Lyrics: Don Black. Book: Meera Syal.

The musical features a reverse-gendered Cinderella story of transformation. Akash is a penniless slum dweller in Mumbai, who dreams of becoming a famous Bollywood star. He meets Priya, a budding film producer and the fiancée of the lawyer who is trying to protect the 'Paradise' slum in which Akash lives. Through Priya and her father, Akash becomes a successful actor and begins a relationship with Priya, but at the price of his own sense of identity and the friends he leaves behind in the slum. Recognizing his own alienation, Akash returns to the slum but realizes he needs to inhabit a middle ground. In a typical utopian ending, he finds a way to maintain his career and his relationship with Priya, while understanding the importance of his former friendships and recognizing his roots. The story is to some extent a metaphor for the experience of colonial displacement of British Asians, who experience displacement in both homeland and home (as *In the Heights* is, in respect of different hybrid histories).

The show played successfully in London for two years, in one of the largest West End houses (the Apollo Victoria). It was much less successful on Broadway where it ran for only 284 performances, though assistant director Lucy Skilbeck remarked that, although the show was reworked for Broadway, the audiences are quite different (Gordon et al., 2016, p. 111). The poor box office returns may have also been affected by a combination of controversial casting practices and a different relationship to the histories and cultural practices of Britain and India.

The argument in relation to *Bombay Dreams* is that the work fails to represent the lived experience of British Asians and, instead, promotes stereotypes based within the Bollywood tradition. Although there is a level of cultural affirmation that results from the fact that the show adopts and embraces Bollywood conventions, that are themselves melodramatic and colourfully escapist, one of the concerns Jen Harvie expressed is that the work is significantly non-Asian in its production (2005, p. 182). Other concerns are with the gender and sexual stereotyping of the Hijra or eunuch character 'as a vehicle of local and sexual colour' and that the musical wants both to embrace the utopianism of Bollywood and to simultaneously present itself as ironic and superior. Harvie concludes that '*Bombay Dreams*' Bollywood two-step went some way towards affirming Indian and British Asian cultural difference, but in a gesture that appears finally opportunistic' (Harvie, 2005, p. 184).

This section has demonstrated some of the complexity of the issues within post-colonial and diasporic theatre. The interactions of history are deeply embedded and societies find it difficult to recognize their own ideological bias, such that it takes many years for the experiences of minority ethnic communities to appear in and alter the mainstream and populist form of musical theatre. In Britain, Bollywood cinema and Caribbean music seem to have offered their respective communities the most public and popular opportunities to dramatize their often conflicted experiences of both 'being British and belonging in the diaspora' (Daboo, 2018, p. 64). In America, numerous musicals continue to raise questions regarding who 'belongs' in a nation determined by immigration. *Allegiance* (2015), for example, depicts the internment of Japanese Americans in concentration camps during the Second World War, following Imperial Japan's attack on Pearl Harbor in 1942. Similarly, there is enormous debate over the 'ghostly presence of the enslaved' in *Hamilton*, given the lack of representation of non-white characters (rather than performers) in the show (Saez, 2018, p. 189). What such productions offer, though, is the opportunity for communities to represent their own life experiences at the local and national level.

Conclusion

How has the way British and American musicals represent themselves, and the other, changed over the course of little over a century? Certainly, each nation has become much more socially and culturally aware of issues of national identity, stereotyping, and particularly, issues of race. Given the diversity of specific contexts, it is not surprising that the ways British and American works represent themselves and each other have become increasingly divergent even in this globalized world, where one might have imagined greater universality. The contexts, challenges, circumstances, education and resources of performances, and the backgrounds of their creative teams, make any kind of universality impossible. However, it is possible for the work of the other to be read, understood, appreciated and successful in other times and places as we have seen in relation to the National Theatre reworkings of the classics. In the same way, Shakespeare's plays and characters now have an almost universal relevance because of the themes they address, rather than because of the locations and specific concerns of the characters. That said, the practices incorporated in new productions and adaptations may remain particular to local or national communities. *Romeo and Juliet*'s themes are understood in many countries – they speak about the challenges of developing community with the 'Other'. However, the representation of that theme shifts in portrayals from Japan to Jerusalem. From the feuding factions among British aristocracy in *The Belle of Mayfair* (1906) to the New York gangs in *West Side Story* (1957), and on to *& Juliet* (2019), these diverse musicals are joined by a universal story as their source material, while remaining relevant to historical and geographical context.

In the course of this chapter, we have discovered how we have represented ourselves and each other and how that interacts with social and political events and anxieties, and that is instructive. Why was London's National Theatre so keen to celebrate American mythologies rather than its own culture in the 1990s? What led American writers to focus on British nostalgia in the early 1960s? Sometimes looking at the 'Other' is a safe way of addressing the issues in our own societies, especially since those concerns can be ignored in musicals about other times and places. Yet, even in musicals about the 'Other', the anxieties and concerns that lie beneath the entertainment are revealed. *In the Heights*, for example, revealed issues relating to gentrification and middle-class property ownership in a love story set in a minority community. What we discover is that even when primarily concerned with race within the nation, these productions also tell us something about national concerns, national identity and the mythologizing of cultures.

Tasks

Select a year and explore what musicals were being presented either in the West End or on Broadway. Consider the historical and political events that were current in newspaper reports and explore how the themes of one of the musicals might have been interpreted in relation to its national and cultural context.

Find one British character in an American musical and one American character in a British musical and compare what stereotypes they might be perpetuating. What does each character offer in terms of representing the other nation?

Discussion topics

Why do you think musical theatre is so invested in ideas of national identity? What is it about the form that speaks so directly to ideas of nationhood? Can you think of any other art forms that are invested in national identity in the same way?

Following the success of *Hamilton*, *The Color Purple* and *A Strange Loop* in America, and *Bombay Dreams*, *Bend It Like Beckham* and *Everybody's Talking about Jamie* in Britain, how successfully do you think diversity is being represented within national identity? Are these individual and unusual works that subvert the mainstream? Or is the (what many might consider) mainstream changing to reflect contemporary concerns?

Further reading – conceptual

Herrera, B. E. (2015) *Latin Numbers: Playing Latino in Twentieth Century US Popular Performance*. Ann Arbor, MI: University of Michigan Press.

Holdsworth, N. (2010) *Theatre & Nation*. Basingstoke: Palgrave Macmillan.

Knapp, R. (2005) *The American Musical and the Formation of National Identity*. Princeton and Oxford: Princeton University Press.

Further reading – case study

Macpherson, B. (2016) 'Some Yesterdays Always Remain: Black British and Anglo-Asian Musical Theatre'. In: R. Gordon and O. Jubin (eds) *The Oxford Handbook of the British Musical*. New York: Oxford University Press, 673–96.

Morra, I. (2009) 'Constructing Camelot: Britain and the New World Musical'. *Contemporary Theatre Review* 19/1: 22–34.

Saez, E. M. (2018) 'Blackout on Broadway: Affiliation and Audience in *In the Heights* and *Hamilton'*. *Studies in Musical Theatre* 12/2: 181–97.

7

'The world was wide enough': From colonial to corporate culture

Lin-Manuel Miranda's *Hamilton* (2015) closes with a duel, a gun battle, between the titular Hamilton and his nemesis, Aaron Burr. After killing Hamilton, Burr reflects upon his actions and notes that 'I should've known the world was wide enough for both Hamilton and me'. The history of colonialism – of acquiring control over other nations – demonstrates that the world is wide enough to contain all kinds of people, ideas and creative arts, even if this is only realized after the event (as with Burr). It is often the case, however, that in the heat of battle, or through blindness or self-interest, the views and behaviours of one nation are imposed on another. Not all interactions between cultures are this confrontational but most colonial impositions, although a response to a drive for economic power, had the effect of a cultural imposition too. More recently the financial system Alexander Hamilton helped to create in America has emerged as globally powerful and one of the drivers of a new kind of corporate culture mirrored in many locations around the world. Disney, that has licensed a recording of the musical for its Disney+ streaming service, is now one of several global media corporations, which have undeniably conquered the world with their popular works. Stage musicals like *Beauty and the Beast* (1994), *The Lion King* (1997) and *Aladdin* (2011), for example, as well as *Hamilton*, position musical theatre as a global entity.

The story of this chapter is a story of continual and widespread movement whether in response to colonialism (driven by adventurers and their search for wealth) or more recently by corporate culture (and its expansionist policies that seek greater financial returns). It documents the dissemination of musical theatre as a global product and as a 'transnational brand' (Savran, 2014). The chapter moves beyond the previous chapters' explorations of the interactions between, predominantly, Britain and America and considers how musicals continue to emerge from these two hubs and engage with ever changing practices of global production and distribution. Responding to the regrets of Burr, perhaps it is time to consider the impact of domination on others.

Musical mobilities

While the global distribution of individual musicals to new worlds is perceived as a distinctly twentieth-century phenomenon, musical theatre has been practised globally since the earliest recorded times. As far as history and anthropology can discover, every culture, from the Ancient Greeks and beyond, has used song and story as a means of educating and entertaining. That said, those examples of cultural practices, though perhaps practised by all, are all different, infused with the experiences and issues, forms of storytelling and musical structures that arose in each location. It is also true that people have always been travellers, and migrations have occurred to find food, shelter and safety. The movement of people has been accompanied by the movement of their artistic practices that then interact with other cultures and so are transformed in a continuous process of evolution into diverse performance patterns around the world.

Nonetheless, there are similarities between cultures. Stories that are based on lived experience, or that are metaphors for it, often find universal forms that tell of love and death, family and sickness, travelling and settling, success and failure. As scholar Marina Warner notes, there are similarities in stories because they tell of shared human experiences, but differences that result from the context in which the story is experienced or told (1995). In her work on fairy tales, she discovered marked similarities in tales from all over the world but found it impossible to know whether the similarities arose because they are based on similar life experiences or because they resulted from migrations. An important point is that there can be no sense of a single 'authentic' or definitive starting point or version of a tale and equally of a cultural practice. Stories, like the nations in which they are developed, remain in constant flux.

Disney's *Aladdin*, for example, the 1992 animated film, 2011 stage adaptation and 2019 live action remake, is an Americanized adaptation of a Middle Eastern folktale. The story is now set in a fictional land called Agrabah, which ignores many of the tropes established in previous iterations of the tale with which it shares its name: its context, world view, politics and morality are American, even though its most well-known literary sources are not. The plot is a rags-to-riches love story that has echoes throughout the world. It has themes of questing, adventure and, of course, forbidden love, with which many can identify in relation to their own local contexts. The story is even utopian in that it suggests that youth, vitality and good fortune will win through, but the characterizations and cultural agendas are distinctly American – it promotes the American Dream. Furthermore, the films and stage musical are exported back around the world where the story will again be interpreted in different contexts.

The same is true, as we have discovered in previous chapters, for musical theatre, whose histories, migrations and transformations this book has been documenting. It is especially true, however, when considered in the context of an increasingly globalized production process in musical theatre. As this chapter will document, the British Empire, notwithstanding the trauma it visited around the world, was the catalyst for the establishment of a touring circuit and the global dissemination of certain types of performance. The roots of contemporary musical theatre, and certainly its world view, stem from an era of colonization and migration, while its music (as documented in Chapter 2) results from forced as well as voluntary migrations and trade within and beyond the Americas. In the last century, as the British Empire declined (at the same time as the colonized subjects of many other European countries also achieved independence), America grew in influence as a result of military power and cultural dominance. Its global influence has become immense, and aside from any discussion of its role in global security and politics, its role as a cultural imperialist must be considered in relation to the trade in 'Broadway' or 'Broadway-style' musicals.

Alongside the transition from physical colonization to cultural expansionism, there have been changes in industry and technology, in travel and connectivity, that have gathered pace exponentially. Meanwhile, global institutions have become established that sit above the nation state that are designed to capitalize on the interrelationships between politicians and states to facilitate 'borderless' trade. The World Trade Organization (WTO) was founded in 1995 to regulate international trade, replacing the General Agreement on Tariffs and Trade – or GATT – that was founded in 1948. The United Nations (UN) was founded in 1945, after the Second World War, and now consists of 193 member states; its mission is to maintain international peace and security. The World Intellectual Property Organization (WIPO) is one of the organizations of the UN, founded in 1967, and exists to promote the ability of creators, owners or producers to exploit intellectual property internationally without fear of piracy. The World Health Organization (WHO) was founded in 1948 to promote better health outcomes and disease control throughout the world, since, for example, a mosquito carrying malaria knows no borders. Finally, some global corporations have also become larger than nation states, the most influential of which are those associated with global technology and media such as Google, Facebook, Apple, Newscorp and Disney.

Meanwhile, American imperialism began in the late nineteenth century and consists of policies aimed at increasing its economic, political and cultural influence beyond its borders. The Mexican-American war (1846–8) and the Spanish-American war (1898) both extended the territories and influence of America, while treaties after the Second World War (1939–45), particularly with Germany and Japan, led to the location of military bases in these countries. The Cold War (approximately 1947–91), the Bay of Pigs invasion of Cuba (1961) and the Vietnam War (1955–75) were all instigated by the global confrontations of communism and capitalism in which America led for the global West, while the recent Iraq wars (1990–1 and 2003–11) arguably resulted from the world trade in oil. However, it is the pervasiveness of American culture, its music, films, television and literature, that is the concern here. As Simon Heffer notes, 'overseas artists must make it in America if they are to go global: what would we think of The Beatles now had America simply yawned and looked the other way in 1964?' (2010). The same could be said for musical theatre, since, as David Savran argues, the 'Broadway-style' musical is now the transnational signifier of a certain type of commercial musical theatre. The phrase refers to the styles and structures that are typically associated with Broadway, meaning 'what theatregoers call a Broadway musical need no longer originate or even play in the United States to glow with an unmistakably U.S. aura' (Savran, 2014, pp. 319–20).

This story therefore begins by looking at colonialism, with Stephen Sondheim and John Weidman's *Pacific Overtures* (1976) as a document of the story of colonization, and the practices of the London-based D'Oyly Carte Opera Company (DOC) as an early model of touring and production. Together, these examples demonstrate musical theatre's influence throughout the English-speaking world up to the mid-twentieth century. Following this, discussions of the role of producers and production processes will be exemplified, especially in relation to the global trade in megamusicals since the 1980s and the work of Cameron Mackintosh, Really Useful Group, Disney and others. We consider the effects on local economies elsewhere in the world, identifying not just Broadway musicals that travel (which might equally begin in the West End) but the Broadway-style musicals being created in Europe, in Asia and elsewhere. This is thus a story of how musicals move and spread.

Colonialism

Disney's 1995 animated film musical, *Pocahontas*, which followed *The Lion King* (1994), is a fictionalized account of English settlers from the Virginia Company arriving in the 'New World' in 1607 and claiming the land as Jamestown. Governor Ratcliffe, the film's villain, is desperate to plunder the land's gold, even if it means killing members of the land's native community (whom he terms 'savages'). Despite many of the other settlers being persuaded to relax their barbaric views by fellow settler John Smith, who falls in love with Pocahontas, the daughter of the Chief of the Powhatan tribe, Ratcliffe remains a brutal emblem of the British Empire. Ratcliffe will stop at nothing for fame and fortune, hoping to return to England as a rich and respected aide to King James I.

Pocahontas depicts a romanticized (and somewhat controversial) version of the impact of colonization, which began as an outward exploration of new lands in the fifteenth century led by several sea-faring nations. Including the British, Dutch, Spanish, Portuguese and French, each nation competed to annexe territories for their own economic gain – conveniently ignoring the inhabitants who were already there. The expansion was, at first, the result of developing trading links led by private enterprise; wealth was vital for continuing the expansion and to finance the wars these companies pursued to secure their primacy. The East India Company, for example, began as a trading company that imported goods from India and was given a royal charter by Queen Elizabeth I in 1600. It was only later that the colonization of lands and British state control of the company led to the establishment of empire, but even within the British Empire, the circumstances of colonization were different in each colony. The arrangements for control and policing, and the establishment of institutions for education and cultural practices, all varied. So, while there are patterns to be perceived in the ways in which British culture spread around the globe, there are also differences to be discovered in the ways in which colonized countries incorporated and resisted cultural domination.

KEY CONCEPT: Colonialism

To colonize another country is to take authority or control over that weaker country – to occupy its territories and to use its resources for one's own advantage. In many cases, the occupation resulted from a desire to exploit either the natural resources or the cheaper labour in the colonized country initially as a means of survival. This kind of practice arguably began before the Egyptian Empire, 3–4 millennia BCE, but for our purposes we will begin in the fifteenth century when seafaring European countries, led by Portugal and Spain, set out to explore the world. Other European nations, predominantly the Dutch, English (later British) and French, were also involved in developing territories in Asia, Africa and the Americas, with Britain building the largest empire the world has ever seen by the late nineteenth century. Russia and Japan were also responsible for considerable colonial expansion of their territories.

Some British colonies were lost very early on. The American War of Independence (1775–83), for instance, marked the start of the United States, when thirteen states defeated the British in 1783 – as depicted in *Hamilton* (2015). Even after this establishment of the United States, British expansion continued in India, Southeast Asia, Africa and even South America, while Canada remained a colony until it became a self-governing dominion within the British Empire in 1867.

In many cases, colonialism continued until after the Second World War (from 1945 until 1960) when colonized nations wrested back control of their own governments. In some cases, it was a peaceful transition, though not in many others. Some territories became autonomous rather than independent with some former British colonies establishing a Commonwealth of Nations. This intergovernmental organization, which was known as the British Commonwealth until 1949, is currently led by the British monarch as its Head of the Commonwealth (Queen Elizabeth II at the time of writing). There also remain Commonwealth realms for whom the British monarch remains Head of State (like Australia), and there are still sixty-one colonies in the world, some of which choose not to separate from their colonizer. Gibraltar, while a unique example for historical reasons, is an example of a territory that has chosen to remain part of the United Kingdom, rather than return to Spanish rule.

A new phase of post-colonialism began when newly independent countries needed to establish their place in the world – each at their own pace. Their identities as expressed in arts and culture were revisited, often through the reinstatement of traditional or indigenous artistic practices, and the vestiges of the imposed colonial cultures were simultaneously present, not least in the architecture of theatres and concert halls, as well as in theatrical genres and the hierarchies of culture. As a result, the post-colonial period is often marked by stages of independent artistic production based on traditional practices, before new hybrid or composite practices emerge that result from the interactions between the influence of the ex-colonizer and the traditions of the former colony. Examples of this hybridity in *In the Heights* (2008) and *Bombay Dreams* (2002) were mentioned in the previous chapter. As with the variety and fluidity of cultural practice within colonized nations, such post-colonial cultural practices emerged differently in different places and times.

This context is perhaps best illustrated, in musical theatre terms at least, by the 1976 American musical, *Pacific Overtures*. The musical documents the arrival of American ships in Japan in 1853, whose goal was to establish trade with the nation. Although the show suggests that America was the first to establish trade with Japan, it was, in fact, Portugal and the Netherlands that had reached the country in the sixteenth century and began trading. However, Japan cut off links with the outside world soon after, and the country remained largely secluded until Admiral Perry's expeditions of 1853 and 1854 brought it to an end. Japan's isolation had begun in the Edo period around 1609 and lasted until Perry negotiated new trading links by 1868, a period that culminated in the overthrow of the Shogun and the restoration of imperial rule to Japan under Emperor Meiji (the 'Meiji Restoration').

CASE STUDY: *Pacific Overtures* (1976)

Music and lyrics: Stephen Sondheim. Book: John Weidman.

When Admiral Perry arrives off Japan in 1853 to open negotiations about trade links, Japan's rulers effectively ignore, rather than deal with, the intrusion and the offer of trade with the Americans. The foreign powers become increasingly belligerent and are followed by the British, Dutch, Russians and French, all hoping to access this new market. The musical demonstrates the clash of cultures, especially in the song 'Pretty Lady' when the daughter of a samurai is assumed to be a geisha and solicited for sex for money. In the final scene, contemporary Japan appears having modernized itself, assimilated many of the capitalist traits it was subjected to, and is now seen to be dominating the market.

Directed by Hal Prince, the original production was nominated for ten Tony Awards, winning for Best Costume Design and Best Scenic Design. In 2002, the New National Theatre of Tokyo presented a production in Japanese with English subtitles, which played in New York later that year. This production was revived again on Broadway in 2004, this time in English, and a new cast recording was released. Weidman revised the book for a 2017 Classic Stage Company revival, directed by John Doyle, which reduced the cast to ten performers and a running time of ninety minutes.

Pacific Overtures is important in this context because of the historical events it documents and the politics of post-colonialism it attempts to engage with. However, it not only explores this in the history it documents, but in the musical and theatrical forms it uses (see Figure 7.1). The original production, although written, directed and produced by a white American team, employed elements from the Japanese tradition of Kabuki, a predominantly Asian male cast (men play the roles of women), a narrator/ reciter, as well as a scenic design and an episodic construction (with some sequences using Japanese bunraku puppets). The orchestra incorporates traditional Japanese instruments, while the lyrics and score use some Japanese musical and poetic structures. The American and European characters are represented as stereotypical characters: the British are embodied in a Gilbert and Sullivan style patter song, the Russians in a folk song, the Dutch in a vaudeville performance. In these ways the team attempted to replicate the form of Kabuki and to tell the story from a Japanese perspective; however, in some respects, this is another form of appropriation as the white creative team adopted a Japanese form and use it to stereotype themselves and others (see Knapp, 2005, pp. 268–80). Unsurprisingly, a filmed version broadcast in Japan received a mixed reception.

Nevertheless, a 2002 Tokyo New National Theatre production played on Broadway in 2004. It moved away from Kabuki and towards Noh theatre, while the comic and satirical Broadway elements that had been designed to treat the

Figure 7.1 Yuki Shimoda (arms out) and unidentified others in the stage production *Pacific Overtures*. 1975. Photo: Swope, Martha. © NYPL.

West as an intruding 'Other' were less exaggerated. The work was therefore less effective for Western audiences, though it made more sense to Japanese audiences (Knapp, 2005, p. 280). Alongside the narrative history of the development of trade with Japan, then, *Pacific Overtures* demonstrates the difficulty of translating works across cultural boundaries, as well as the importance of locating an 'Other' as a perspective for critiquing and understanding ourselves.

Culture within colonialism

British workers living in far-flung locations around the Empire were not without opportunities for watching, and indeed taking part in, theatre performances. The first British theatre was built in Calcutta (now Kolkata, India) as early as 1775, and diasporic communities (see Chapter 6) across the globe were able to watch professional touring companies who travelled from city to city performing for eager audiences. Such shows, like letters and newspapers, provided a connection with home, even if that home had been left many years earlier. They provided a social space of interaction for the community and may even have had a role in unifying the empire (Becker, 2014, p. 701). Although these performances were ethnically segregated at first, gradually the doors were opened for members of the Indian elite to attend if they had sufficient English language skills and an interest in the colonial culture. This was later expanded when the Indian community, who were banned from attending amateur theatre in Simla, established their own amateur company before joining the British company in the mid-1930s – perhaps an example of the changing relationships between colonists and the colonized at this time. Moreover, members of the Indian community even established their own indigenous language theatre companies modelled on the British theatre practices and architecture. Attending (and even staging) amateur theatricals, as well as professional theatre performances, allowed performers and audiences to take part in what they considered to be a 'civilizing' experience and to remove themselves from their colonial duties and identities. When the show being toured was a recent hit musical comedy from London, there was the added bonus of feeling part of a 'West End' experience, especially when musical comedy featured the latest inventions, fashions and fads in the early decades of the twentieth century. Indeed, the shows that toured played on the branding of success in the West End – a feature that will recur in the twenty-first century in relation to 'Broadway' shows.

Tours to the colonies had begun earlier in the nineteenth century for plays, especially by Shakespeare, yet it was the D'Oyly Carte Company (DOC) that established the practice of world tours for comic opera that would be followed by musical comedy. Although stars may not want to take the time to travel the globe, bearing in mind that it took several weeks to travel to India by ship, the economics of theatrical production meant that it became increasingly common for lesser-known actors to tour, mostly actors who did not have the prestige to refuse work abroad. The cost of licensing and rehearsing a play script, creating sets and costumes and arranging the production meant that the set-up costs of mounting a new work could be recouped and profits made over a longer period if the show travelled. Rather than reaching only one audience, the show was then able to play to many new audiences around the world. On such tours of the colonies, the company might travel with several shows so that they could play a different show to the same audience on different nights of the week (known as playing in repertory – or in rep). This maximized the producer's profits, though this was offset by the time taken to travel between locations, such as between India and Africa or Australia by ship. This whole enterprise was facilitated by the development of copyright laws in national locations and later by the WIPO that provided global protections for copyright works.

KEY CONCEPT: Intellectual property

'Intellectual Property' is a term that encompasses protection for creators of trademarks, patents, trade secrets and, most importantly for arts practitioners, copyright. Copyright laws protect the creators of works that are written/published in a tangible form from having their work copied, sold, distributed or performed. An economy has developed where producers pay a license (often in the form of a royalty) to the writers for permission to perform a show. Such systems are expensive to police, so licensers like Concord Theatricals or Music Theatre International (MTI) only allow performance companies to access copies of a script and/or score on signing a contract. This means that licensers can ensure the quality of a production and, in some works, legally stipulate that original choreography is performed (though often with optionality). For example, Jerome Robbins's choreography for *West Side Story* (1957) and *Fiddler on the Roof* (1964) can be presented in full, in part or ignored entirely in all amateur and professional productions of these shows.

Permission in the form of an agreement or license is also required to adapt a work (such as a novel to a musical), to record (music or to read a play text on a recording) and even to play recorded music in a public location (e.g. shops and cafes pay a license to play live or recorded music). The money raised covers administrative costs, but also the writers and performers benefit in royalties, which, in many cases, is how they earn a living. Just think of the amount of money in royalties a composer like Andrew Lloyd Webber has earned from the global distribution and performance of songs like 'Memory' and 'Any Dream Will Do', whereas it can be a lifeline for new composers trying to establish themselves. Although the exact year differs in different countries, the copyright of a text (song, play, musical etc.) tends to expire seventy years after the writer's death, with shorter periods for the creators of recordings and films of those texts. This means that, despite the works of Gilbert and Sullivan being licensed by the DOC to both professional and amateur companies since the 1880s, these works have been in the public domain (meaning license-free) since the mid-twentieth century.

The first production of *HMS Pinafore* (1878) by W. S. Gilbert and Arthur Sullivan was a huge hit in London, which quickly led to many American companies performing edited and unofficial productions of the show to the annoyance of the authors and their producer, Richard D'Oyly Carte. While there was an International Copyright Law in place, which offered signatory countries the equivalent of national protection, America was outside of the law's jurisdiction. Consequently, *HMS Pinafore* needed to be published and produced in America, as well as in London, to secure copyright protection and avoid pirated versions. It was not until 1891 that America began offering any kind of national treatment to international productions, and so the DOC's next production was written and produced in knowing response to the 'piracy' that had plagued their past productions. Indeed, *The Pirates of Penzance* (1879) opened in Paignton, Devon, on 30 December 1879 to secure copyright protection in Britain, before opening at the Fifth Avenue Theatre in New York on 31 December 1879, a day later, to secure copyright in America. It then had an official opening in London in April 1880, making it the only Gilbert and Sullivan opera to officially open in New York before playing in London. Indeed, the use of the word 'pirate' in copyright is thought to stem from this particular show.

DOC did not publish the full vocal score to avoid unauthorized versions of *The Pirates of Penzance*, as occurs with most contemporary musicals today, but it licensed the rights to mount productions in America and New Zealand. At any one time, D'Oyly Carte could have several productions of the same show running in London and New York, one or two national tours, plus other licensed productions in New Zealand or Australia and other companies touring America, South Africa and occasionally Europe. By the late nineteenth century, D'Oyly Carte had transformed musical theatre into a transnational operation in which productions became capitalist products to be sold and globally distributed.

There is an unusual situation with Gilbert and Sullivan's *The Mikado* (1885). Gilbert set the piece in Japan so that he could satirize Victorian conventions by disguising the British institutions and relocating them to the fictional town of Titipu in Japan. When the work first toured, it was not considered acceptable in Japan, since any negative caricature of the Emperor (or Mikado) was an offence. Negative reports from Japanese visitors who saw the work in London meant there was already an aversion to the work. Nevertheless, it arrived in Yokohama in 1887, with a changed title and references to the Emperor removed, and was performed only for expatriates in the foreign concession (land controlled by an external country/individual).

A Savoy Opera troupe was refused permission to perform the work in Japan in 1923, since the work was considered an imperial spoof, though it was performed for American troops by a Japanese company at the Takarazuka-Geikijo theatre in Tokyo during the occupation of Japan in 1946 (Raben, 1998). There have been further attempts to bring the work to Japan since the mid-twentieth century, including when a Japanese resident of Chichibu linked the work to a peasant rebellion and tried to prove the link between Chichibu and Gilbert's fictional Titipu (Enbutsu, 2000). Although the link was disproved, the work was finally performed in a Japanese translation in Chichibu in 2001, in a production by the Tokyo Theatre Company using wardrobe and wigs from Kabuki opera. Since then, the Japanese translation has been used on several occasions, including at the International Gilbert and Sullivan Festival in England in 2006. This work, which has been consistently performed for over 130 years, demonstrates some of the issues with translating materials between cultures without understanding the offence that might be caused.

CASE STUDY: *The Mikado* (1885)

Music: Arthur Sullivan. Lyrics and book: W. S. Gilbert.

Known also as *The Town of Titipu*, this comic opera was the ninth collaboration between Gilbert and Sullivan. The son of the royal Mikado, Nanki-Poo disguises himself as a peasant, in this case, a wandering minstrel – to go out into the city. He wants to escape an arranged marriage to the elderly Katisha, a lady of his father's court. He and the beautiful Yum Yum meet and wish to marry, but she is already engaged. Her betrothed, Ko-Ko, had been destined to be executed but is reprieved and promoted to Lord High Executioner. When a royal decree is issued that insists that someone from the city be beheaded, Ko-Ko (who must find a candidate) persuades Nanki-Poo, who is in despair and contemplating suicide over his love for Yum Yum, that he should volunteer. To persuade him, Ko-Ko even suggests that Nanki-Poo marries Yum Yum and only afterwards is beheaded so that she will be free to marry Ko-Ko and the Mikado's edict will have been carried out. A different law is then discovered, confusing matters further, in which, if a man is beheaded, his wife must be buried alive. Yum Yum, unsurprisingly, has second thoughts causing despair for Nanki-Poo who wishes to be executed instantly.

> Ko-Ko, who must complete an execution on pain of being executed himself, suggests that the pair get married and go into hiding so he can pretend that an execution has taken place. However, when the Mikado arrives, with Nanki-Poo's intended, Katisha, and they discover that his son has been executed things get even worse. Nanki-Poo will not come out of hiding until it would be impossible for him to marry Katisha, or for Yum Yum to marry Ko-Ko, so Ko-Ko agrees to marry Katisha. Then Nanki-Poo and Yum Yum come out of hiding and all ends happily.

Following the success of these tours of comic opera, successful musical comedy shows began to travel to the colonies (and former colonies), with, for example, George Edwardes' production of *A Gaiety Girl* (1893) – a show introduced in Chapter 1 – touring to Broadway, provincial America and Australia. *Our Miss Gibbs* (1909) followed an even larger circuit over the next few years, taking in the British provinces, plus Cape Town, Bloemfontein, Kimberley, Johannesburg, Pretoria, Bulawayo, Lucknow, Allahabad, Cairo, Alexandria, Calcutta, Rangoon, Bombay, Manila, Hong Kong, Shanghai, Tientsin, Yokohama and finishing in Australia and New Zealand (Becker, 2014, p. 704). This route had been followed by theatre managers since the late 1870s, when it was successfully followed by producers of musical comedy. Shows could play several weeks in cities with the largest diasporic communities, such as Bombay and Calcutta, and only a day or two where the community was smaller. Theatre managers in the colonies were also developing successful businesses, including Maurice E. Bandmann, who built, part-owned or ran several theatres in both Bombay and Calcutta. Bandmann (his name sometimes appears as 'Bandman') then established an opera company that was licensed to perform musical comedies in Asia, but also in South America and Canada. Known as the Bandmann Circuit it 'extended from Gibraltar to Tokyo and included more than two dozen towns and cities across the Asian continent as well as occasional forays to the West Indies and even South America' (Balme, 2020, p. 2). According to an obituary in Singapore's *Straits Times*, Bandmann 'inaugurated the system that will remain as a monument to his memory in theatrical circles' (quoted in Balme 2020, p. 1), having a huge impact on the global spread of musical theatre.

The cultural dimension of globalization

The trade routes Europeans opened up in the sixteenth century were not new; some had existed since antiquity, with some academics suggesting that there has been such a thing as 'world economics' and embryonic capitalism since the Middle Ages. There is also a debate about where the centre of such capitalist and world economics might have been located, with some arguing that the centres have included Genoa, Holland, Britain and now America, while others suggest that Asia was the centre of the global economy until the mid-eighteenth century, rather than Europe. Whatever the debate in history, however, we move now to the globalized present and an age of interconnected, even homogenized, cultures.

KEY CONCEPT: Globalization

'Globalization' is a term that describes a set of changes that began to occur in the early 1970s, though global trade flows, tours of performances and other interactions were already in existence (as we have seen). The development of the specific form of globalization that arose in this period required certain features to be in place: the easy and safe movement of money following deregulation and neo-liberalization; technological development in communication (including mobile telephones and later the Internet); and increased roles for intergovernmental and world organizations. Alongside these features that promote global trade, certain issues, such as the sustainability of the environment and some aspects of healthcare, may be best dealt with at the global level.

In response to the global pandemic of Covid-19 in late 2019/ early 2020, the WHO acted as a central point overseeing the flow of information, the availability of statistical information, the sharing of strategies and guidance, plus documenting the development and trials of vaccines. While each government responded to the health crisis as it pertained within their state, including raising and lowering the levels of lockdown or tracing the sources of infections within communities, the global dimension proved invaluable. On the other hand, flows of goods and people were seriously hampered, revealing the complexity of existing physical networks and practices (such as 'next day delivery', as well as live performance, tourism and business travel). This global network has proved to be less effective in these circumstances. Meanwhile, technological flows expanded exponentially with online meetings, conferences and even performances being created for this new reality. Some academics suggest that the effect of global capitalism is to produce an amoral society that cares more about profit and efficiency than human or environmental sustainability and that the link between capitalism and globalization reduces accountability, ethics and morality (Steger, 2017, p. 92). This has also been argued in relation to Covid-19 with some commentators suggesting that travel restrictions, for example, were lifted before the pandemic was controlled, basing decisions on economic rather than health requirements. In sum, globalization is a fluid and dynamic process that is always in a state of transformation.

The practice of international touring can be traced to the model used by Gilbert and Sullivan and the DOC. The company that owns the copyright for the work, and has mounted a production, contrives to maintain control of most aspects of production in performances around the world. However, as we have seen above, some productions were licensed to local and international producers (such as Maurice Bandmann) to mount their own productions. There are thus different models, even within the work of the DOC, with some productions sent out with original or replica staging, and others licensed for local producers to create new versions of the works ('the work' in these cases mostly being the script and score). In touring versions, the performers travel with the work, while in the licensed model 'the work', meaning the script, score and sometimes the choreography and design, is consistent, and local performers are employed, and a local director and producer create a new production. When local people are employed there is a greater trickle down of money than in the touring versions that have the attraction of advertising themselves as 'original' Broadway or West End productions. As we will see, a new franchise model was introduced in the late twentieth century that altered the model again. In the meantime, these two types of practice continued well into the twentieth century as J. C. Williamson Ltd., for example, imported replica stagings of original

Broadway productions (usually with imported stars) across Australia during the twentieth century (continuing earlier traditions long after the death of Williamson in 1913). Elsewhere, however, companies were able to license the same works and create new versions. The relative value of these productions is potentially different, therefore, with a premium in some countries being paid for the ability to market the source of the production.

Jump forward to the 1980s and the origins of the so-called McMusical, or what Dan Rebellato terms 'McTheatre', are based on the idea of a franchise model associated with the fast-food chain McDonalds (2009b, p. 12). Consider how, in most areas of the world, for example, a McDonalds' Big Mac follows the same recipe – no matter where it is served or who it is cooked by. It is this model, and the global empire of McDonalds, that McTheatre is said to mimic. In particular, the McMusical is often associated with the production practices of Cameron Mackintosh and Andrew Lloyd Webber's Really Useful Group (RUG), plus Disney Theatrical Productions (DTP) in America, where the entire production, overseen by directors and supervisors, is transferred onto performers in territories around the world. The critique of this system is that the money flows back to the originating production company in London or New York and that the performers in the franchised productions around the world are little more than puppets. However, each of the above companies operates different structures for their globalized networks and their production strategies are not as homogenized as they might first appear.

KEY CONCEPT: Theatre production and producers

Until the very recent past, musicals were developed by one or perhaps two producers. Charles Frohman and George Edwardes have been mentioned elsewhere for transferring early musical comedies between Britain and America. George White and Florenz Ziegfeld were also significant in America in the first half of the twentieth century. David Merrick, who was responsible for *Gypsy* (1959), *Hello, Dolly!* (1964) and *42nd Street* (1980) on Broadway, was one of the last producers to generate a production from an initial idea to full performance (Adler, 2011, p. 359). More recently, producers shepherd productions that artists bring to them. Rocco Landesman was the producer responsible for the development of *Big River* (1985) and, later at Jujamcyn, *The Producers* (2001) in New York, while director Hal Prince also started his career as a Broadway producer. Australian-born (but British-residing) Robert Stigwood was originally a music producer, but later moved into theatre and film production, where he was responsible for stage versions of *Hair* (1967), *Jesus Christ Superstar* (1971), *Pippin* (1972), *Evita* (1978) and *Sweeney Todd* (1979) on both sides of the Atlantic. Newer international producers include British-born Judy Craymer (*Mamma Mia!* [1999]) and Sonia Friedman (*Sunny Afternoon* [2014]), plus Daryl Roth (*Kinky Boots* [2013]) and Jeffrey Seller (*Hamilton* [2015]) in America.

The producer is responsible for gathering together a creative team, raising the finance for a project, and then for ensuring the project sticks to time and budget. They must consider pre-production costs, including the costs of writers and those designing and creating sets and costumes, as well as any running costs, such as salaries, royalties, advertising, insurance and theatre rental, before deciding how much investment they need to raise to capitalize a show. Successful shows with small capitalization costs result in rapid recoupment – at which point the show makes a profit. Steven Adler records that the Broadway production of *RENT* (1996) recouped its (very small) costs in about fifteen weeks and *Avenue Q* (2004) in about forty weeks. Jeffrey Seller's 2002 Broadway production of Baz Luhrmann's *La Boheme*, however, eventually cost $9 million – losing $6 million in the process (Adler, 2011, pp. 356–7). *Spider-Man: Turn Off the Dark* (2010), a now infamous Broadway flop, was also in previews for 182 performances and cost a staggering $75 million to produce, losing a significant portion of investment when it closed.

Two things have changed in the recent past. First, the cost of staging productions is now so high that it is rare for a single producer to mount a show without a series of partners, many of whom are simply investors. Second, the process of an out-of-town try-out, an American tradition where productions played several venues to iron out the wrinkles before arriving in New York, has been replaced by partnerships with not-for-profit theatres. Such theatres have helped develop several new musicals and have reaped the (financial and reputational) rewards that then support their other work if such musicals are successful. The Public Theatre in New York led by Joseph Papp is a significant venue of this kind, with *Fun Home* (2015) and *Hamilton* (2015) as recent successes, and *Hair* (1967) as one of its early productions. Elsewhere, *Les Misérables* (1985) was a partnership between the Royal Shakespeare Company and Cameron Mackintosh in London, while Broadway's *Big River* (1985) resulted from a partnership between Rocco Landesman, American Repertory Theatre (ART) and La Jolla Playhouse. The ART has also been fundamental to developing a range of new musicals, many of which transferred to Broadway, including *Once* (2011) and several productions staged by artistic director Diane Paulus, such as *Finding Neverland* (2014) and *Jagged Little Pill* (2018).

Global producers and international productions

Cameron Mackintosh made his name as the producer of *Cats*, with Andrew Lloyd Webber, in 1981. Together, they brought in Dewynters to market the show and, in turn, transformed the way musicals were advertised. This company, which remains the leading West End advertising and design agency, created a single visual image to 'brand' the show (rather than sell the show by advertising star names or the opinions of critics). Like the iconic 'Golden Arches' associated with McDonalds or the Starbucks Mermaid, *Cats* was sold through the image of an internationally recognizable set of yellow cat's eyes (whose pupils were represented by silhouettes of dancers). This was followed with productions like *The Phantom of the Opera* (1986) and *Miss Saigon* (1989) featuring similarly wordless logos. These logos have the advantage of not requiring translation and being identical throughout the world. In turn, the product itself is branded as a West End or Broadway replica. Producers can then also capitalize on selling associated merchandise that supports the advertising, while also generating an additional income stream. This kind of branding has arguably had as much of an impact on the globalization of musical theatre as the content of the shows.

Although his company now presents work around the world, Mackintosh has continued to maintain a personal approach to production that allows him to have a hands-on say in the development of new musicals. Mackintosh sends his creative and production teams to work with companies in local contexts to develop the shows as global products that are almost identical. The show must look and sound like the original, in all except language, though there are necessarily local changes resulting from the translation of cultural practices. *Les Misérables* (1985), for example, had been translated into twenty-one different languages by the show's twenty-fifth birthday and had played in forty-two different countries (Masters, 2010).

By contrast Lloyd Webber and Tim Rice had set up New Talent Ventures resulting from the success of *Joseph and the Amazing Technicolor Dreamcoat* in the early 1970s. That company released the album of *Jesus Christ Superstar* in 1970 (see Figure 7.2), which sold particularly well in America. Robert Stigwood took over producing at that point and increased the capital investment and the aspiration of the show, which opened on Broadway in 1971. It was then produced in California before arriving in London in

Figure 7.2 Composer Andrew Lloyd Webber, producer David Geffen and Trevor Nunn at a recording session for the cast album of the Broadway production of the musical *Cats*. 1983. Photo: Swope, Martha © NYPL.

1972 and a film version was directed by Norman Jewison in 1973. It was between the album release and London stage opening of *Evita* (1978) that Lloyd Webber formed his Really Useful Company. *Cats* followed in 1981, which, building on its success in London, not only opened in New York but was the first production Lloyd Webber's Really Useful Company licensed to Friedrich Kurz in Hamburg for a German language production. The show had reportedly brought £20m to the city by 1988 and the producer was involved in transforming the red-light district into a theatre district. As a result of the employment of performers and the investment in theatres, this production began the process of revitalizing musical theatre in Germany, to the extent that the local council built a new theatre in Bochum for *Starlight Express* (1988) (where it still plays today).

CASE STUDY: *Cats* (1981)

Music: Andrew Lloyd Webber. Lyrics: Adapted from T. S. Eliot's *Old Possum's Book of Practical Cats.*

The concept musical takes place at a gathering of Jellicle Cats, called the Jellicle Ball. The cat community decides which of them should ascend to the Heaviside Layer, effectively to be reincarnated. The interest, however, lies in the characterizations arising from the poetry and from Lloyd Webber's accompanying music, as well as in the work of director Trevor Nunn and choreographer Gillian Lynne in creating the structure and characters. Each of the cats has an opportunity to be showcased at the Jellicle Ball, including the Rum Tum Tugger and Mr Mistoffelees, before the decision is made. The cat chosen is Grizabella, a former glamour cat, who sings the hit song 'Memory' before being chosen and ascending to the Heaviside Layer.

Despite a loose plot and lack of clear protagonists, *Cats* ushered in an era of blockbuster musicals for families and tourists. It won Best Musical awards at both the Laurence Olivier Awards (London) and the Tony Awards (New York) and ran for twenty-one years in the West End, as well as for eighteen years on Broadway. It has been translated into over twenty languages and remains a popular hit around the world. It was adapted as a feature film in 2019, which infamously used CGI and reportedly lost up to $114 million at the box office.

Although the Really Useful Company began as a theatre production company, with Lloyd Webber owning separate companies to manage his personal finances and music publishing, the whole conglomerate was brought together as Really Useful Group (RUG) in 1985. This group now has many other branches and activities that include ticket sales, theatre ownership, film production and magazine publishing. It was also in the mid-1980s that RUG broke into the Asian market through a link with the Shiki Theatre Company in Japan, where *Evita* and *Cats* first toured. Whereas Mackintosh maintains a centralized operation, RUG has gradually built up 'hubs' in Singapore, Hong Kong, Sydney, Frankfurt, New York and Los Angeles, with its head office remaining in London. From each of these nodal points, productions can be developed and overseen, creatives and performers auditioned and employed, and appropriate marketing and translation strategies agreed, but crucially the company generally works in collaboration with local producers.

The common features of the global musicals of Cameron Mackintosh and RUG are that near-identical productions are offered to audiences around the world in what some might regard as a democratizing process that allows audiences to see a lightly adapted or translated version of the same show as appeared on Broadway or in the West End. The idea of the 'Broadway' musical as a brand emerged to describe such shows, even when these musicals originated in Britain, leading to these shows being perceived around the world as 'Broadway' musicals. Indeed, as David Savran has argued, although the shows are branded as being from New York, they need to be analysed from a transnational perspective 'that emphasizes interconnectedness and the cross-border fluidity of cultures and species of capital' (2014, p. 318).

The Disney Corporation was the next company to become a key player in this global enterprise. By 2014, Disney had become one of the largest media conglomerates in the world (with others including Time Warner, Google and Newscorp). The company signed a forty-nine-year revenue-based lease for the New Amsterdam Theatre on 42nd Street in 1995 and spent $8 million renovating the venue. The company also made a commitment to make a substantial investment in renovating Times Square to become a cultural quarter. Since the 1970s, 42nd Street and Times Square had been populated by strip clubs, pornography cinemas and other non-family friendly establishments, meaning Broadway theatres were not always considered safe environments for children. Disney's investment led to other conglomerates populating the area, with 42nd Street, today, being home to Ripley's Believe It or Not, the Madame Tussauds wax museum, various cinemas and other attractions. Some people believe the clean-up effectively rendered the theatre district of New York corporate and middle-class (see, for example, Adler, 2004), but it has become the heart of a vast global operation.

Disney has also led the way in developing new global productions based on its own intellectual property. As addressed in Chapter 3, the company developed *Beauty and the Beast* (1994) from its own 1991 animated film, followed by *The Lion King* (1997 [1994]). More recent Broadway productions include *Aida* (2000) through their own subsidiary Hyperion Productions, plus the stage adaptations of films like *Tarzan* (2006 [1999]), *The Little Mermaid* (2008 [1989]), *Newsies* (2012 [1992]) and *Aladdin* (2014 [1992]). Disney Theatricals can develop large-scale productions by managing the finance through the film studios, leading to a cross-fertilization of product between studios, theme parks, theatre, ABC television and the merchandising arms of the company. This concept is known as synergy, in which products are sold in relation to each other, under umbrella franchises (like *The Lion King*), and sold and advertised across the Disney product line (from toys to television).

By 2014, *The Lion King* had generated more than $6.2 billion worldwide. This means that DTP is less susceptible to the costs of producing stage musicals since they can recoup those costs around the world or spread them across other parts of the company. Not only has *The Lion King* been a major hit in London and on tour in Britain, it (and other Disney musicals) has played in Germany, Japan, Australia, Spain, Mexico, Canada, Brazil, South Africa, Russia, Italy, China, Argentina, Denmark, Sweden, Finland, Malaysia, Indonesia, the Philippines, Estonia and South Korea. The company used *The Lion King* to brand a production in its Shanghai Disneyland theme park in 2016, but there were cultural differences that meant the production only ran for a year (Bennett, 2020, p. 449). DTP has also branched out into partnerships with other producers, including Cameron Mackintosh for *Mary Poppins* (2005 [1964]), the first Disney adaptation to originate in London, and others for *Sister Act* (2011 [1992]) and *Peter and the Starcatcher* (2012), a play by Rick Elice.

One of the key changes in practice since Cameron Mackintosh began producing is that musicals are now co-produced by many companies because the level of financial investment required is so much greater. Mel Brooks's musical, *The Producers* (2001), demonstrates an older model of production similar to that followed by DOC in the late Victorian period, when a producer could raise funds from individual 'angels' to mount a show. In the case of Bialystock and Bloom (the musical's fictional producers), the funds came from many 'little old ladies'. As an independent producer, Cameron

Mackintosh also used groups of investors to finance his early shows, as did his contemporaries. This has changed and, because of the incredible costs of production, it is now almost impossible to raise the necessary funds or take the risk of launching a new production without significant investment that comes from large-scale funders, financiers and many (sometimes internationally diverse) co-producers.

(Far) Beyond Broadway

The globalized networks described so far have cemented musical theatre as a transatlantic, but also transnational, form. Musicals are now co-produced by many (often international) companies and might also be produced in one of any number of territories and result from transnational collaborations. This process began with the investment of European producers in theatres and imported musicals in the late twentieth century, but more recently the local economies and infrastructure in (especially) Germany, Austria, the Netherlands, Japan and South Korea have developed to the extent that producers are able to generate their own new productions in a Broadway style, as well as mounting imported productions.

In Japan, performers are often employees of a parent company with whom they train and for whom they work consistently. This practice is built around a corporate industrial model that began, surprisingly, with railroad companies. Ichizo Kobayashi began producing shows with an all-female theatre troupe in 1914, partly to stimulate use of its Hankyu train line whose terminus was at Takarazuka. The shows were so popular that within ten years the company had its own theatre in Takarazuka. They also own the Takarazuka Geikyo Theatre in Tokyo (where *The Mikado* played to American service men during the Second World War). Short runs of shows are programmed years in advance in this model, which contains no flexibility to extend the runs of popular shows or indeed to produce the open runs of shows that are seen in the West. The shows themselves have been influenced by Western musical theatre practices and Hollywood film musicals, often being extremely melodramatic and escapist in style and content, as well as being performed entirely by women. The 'male' performers develop a low vocal range and a physical style that is gendered as male. Both male and female principals become huge stars to the (largely female) audiences. It may be the strength of these female performers, in contrast to their conservative narratives, that appeals to modern Japanese women. By contrast, the Shiki Company, with whom RUG first worked in Japan, has moved to a Western model with open-ended runs and the employment of freelance professionals – a fairly recent category/development in Japan. This means that Western shows can be mounted and those that are successful simply continue, while those that are not close. This is the same flexibility that Western productions enjoy, allowing the company to maximize the profits from successful shows, and minimize losses from those that are not drawing audiences. Takarazuka, by contrast, maintains its performers on permanent contracts and programmes a regular offering in its theatres.

South Korea's engagement with musical theatre began in 1960 as a competition with large-scale events mounted in North Korea. Nationalist entertainment events based on folk legends were mounted by a company called Yegrin (that later changed its name to Seoul City Music Theatre). These shows had a political motivation and were overseen by the government. However, as South Korea became increasingly independent of the North, and was more influenced by America, the Seoul City Music Theatre began to stage 'Broadway' shows such as *Fiddler on the Roof* (1964). By the 1990s, the company had become the Seoul Music Company, and Yegrin was the name of a musical award. Meanwhile, in the 1980s, and given the economic boom, the Hyundai Theatre began to stage Western works such as *Jesus Christ Superstar* (1971), *West Side Story* (1957) and *The Sound of Music* (1959), paving the way for new collaborations with Western producers.

Seol and Company was founded in 2001 to focus on importing Broadway-branded musicals, even if the musicals were actually European. The first Korean language version of *The Phantom of the Opera* (1986) opened in 2001, followed by *Cats* (1981) in 2008, through an agreement to mount RUG productions, though they have also produced American musicals. Following the development of physical infrastructure and performer training for these shows, new Korean product was developed, while the English-speaking performers from Korean productions were able to work internationally. Arts Communication International (ACOM) was founded in 1991 and developed a new corporate culture and better pay rates for performers, increasing the professionalism of local productions in works that focused on national identity. Their most famous musical to date is *The Last Empress* (1995), a work that was exported to the Lincoln Center, New York, in 1997 and played in the West End in 2002. This was the start of a process that has, most recently, seen South Korean money involved in the development of an 'out-of-town' opening in Seoul for a production of *Dreamgirls* (1981) in 2008

(Lee, 2017). This production played the Apollo Theatre in Harlem and toured America with an African American cast in 2009. The show was produced by John F. Breglio, and his company Vienna Waits Productions, in partnership with Chun-soo Shin and Open the Door (OD) Musical Company (see Lee 2017, for more on the development of Korean musicals).

Vereinigte Bühnen Wien (VBW) in Vienna and Stage Entertainment in the Netherlands have also built on the professionalism of performers, and the development of infrastructure for large-scale musicals, to create their own new musicals in the Broadway style. In 2010, Fred Boot, once an employee of Stage Entertainment, began his own company that produced the innovatively staged nationalist story of *Soldier of Orange*. A new theatre was built in an airport hangar at the former military airport in Valkenburg to house the production, in which audience members sit in a rotating auditorium with scenes taking place around the circular seating formation. Elsewhere, Joop Van den Ende, who founded Stage Entertainment in 1998, is another example of a producer who has invested in West End and Broadway productions in partnership with many international companies, including RUG, Disney and VBW, and who has been active in European theatre ownership and production. Since his retirement in 2016, however, and the sale of Stage Entertainment, the company's operations have changed (Thierens, 2017).

The German market for musicals is somewhat unique, given that, as we saw in Chapter 1, musical theatre (as we know it today) grew out of the Austrian (German language) operettas that toured internationally in the 1800s. However, as Frédéric Döhl documents, while there is 'a rich diversity of professional musical theatre within a strong theatre system' in Germany, the market for musicals is very different from other territories in terms of structure and output (2020, p. 427). Public theatres that receive significant amounts of public funding attract older musicals and revivals, especially those with quasi-operatic or symphonic scores, such as *Passion* (1994) and *The Light in the Piazza* (2005). On the other hand, commercial theatres mostly host international productions, predominantly from RUG, at first, and more recently from Disney. Just as in Korea, the theatre districts, trained performers, increased professionalism and the success of the form have led to the development of local productions. In the German-speaking world, the most successful have been *Elisabeth* (1992), *Tanz der Vampire* (1997) and *Mozart!* (1999), each produced by Stage Entertainment, while many American musicals have been too removed thematically to resonate with German creatives and audiences (Döhl, 2020, p. 432).

These are just a few examples, since there are, of course, many other countries and cities throughout the world in which musical theatre is prospering.

Conclusion

Over the last century and a half, the interest in musical theatre has grown exponentially around the world. Beginning with tours of comic operas and musical comedy, the interest has developed beyond what was initially a colonial audience for shows from London and New York performed by Western performers. Now, although the production is branded as a 'Broadway' show and replicates the plot, songs, scenery and actions of the original production, the work is likely to be translated and performed by local performers and may have been developed in London or New York or, indeed, elsewhere. The costs of such productions have risen to the extent that such global opportunities are necessary to fund the Broadway or West End development, pre-production and costs leading up to the premieres. Cultural tourism has accelerated to the extent that, not only do Broadway and West End producers actively promote their products to tourists, but they also serve to enhance tourist destinations around the world (Bennett, 2005).

Of course, there are issues with this global market, not least of which is the cultural reception of stories developed in America or Britain in other markets. Although shows are translated and adapted in each location there can be awkwardness if there is insufficient awareness of local concerns and practices. Perhaps more fundamental is the issue of whether such global transfers flatten out the independence and creativity of local theatre makers. Performers are required to reproduce rather than create performances, music falls into a generic 'soft rock' or symphonic sound that is assumed to appeal to all, while voices and acting styles become institutionalized and similar. On the other hand, there is no question that these productions have led to the development of training opportunities, professionalization of staff in all areas of theatre, the opening of theatres, the production of new musical theatre works arising in regions around the world, and benefits to the economies of the cities concerned (as well as the producers themselves, of course). There can be no simple binary conclusion, therefore, about the effects of globalized musicals, since the global reach of Broadway and

Broadway-style musicals has impacted on and informed the aesthetics, practices and marketing of musicals not only on Broadway and in the West End, but also in Europe, Asia and across the globe.

This is not the end of the story, however. In recent decades, the above complexities have been somewhat altered by the Internet. As addressed in Chapter 3, the Internet has drastically changed how musicals are created and consumed. Fans can now access the paratexts that frame a musical, whether a cast recording or fan art, from anywhere in the world with Internet access. This has also led to the development of several Internet musicals (see Hayashi, 2020). Team Starkid, for example, has developed several low-budget stage musicals in Chicago that were then filmed for YouTube. Inspired by Josh Whedon's earlier YouTube musical *Dr. Horrible's Sing-Along Blog* (2008), the team has generated an international fan base for their parody musicals, including *A Very Potter Musical* (2009) and *Twisted: The Untold Story of a Royal Vizier* (2013). These works, plus those by similar groups like AVbyte, transcend national barriers as productions that can be enjoyed at any time or day, with unlimited access, for free.

This global model was followed in 2020 when institutions such as the National Theatre in London streamed existing recordings of their stage productions during the Covid-19 pandemic. Under the heading of NTLive, the National Theatre had streamed live performances to international cinemas since 2009. During the pandemic, however, existing recordings were streamed for limited amounts of time on YouTube, often designed to accept donations in lieu of a ticket price, though producers and theatres soon started to develop paid online content. The Other Palace in London, for example, curated an online production of *Songs for a New World* (1995) in July 2020, from the separate homes of its four performers. Elsewhere, *Ratatouille the Musical* was crowdfunded and developed remotely during the pandemic. Following an Internet meme from Emily Jacobsen on TikTok, other users added their own elements of a hypothetical *Ratatouille* musical to their social media accounts, which was later professionally curated as a benefit concert, again online, in January 2021 to raise money for the Actor's Fund. As the twenty-first century develops, then, boundaries of time, space and finance continue to erode in relation to musical theatre. Performances transcend physical theatres, and, with this development, musical theatre plays even further to a globally interconnected world.

Tasks

Discuss the history and current state of a megamusical like
Les Misérables (1985) as a transnational brand. How does the
production conform to the idea of globalization? What are the pros
and cons of this type of production model? How have the once
'identical' production and performance values of this musical
altered in the twenty-first century?

Select a city not discussed in this chapter, say Paris, Berlin or Toronto.
How has the globalization of the theatre industry impacted that
theatre community? Have hybrid or composite works been developed
in that city that reflect the nation or culture? If not, why not?

Discussion topics

Can a musical exclusively be described as British or American and, if
so, what criteria might you use to denote its nationality? Is *The Lion
King* (1997) an American musical, for instance, when it integrates so
many styles and influences from across Africa and Asia?

What are the consequences of globalization for other aspects of
production, such as performance practice, vocal and musical style, and
sound design? How might performing in a long-running production of
Cats (1981) differ to that of starring in a new play, for example?

Further reading – conceptual

Balme, C. B. (2020) *The Globalisation of Theatre 1870–1930*.
   Cambridge: Cambridge University Press.
Bennett, S. (2005) 'Theatre/Tourism'. *Theatre Journal* 57: 407–28.
Poore, B. (2016) *Theatre & Empire*. Basingstoke: Palgrave
   Macmillan.

Further reading – case study

Döhl, F. (2020) 'The Third Biggest Market: Musical Theater in
   Germany since 1990'. In: J. Sternfeld and E. L. Wollman (eds) *The*

Routledge Companion to the Contemporary Musical. London and New York: Routledge, 427–44.

Kim, H. (2016) 'Celebrating Heteroglossic Hybridity: Ready-to-Assemble Broadway-Style Musicals in South Korea'. *Studies in Musical Theatre* 10/3: 343–54.

Savran, D. (2014) 'Trafficking in Transnational Brands: The New "Broadway-Style" Musical'. *Theatre Survey* 55/3: 318–42.

'Journey to the past': From revival to revisal

If you were to ask a young musical theatre fan to discuss the stage musical *Chicago*, it is likely they would conjure images of female dancers in black lingerie, plus male dancers with rippling muscles, on an open stage with minimal set and an onstage band. Missing from these descriptions of the 1996 Broadway production, which is still running in New York at the time of writing, is any acknowledgement that this iconic production is, in fact, a revival. Despite the musical's juggernaut success in the 1990s, which spawned various international productions, and an Oscar-winning film version in 2002, John Kander, Fred Ebb and Bob Fosse's musical *Chicago* was first performed in 1975. The production starred Gwen Verdon and Chita Rivera, as femme fatales Roxie Hart and Velma Kelly, and was directed and choreographed by Fosse. The 1996 revival was directed by Walter Bobbie and choreographed 'in the style of Fosse' (who had died in 1987) by Ann Reinking, Fosse's former partner. Reinking also played Roxie in the revival, having replaced Verdon as Roxie in the original production (as documented in the FX television drama *Fosse/Verdon* [2019]). There was also a London production in 1979, choreographed by Gillian Gregory (rather than Fosse). However, both have been superseded in many people's memory by the 1996 revival production that is currently the longest-running American musical in Broadway history. *Chicago* is thus one of many musicals that has found further (if not more) critical and/or commercial success as a revival. Bill Kenwright's 1988 revival of Willy Russell's *Blood Brothers*, for example, ran for twenty-four years in the West End, having only played for six months during its original London run in 1983. Similarly, the provocative revue, *Oh! Calcutta!*, played for nearly thirteen years on Broadway from 1976 to 1989, having originally played for a comparatively short three years in 1969.

The revival and recreation of musical theatre works therefore continues to prolong the life of individual shows and also musical theatre as an art form.

This final chapter traces a transatlantic history of musicals in *production*, many of which are revived or transferred between London and New York. Existing shows reappear, often in entirely different packaging, attract new audiences and nostalgically engage past ones. Works are re-envisaged for new contexts, and new themes emerge as a result of altered social, political, historical and geographical contexts. The importance of context is revealed in works that are themselves 'unfinished' products (to use Bruce Kirle's term), able to be re-envisaged by creative teams, the audiences who view them with new expectations, or an altered world view (2005). They are also altered by new performers who revisit these shows year after year, whether professionally or through amateur performance.

KEY CONCEPT: Revivals and revisals

The purpose of a revival is to re-envisage an existing text for a new time or place so that new performers and directors can say something new about the work or about the world through the work. The term 'revival' stems from the word 'revive': to regain consciousness or to bring something back to life. After the original production of a show has closed, years, or even decades, later a producer or director may decide to re-examine that musical because they believe it has something to say to a contemporary audience or that they have a concept for staging it again in a new production.

Revivals are not transfers of productions that run concurrently in new cities, however. Broadway hits like *Hamilton* (2015) have not yet been revived, simply replicated in London and various other cities. While it is interesting to consider how a production might be received differently in each city, and each socio-cultural context, the production itself remains the same; it has not been reinvented or reimagined by a new director and creative team. Revivals retain the original book, music and lyrics to a large extent but are new productions of those texts, typically with new direction, choreography, scenic design, lighting, costumes, venue and performers. Revisals, by contrast, have at least some of the book, music and/or lyrics rewritten, reduced or expanded with new material for a different audience, time and place.

Reviving *Gypsy*

There are no definitive rules or formulas for producing a revival, yet a key feature is that each production is a new interpretation by the creative team and performers, which, given the difference in time between the original and revival productions, is also likely to be interpreted differently by audiences. Musicals, in this sense, are 'works-in-process' that may 'assume lives of their own that can be quite independent from the original intentions of their authors' as they continue to be produced and performed for live audiences (Kirle, 2005, p. 1). In the hands of new directors, casts and receiving audiences, musicals alter over time due to their inherent liveness and ability to be reimagined in new contexts. The liveness of productions, and their 'unfinished' state, is the significant difference between stage and screen (or film) musicals.

CASE STUDY: *Gypsy* (1959)

Music: Jules Styne. Lyrics: Stephen Sondheim. Book: Arthur Laurents.

This classic Golden Age musical depicts the real-life relationship between famous striptease performer, Gypsy Rose Lee, and her overbearing mother, Mama Rose. Set during the 1920s and 1930s, the musical sees Baby June, Rose's youngest daughter, find mediocre success on the vaudeville circuit, with help from Herbie (the act's manager and Rose's partner). When June abandons the act, and elopes with dancer, Tulsa, Rose thrusts her shy and reluctant daughter, Louise, into the spotlight. As the new act – 'Madame Rose's Toreadorables' – is booked into a burlesque house in Act 2, Louise steps in for a missing performer and finds herself a new career: stripping. Louise develops a successful career as Gypsy Rose Lee without her mother's help, leaving Rose to consider her manipulative actions in the iconic number, 'Rose's Turn'. In a scene that has been performed in various ways over the last six decades, the musical closes with Louise supporting her frail mother as an act of reconciliation.

Figure 8.1 Tyne Daly performing 'Rose's Turn' in a scene from the Broadway revival of the musical *Gypsy*. 1989. Photo: Swope, Martha. © NYPL.

The difference between a revival and a replication can sometimes be confusing. The musical *Gypsy*, for example, has been revived four times in New York since the original 1959 production, which starred Ethel Merman as Mama Rose. Each new production was performed in a new venue with a new design and a different actress playing Rose: 1974, Angela Lansbury; 1989, Tyne Daly (seen in Figure 8.1); 2003, Bernadette Peters; 2008, Patti LuPone. (The role has also been played by Rosalind Russell on film [1962] and Bette Midler on television [1993].) The 1974 Broadway production was a transfer of the 1973 London production: essentially the same show, with small adaptations for the American market. However, each of these Broadway revivals has recreated Jerome Robbins's original choreography, with three out of four of these productions also being directed by the musical's librettist, Arthur Laurents (all except Sam Mendes's 2003 production). These revivals are likely to have been similar to each other in some respects, given the level of continuity between them in direction and choreography, but each production re-envisaged the show after a considerable period of time. However, Mendes's production is definitely new, and noted for Bernadette

Peters's performance, which, according to Ben Brantley in *The New York Times*, broke the mould that had been created by Merman in 1959. Peters's 'brisk sweeping away of preconceptions' allowed Rose to emerge 'with her monumental willpower intact. But something new and affecting is simmering within the character, a damning glimpse of self-awareness' and that she might 'deflate into a small and bitter creature' (2003).

In Britain, an entirely new production was developed by director Jonathan Kent and choreographer Stephen Mear for Chichester Festival Theatre in 2014. Transferred in its entirety to London the following year, this version won four Olivier Awards in 2016, including Best Musical Revival and Best Actress in a Musical for Imelda Staunton as Rose. Writing in *The Guardian*, Michael Billington reminds us that Rose is '"a showbiz Oedipus", as Sondheim called her, wrapped in self-delusion' (2015). In this production, it is self-delusion and her hunger for stardom that leads to Rose's ultimate breakdown as 'a mink-wrapped Staunton grotesquely mimics the strip-teasing motions of her now celebrated daughter, Gypsy Rose Lee' (2015). Leslie Felperin, in *The Hollywood Review*, remarks on the different performances of Rose: 'Petite and pugnacious, Staunton's dowdier Rose is not a frustrated glamor puss like Rosalind Russell's version in the 1962 film adaptation, nor a fragile flower like Peters. Instead, her Rose is a yapping, growling mutt: half terrier like the Yorkie tucked under her arm, half pitbull' (2015). The different revival productions of *Gypsy* are not just memorialized in the work of directors and choreographers, then, but in the ongoing comparison of leading performances – what scholar Marvin Carlson describes as the 'haunted body' (2001). It is also apparent that even a replica production can be transformed by recasting principal, and especially star, performers.

1970s American revivals

While it may now be commonplace for audiences to attend musicals that they have seen before, the regular practice of reviving existing works developed largely in the mid-twentieth century. Miranda Lundskaer-Nielsen has argued that this is due, in part, to the 'youth of the genre: unlike drama and opera, musicals are essentially a twentieth-century art form' (2008, p. 110). Many musicals that opened before the 1940s, and thus before the American 'book musical', replaced the more diverse and diverting musical comedy, feature loosely constructed narratives with local, comic or topical references that are often too tied to their originating time period to make sense to, or amuse, audiences today. Dominic Symonds has noted how various early forms of musical theatre, including the amateur Varsity shows in America, were so tied to their cultural context that they would be considered 'contemporary, if self-obsessed, burlesques' today (2015, p. 42). Many later musicals, however, like *Gypsy* above, were presented unaltered several decades after they were first performed, meaning the work's characters or narrative addressed universal themes that spoke to contemporary issues.

Many musicals are also revived, not because their content speaks to contemporary issues but because the show acts as an escape from often troubling cultural contexts (e.g. war). This is true of many earlier British revivals of works by Gilbert and Sullivan, Lionel Monkton, Noel Coward, Noel Gay and Ivor Novello (among others) before, during and after the Second World War. Coward's *Bitter Sweet* (1929), for instance, transferred to Broadway in 1929, was revived in 1934, before returning to London in 1988. Likewise, Novello's *Glamorous Night* (1935) was revived in 1975 and Gay's *Me and My Girl* (1937) was revived in 1941, 1945 and 1949, plus briefly in 1952, and then revised in 1985. These shows were old-fashioned mementoes of the past, designed to provide a sense of comfort and escapism from the troubling contemporary world.

Musicals are not only written in response to their socio-cultural and political context, then, but revived and revised in relation to it too. After all, what better way to escape the troubles of the modern world than to attend a performance of a popular musical from the past? That these musicals survived as revivals, without revision, until short runs in the 1970s or 1980s demonstrates that it is only possible to revive musicals successfully if they can be understood and appreciated within the current context – even if that is the need for escapist entertainment. To be appreciated, the revival must speak to local, regional, national or international social and political concerns, especially in new ways so that the musical has a new currency in the time and place of the revival. For most of these older British musicals, that time seems to have past – though, as discussed further below, *Me and My Girl* is an obvious exception to this.

To cross the Atlantic, again, the trend of frequently reviving existing American musicals started in the 1970s. This was a time of progression and change in America, but was also, according to James Lovensheimer, 'dark and troubled' (2019, p. 59). While the youth-led counter-culture movement (that included civil rights, gay rights and women's liberation) had gained momentum during the 1960s, and continued throughout the 1970s, the assassination of Martin Luther King, Jr. (1968) and the election of President Richard Nixon (1968) were signs of a conservative backlash in favour of traditional family values. This was also a decade of racist-based zoning laws, neighbourhood racial ordinances and segregation throughout the nation. Americans were involved in the Vietnam War until 1973, plus the Watergate scandal began in 1972 and led to the impeachment of Nixon in 1974. High inflation accompanied Nixon's dismantling of the limited social welfare provision, though he did try to pass an affordable health care bill. America, a nation in which its youth were attempting to moving towards an increasingly liberal and racially diverse society, and towards racial and gender equality (as later reflected in the nostalgic 1988 film *Hairspray* and its 2002 stage adaptation), also swung to the right.

Although increasing diversity was reflected in the popularity of transatlantic musicians like Diana Ross, The Beatles and later Michael Jackson, 1970s popular culture was more broadly hit by a wave of nostalgia in response to the rise of 'The New Right'. Through films such as *American Graffiti* (1973), television shows like *Happy Days* (1974–84), and pop artists like the Everly Brothers, American popular culture frequently looked back on itself through a cultural fascination with the seemingly simpler 1950s. For example, the 1978 film adaptation of *Grease*, loosely based on the 1972 stage musical, featured a carefree impression of 1950s (white) teenagers rock 'n' rolling to jukeboxes, visiting drive-in movie theatres and slurping milkshakes. In the film's high school dance scene, the students adorn their school gymnasium with paper decorations, dance in circle skirts or ruffled shirts and bop along to Johnny Casino and the Gamblers (the fictional band played by Sha-Na-Na, the 1950s-style doo-wop group that were part of the 1970s Rockabilly revival movement). In its narrative, setting and presentation, as well as its heteronormative happy ending, *Grease* encapsulates the broader cultural turn towards nostalgia and family values that occurred during the 1970s.

But, why did this happen in the 1970s? What was it about American culture during this time that generated this sweep of nostalgia? For Jessica Sternfeld and Elizabeth L. Wollman, nostalgic musicals tend to have an 'especially strong impact during or immediately after periods of national hardship' (2011, p. 120). Musical comedies like *Mamma Mia!* (1999 – opening on Broadway in October 2001) and *Hairspray* (2002) provided comfort to New York audiences after 9/11, just as *Oklahoma!* (1943) provided a reassuring account of American nationhood during the Second

KEY CONCEPT: Nostalgia

In seventeenth-century Europe, medical student, Johannes Hofer, coined the term 'nostalgia' to describe the sense of homesickness (*heimweh*) experienced by Swiss soldiers away from home at war. The English translation 'nostalgia' is used now in a variety of contexts with a revised meaning: it describes happy memories of former, somewhat idealized times, and no longer contains the sickness, longing or distress that characterized the original medical condition. Some people may feel nostalgic for a particular time period, perhaps the one they grew up in, or even nostalgic for a film or pop song that evokes happy memories. Nostalgia is more than simple remembering, however, since the term refers to the selective resurrection of faded, and often wildly inaccurate, images that are either culturally shared (such as the idea that everyone had greased hair in the 1950s) or subjectively determined (perhaps a particular love for Roald Dahl novels). Nostalgia is thus a revision of the past, in which nearly all negative attributes have been removed, that provides positive and comforting (if false) memories.

World War. Americans were already fighting and dying in Vietnam when Nixon was elected in 1968. He then approved an incursion into Cambodia in 1970, which led to protests around the country, on top of the already active anti-war movement. The Paris Peace Accords of 1973 led to America's withdrawal and the war finally ended in 1975. For those audiences who wanted to engage with politics, these events were directly referenced in *Hair* (discussed in Chapter 4), and opposition was also expressed, for example, in 'All the Children in a Row' from Kander and Ebb's *The Rink* (1984). These were not, of course, nostalgic musicals.

Meanwhile, as the Baby-Boomer generation (those born between 1946 and 1964) sought to fight oppression and inequality through the 1960s counter-culture movement, nostalgic texts appealed to those who felt alienated by cultural change. Individuals who had survived one (or even two) world wars, a generation with enough disposable income to attend a Broadway show, could turn to musical theatre revivals to relive comforting experiences from their youth. Although 1970s popular culture traded more in cultural nostalgia (through its depictions of the 1950s), Broadway musicals tended to elicit personal nostalgia for revisiting tried-and-tested favourites. Audiences left theatres humming the same tunes they had first hummed several decades before in a way that brought them joy.

This might explain, then, the profusion of American Golden Age musicals that began to return to the Broadway stage in the mid-to-late 1970s as popular favourites. In 1979, for instance, the first open-ended revival of *Oklahoma!* opened on Broadway, having only previously been seen on Broadway during its monumental five-year original run in 1943 and for two short celebratory runs in the early 1950s. Similarly, many of Rodgers and Hammerstein's other musicals were revived during this decade, including a major production of *The King and I* (1951) in 1977 in which Yul Brynner reprised his Tony Award–winning portrayal of the King. The show continued until 1985 and included a tour to London during this period. When Brynner died four months after completing his eight-year revival run, he had played the King for 4,625 performances across his lifetime (including five years in the original production in New York and on tour). In addition, *Man of La Mancha* (1965) had been revived twice on Broadway by the end of the 1970s, with Richard Kiley reprising his role of Cervantes/Quixote in limited engagement runs in 1972 and 1977. While new musicals like *Company* (1970) and *A Chorus Line* (1975) challenged Broadway traditions during this decade, an increasing number of Broadway producers were turning to the past to mount theatrical experiences steeped in nostalgia.

Rather than reimagining the production for new audiences, a dominant trend in revivals of these musicals was to replicate the staging of the original production. Replica productions reinforce the idea that 'the attraction to revivals is grounded in individual memory and familiarity' (Rugg, 2002, p. 46). What was once popular is desired to be seen again, or so producers hope, and so productions are remounted to replicate the original experience as closely as possible. The 1970s American musical thus generated a trend that remains globally popular today. Whether aiming to replicate or reinvent, revivals enable individuals to relive an experience, pass that experience on to younger generations, or simply experience a musical they were too young to see the first time around.

My Fair Lady (1956) in 1976 and *Man of La Mancha* (1965) in 1977 both replicated earlier productions, as did the 1975 revival of Jerry Herman's *Hello, Dolly!* (1964). The performers were entirely new, but the look and feel of the musical remained the same. Interestingly, producer David Merrick developed an African American version of the show when box office receipts had flagged in 1967 after three years running with Betty Grable in the lead. The new version, starring Pearl Bailey and Cab Calloway, won Bailey a special

Tony Award and ran until 1970. When the show was revived in 1975, Bailey again played the lead. Having been staged starring African Americans amid the civil rights movement in 1967, this revival recaptured a specific part of the musical's performance history for a new set of theatregoers. That said, despite seeming to embrace diversity, this production could also be read as accentuating the inherent whiteness of the show. The original Broadway production was replicated, once again, in 2017, with (white American) Bette Midler as Dolly, recycling the original design, orchestrations, and even the original poster design and cast recording artwork, thus returning the show to its white conservative origins.

Similarly, the 1976 revival of *Fiddler on the Roof*, which played on Broadway originally from 1964 until 1970, was designed as a star vehicle for Zero Mostel, the original Tevye, to return to Broadway. With Jerome Robbins recreating his original direction and choreography, this production typifies a type of revival that responds to the innate sense of loss generated by the ephemerality of live theatre. Unlike redistributing a film to local cinemas, selling DVD and Blu-ray copies, or downloading a recording, theatre only exists in a live venue, with human performers, for a limited period of time. If an audience member misses a production during its initial run, the only way to experience it is as a revival, whether amateur or professional, or through its related paratexts (such as the cast recording or film version).

New models and styles

Since the 1970s, musicals have remained, returning to Kirle, 'works-in-process': open to imagination and alteration. Throughout the recent transatlantic history of musical revivals, however, any notable changes to the original staging or performance of a work have often been questioned by critics and audiences. For instance, should Tevye be an extrovert figure in *Fiddler on the Roof* (as Mostel had played him in 1964) or a more restrained character (as Alfred Molina presented in David Leveaux's 2004 production)? Similarly, does this musical require a detailed scenic representation of the village of Anatevka, as in Trevor Nunn's 2018 London revival, or can it be presented on an almost bare stage (as both Leveaux [2004] and Bartlett Sher [2015] have done)? Likewise, what language is the show to be performed in? In addition to being translated into multiple languages internationally, *Fiddler* has played in New York in both English (all major productions since

1964) and in Yiddish in Joel Grey's 2018 production at the Museum of Jewish Heritage, which later transferred to an off-Broadway theatre. These rhetorical questions speak to what Lundskaer-Nielsen notes as the difference between a 'show' and a 'production' (2008, p. 113). After all, the memorable staging or performances featured in the original production of many musicals often become as much a part of the expected performance text as the lyrics or the dialogue. *Les Misérables* (1985), for example, is as identifiable by the original production's use of a revolving stage, or a group of performers marching in a triangular formation in 'One Day More', as it is by the inclusion of characters like Jean Valjean, Eponine and Javert. Certain aspects of a production's staging, choreography, design and so on, overtly 'ghost' future productions of the musical by remaining in the minds, or expectations, of future audiences.

KEY CONCEPT: Ghosting

In his book, *The Haunted Stage: The Theatre as Memory Machine* (2001), theatre scholar Marvin Carlson suggests that the theatregoing experience is always 'ghosted by previous experiences and associations' (2001, p. 2). In short, every theatrical experience conjures for an audience, whether consciously or otherwise, previous experiences that affect the way in which they interpret the current performance. For instance, fans of *Legally Blonde*, the 2001 Hollywood film, may have interpreted the 2007 stage version differently to those who have not seen the original source material (particularly when key scenes are recreated on stage). Similarly, those who saw actress Idina Menzel in *RENT* (1996) or *Wicked* (2003) on Broadway, or in hit Disney films like *Enchanted* (2007) and *Frozen* (2013), may have interpreted her 2014 performance in *If/Then* through the lenses created by those past performances. Likewise, those who saw *Cats* (1981) during its original West End run at the New London Theatre (renamed after *Cats* choreographer Gillian Lynne in 2018) may recall this experience when attending a future performance, of a different show, at this venue. In turn, the theatrical text, the performer's body, the performance venue and other aspects are ghosted by expectations generated in the past. When audiences take their seats to experience a 'new' performance, a range of associations are inevitably invoked that haunt the onstage action and the experience they have in that theatre.

This raises the question of whether these musicals should retain these qualities in all future productions. If musicals are to be upheld as 'works-in-process', then absolutely not! It cannot be taken for granted that most mainstream revivals, like their original productions, will be staged in conventional, often proscenium arch, theatres in either the West End or on Broadway. One might imagine a revival of a musical to be of a similar scale in production to the original, with similar actors and performance styles, yet with enough fresh aspects (however subtle) to be considered a 'new' production; however, this is not always the case. Instead, many revivals are staged, both aesthetically and in terms of venue, in ways far different from the original production. The cast size, orchestra, staging, venue and design may be reduced, or expanded, and presented in ways that challenge the assumption that the first production is the model for future versions.

We should, of course, mention that this is most prevalent in amateur productions, whether by college, school or community groups, in which the visual and aural aesthetics are often vastly different to those in professional productions. As Stacy Wolf describes in relation to the abundance of American musicals performed in amateur settings, musicals 'cut across economic, racial, and geographic divides assuming the status of a national folk practice' (2020, p. 4). Despite companies licensing the same script and score of, say, *Fiddler on the Roof*, the resultant casting and productions are unimaginably diverse. Before considering how a musical's 'written text' might be revised as it is restaged (a revisal), then, it is important to understand how the 'performance text' of a musical is often altered through the selection of several aesthetic tropes. Not only do specific revival productions travel the world, but also a variety of different models for reviving works have been generated on either side of the Atlantic that have quickly impacted the ways in which existing works are restaged.

Concert and small-scale productions

The conscious reduction of musicals in terms of venue and aesthetic scale is now common practice in musical theatre. Musicals are regularly 'sized up' during their development phase – from rehearsed reading to workshop to production – only to be later staged at the same scale or 'sized down' in reduced productions. This is not to say that productions are never expanded in revival, however. Lionel Bart's musical *Oliver!* (1960), which transferred to Broadway in 1963, was replicated in London in 1977, even down to the use of the same sets. Cameron Mackintosh then produced a much larger, more spectacular version for the London Palladium in 1994, directed by Sam Mendes, which was renowned for being lavish and cinematic as a response to audience awareness of the 1968 film. Then, in 2009, Rupert Goold scaled the show up again for the even larger stage at the Theatre Royal, Drury Lane. Despite the design being heavily based on the 1994 production, the 2009 revival was expanded, with extra dance arrangements added, to take full advantage of the much deeper stage.

It is considerably more common, however, for productions to feature a smaller cast, staging and often venue when revived. A prime example of this is in the creation of the 'Encores! Concert Series' in 1994. Produced by and at the New York City Center, the concert series is dedicated to staging rarely performed American musicals (often with their original orchestrations). With minimal props, staging and costumes, the series (and its related off-shoot programmes like 'Encores! Off Center') has produced over 100 different revivals since the 1990s. Having produced nearly twenty new cast recordings, plus numerous Broadway transfers, Encores! has become an important institution for the revival of, presumably, 'forgotten' musical scores. The record-breaking revival of *Chicago*, for instance, as introduced at the start of this chapter, was Encores!'s first Broadway success. With its simple sets, slinky costumes and high-octane performances, the Encores! concert presentation of *Chicago* in May 1996 transferred to Broadway later that year relatively unchanged. The musical's exploration of 'criminals-as-celebrity', and its critique of the media and the legal system as ripe for manipulation appealed to audiences far more in 1996 than they had in 1975, with the O. J. Simpson trial in particular, gaining much media attention. In turn, the musical's themes spoke more directly to the cultural context surrounding this production, with audiences flocking to see such a simple and overtly sexual revival. The production then played internationally, including for nearly fifteen years in the West End, and has become the somewhat standard production of *Chicago* in the twenty-first century. Since then, productions of musicals as diverse as *Wonderful Town* (1953) in 2000 and *Sunday in the Park with George* (1984) in 2016 have transferred from City Centre to Broadway, making the Encores! concert series a key contributor to the revival of American musicals in New York (and sometimes elsewhere).

In the UK, a series of semi-staged readings of shows that had played in the West End between the 1950s and 1970s was mounted in the 2000s. All readings were directed by Stewart Nicholls, of Just the Ticket Productions, in collaboration with the Theatre Museum (a now closed venue that was conveniently located in Covent Garden, in the heart of the West End). Among the revivals were semi-staged readings of *A Girl Called Jo* (1955), *Follow That Girl* (1960), *Zip Goes A Million* (1951), *Vanity Fair* (1962), *The Amazons* (1971), *Grab Me A Gondola* (1956) and *Ann Veronica* (1969). These were followed by a fully staged small-scale revival of *Gay's the Word* (1951) in 2012, which transferred from the Finborough Theatre to the Jermyn Street Theatre (another London fringe theatre). The Finborough Theatre later hosted and co-produced *Free as Air* (1957) in 2014, in collaboration with Katy Lipson, which only further established the Finborough as a venue that championed British musicals. Five of these performances produced cast recordings of these 'forgotten' works, including a 2012 recording of *Gay's the Word* with actress Sophie-Louise Dann.

In other London fringe venues, most of the musicals produced are American revivals or new British work. The Southwark Playhouse, for example, which opened in 1993 with a mission to provide opportunities for the best emerging practitioners and companies, has more recently hosted productions of several American (often cult) musicals, including *Dogfight* (2012) in 2014 plus *Side Show* (1997) and *Grey Gardens* (2006) in 2016. Each performed in the venue's 240-seat main auditorium, the Large; these productions are often inventive and highly stylized reinventions of musicals that were first lavishly staged on Broadway. Notably, in May 2014, Paul Taylor-Mills's production of *In the Heights* (2008) played for a month at the Southwark Playhouse, before transferring to the (newly built) Kings Cross Theatre in October 2015. This production ran for over a year in this larger venue, on a traverse stage, where it earned three Olivier Awards in April 2016. (At the time of writing, this is the only musical to have been transferred from the Southwark Playhouse to a larger West End venue.)

Similarly, the Menier Chocolate Factory, an even smaller London fringe venue, has produced various musical revivals since opening in 2004 (under artistic director David Babani). British musical revivals include *Talent* (1979) in 2009, *The Invisible Man* (1993) in 2011 and *The Boy Friend* (1954) in 2019 (a Toronto transfer was planned for 2020 but cancelled due to the Covid-19 pandemic). Unlike the Southwark Playhouse, many of its American musical revivals have transferred to the West End and even Broadway. The 2008 Menier productions of *La Cage aux Folles* (1983) and *A Little Night Music* (1973), for instance, both transferred into the West End, before transferring to Broadway in 2010 (with both productions winning Tony Awards that year). While revivals of American musicals continue to be produced in New York, half of the nominees for 'Best Revival of a Musical' in 2010 had first been staged in an intimate fringe venue on the other side of the Atlantic. Likewise, the 2015 Broadway revival of *The Color Purple* (2005) was first staged at the Menier Chocolate Factory in 2013. With British newcomer Cynthia Erivo as Celie, a composite set was constructed from wooden planks, several chairs and minimal props that created an entirely different visual landscape to the original Broadway production's lavish, and somewhat realistic, staging. This production did not transfer into the West End, however, but subsequently returned to Broadway in an expanded, though still minimalist, version of the Menier staging in December 2015. With Erivo reprising her role and winning the Tony Award for Best Actress in a Musical for her performance, the production starred singer Jennifer Hudson as Shug Avery and television actress Danielle Brooks as Sofia. In this example alone, then, the revival of musicals in smaller, more transferrable, productions has led to a fascinating web of transatlantic exchange. Shows often start in one city, are revived in another and then reappear in the original city in a re-envisioned production several years later.

KEY CONCEPT: Tony (US) and Olivier (UK) awards

Annual award ceremonies are a staple part of the entertainment industry. Oscar, Grammy and Emmy are household words across America, just as BAFTA and BRITS are in Britain. Those terms recognize excellence in film and music, however. The equivalent awards in theatre are the 'Tonys' and the 'Oliviers'. The American Tony Awards, named after Antoinette 'Tony' Perry, the co-founder of the American Theatre Wing, were inaugurated in 1947. Meanwhile, the Olivier Awards in Britain were known as the Society of West End Theatres Awards (SWET Awards) from 1976 until 1984, when the title was changed to honour the actor Laurence Olivier. Designed to celebrate new work each Broadway season, the Tonys are now a major televised event that is broadcast in June, typically from New York's Radio City music hall. While key awards like Best Play or Best Musical have been awarded since the 1940s, the Tony Award for Best Revival was first presented in 1977, reflecting the nostalgic turn of the 1970s. In 1994, however, this award was divided into two categories (Best Revival of a

Musical and Best Revival of a Play) and remains in that form as of this writing. In Britain, as in America, the celebration of revivals did not occur until sometime after the awards were first presented. Musical revivals were first awarded under the Outstanding Musical Production category in 1997 and, in 2008, this became the Best Musical Revival award, as it is today. Unlike the Tony Awards, which are broadcast on television network CBS, the Olivier Awards have been broadcast by different television companies (and some years have only appeared on radio). Recently, ITV has broadcast the awards from the Royal Opera House (2013–16) and the Royal Albert Hall (2017–).

Actor-musicianship

Since the millennium, the idea of a musical theatre performer being skilled in three disciplines (singing/acting/dancing) has expanded: it is now beneficial to play an instrument too. Recent productions like *Natasha, Pierre & The Great Comet of 1812* (2016), for instance, have no pit orchestra, as is often expected in a musical, but feature a troupe of onstage actor-musicians who play both the characters and the score (both accompanying themselves and other actors). This aesthetic shift has developed out of several theatrical trends, including a British jukebox musical called *Return to the Forbidden Planet* (1989) in which the spacesuit dressed cast perform rock 'n' roll numbers, and is often used in new musicals for a clear dramaturgical (or diegetic) purpose. The children of *School of Rock* (2015), for example, are forming a rock band, just as Guy and Girl fall in love through their shared passion for writing music in *Once: The Musical* (2011). When it comes to revivals, however, the actor-musician model is typically applied to musicals that were originally written for a separate, off-stage orchestra. While this choice ultimately reduces production costs, the most effective examples of actor-musicianship come when the director develops a clear dramaturgical reason for using instruments on stage. Enter John Doyle.

The Watermill Theatre in Newbury, Berkshire – a 220-seat regional theatre about 60 miles west of central London – was put on the map in 2004 when its production of Sondheim and Wheeler's *Sweeney Todd* (1979) transferred into the West End (and then to Broadway in 2005). Directed by Doyle, with orchestrations and musical supervision by Sarah Travis, the production reduced the original twenty-six-piece orchestration to ten onstage actor-musicians. In a minimalist staging with little more than a multipurpose coffin on stage, Doyle's production emphasized the musical's narrative of having to make do with what is at hand (be that a barber's razor to kill or feeding human flesh to customers) with actors presenting Sondheim's complex score as simply as possible. Actor-musicianship was a practice that had been developing in Britain throughout the 1980s and 1990s in Doyle's work, as well as in devised shows and pantomimes by other directors, but Doyle developed this approach to revivals. As Doyle himself added, 'all I do is take old shows and treat them as if they had just been written. I treat every single production as an experiment' (Gardner, 2008). This experimentation continued with Doyle directing two further Sondheim musicals, including a production of *Merrily We Roll Along* (1981) at the Watermill in 2008.

In his 2006 Broadway production of *Company*, for example, during 'It's the Little Things You Do Together', Doyle had Joanne, Bobby's older and cynical friend, clink her glass with the metal bar used to play a percussive triangle. Unlike the other performers on stage, who played instruments which, arguably, require more skill, actress Barbara Walsh leaned against a grand piano, adding only simple sounds to the otherwise complex orchestration. In doing so, Doyle exploited the assumptions made about certain instruments (the ease of playing a triangle) to highlight the character's (outwardly) laconic persona; Joanne considers herself to be more important than those around her and demonstrates this through a lack of physical (and musical) effort. While this character trait was also highlighted in the actress's vocal and physical performance, this aesthetic choice enhanced the characterizations of Sondheim and Furth's musical in new and original ways. Likewise, Bobby, played by Raúl Esparza, was the only character/actor not to play an instrument throughout most of the production (as an indicator of his separation and isolation from those around him). In the final scene, however, Bobby lifted the lid of the onstage piano, sat down and accompanied himself as he sang his eleven-o'clock number, 'Being Alive'. As a metaphoric representation of having come to terms with being single, Bobby joins the other characters (all of whom are, presumably, already self-assured) and, finally, fulfils the production's performative norm of playing an instrument. In selecting who plays which instrument, when and where, Doyle enhances the drama through actor-musicianship – the practical operation and orchestration of which was, again, carried out by Sarah Travis. The orchestra is not simply reduced and put on stage but reconfigured as part of the drama to enhance certain narrative elements and emphasize certain character traits.

CASE STUDY: *Company* (1970)

Music and lyrics: Stephen Sondheim. Book: George Furth.

This early concept musical centres on Bobby, the single protagonist, celebrating his thirty-fifth birthday. Through a series of scenes (or vignettes) with his married friends, told in no particular order, Bobby considers what it is to be married, and what it is to be single, in 1970s New York. Featuring popular numbers like 'The Ladies Who Lunch' and 'Being Alive', *Company* was one of the first musicals to deal with adult relationships in a mature and contemporary way. Still performed five decades later, including the 2011 New York Philharmonic production with Neil Patrick Harris, the musical's gender politics were recently critiqued in Marianne Elliott's revised 2018 London production. With Rosalie Craig as Bobbie, now a female protagonist, the production featured a revised text by Sondheim and several other gender-swapped characters (including Paul and Amy becoming Paul and Jamie, a gay couple). Not only did the production now feature a more diverse representation of sexuality, the musical took on new meaning with a female protagonist battling against her ticking body clock, should she wish to have a child.

Opera House productions

Musical theatre has always had a problematic cultural identity with many scholars describing the form as 'middlebrow'. David Savran claims that musicals are not lowbrow enough to sit alongside reality television or pop music, nor are they highbrow enough to attract Shakespeare or fine art enthusiasts, and so musicals typically fall somewhere between these two categories (2004). That said, musical theatre has a long-standing association with opera, a highbrow art form, in which shows like *Porgy and Bess* (1935) are often considered operas. In recent years, this association has manifested itself in the revival of musicals in major opera houses. In particular, the musicals of Sondheim or Rodgers and Hammerstein, most of which are considered sophisticated or mature works, have received large-scale productions with full symphonic orchestras. The English National Opera (ENO), for example, based at the London Coliseum, regularly programme musicals as part of their summer season. Although Gilbert and Sullivan's operettas have long been part of the ENO's repertoire, as with many opera companies, the ENO started to produce (typically American) musicals in the late 1980s. In 2015, after decades of cuts to the venue's income from government subsidies, this was developed into a West End partnership, with producers Michael Grade and Michael Linnet. In turn, the ENO started to produce in-house productions of popular musicals to sustain their more experimental operatic work. From Glenn Close in *Sunset Boulevard* (1993) in 2016 to Alfie Boe in *Carousel* (1945) in 2017, this trend has blurred the presumed gaps between musical theatre, opera and, in these cases, international stars, musical theatre performers and opera singers. With the transfer of Meat Loaf jukebox musical *Bat Out of Hell* (2017) continuing to diversify this historic venue's audience demographic, the London Coliseum is a recent example of where performing musicals in unlikely venues can lead to fascinating results.

A musical that perhaps best summarizes the fluid boundaries between musical theatre and opera (especially transatlantically) is *Sweeney Todd: The Demon Barber of Fleet Street* (1979). Revived by the Houston Grand Opera in 1984, the musical's first operatic staging, with direction by Hal Prince (the original Broadway director), *Sweeney Todd* has an established history of being revived both as a 'musical', in mainstream commercial theatres (like in the West End), and as an 'opera', in opera houses. The musical has been produced by multiple opera companies around the world in the last two decades, with Chicago Lyric Opera (2002) and Glimmerglass Opera (2016) both having produced the show in America. In 2014, Welsh bass-baritone Bryn Terfel (who had played the title role in numerous opera productions) joined British actress Emma Thompson in Lonny Price's 2014 semi-staged production with the New York Philharmonic. Price first staged *Sweeney Todd* in 2000, with George Hearn and Patti LuPone, and returned to the piece at Avery Fisher Hall (part of New York's Lincoln Center) with a staging that actively acknowledged the implicit divide between opera and musical theatre. As the production opened, the performers entered as though for a staged reading, or concert performance, holding folders of sheet music and standing behind music stands. However, the cast soon began to deconstruct such formal trappings and physically broke concert conventions. Vases were pushed from their podiums, sheet music was strewn on the floor and the performer's formal evening wear was ripped and tattered. As the number became more frenzied, with the cast describing the protagonist's evil deeds, posters covered in bloody handprints were displayed. Finally, a grand piano was lifted by the cast, upturned and dropped to the floor as Sweeney entered. This sequence, while highly metaphoric, reflects the assumed distance between musical theatre and opera by treating Sweeney Todd, the character, as someone who (quite literally) upturns the traditions of the opera house. The expectations of opera are presented, only to be distressed and deconstructed as the performance begins. It might also highlight several transatlantic crossovers and/or contradictions. The musical is set in gloomy Victorian London, though written by Americans, and is here performed by a blend of British and American performers in New York. Although this is but one extreme example, it speaks more broadly to the multiple types of revival that exist in musical theatre today. This is highlighted even further by Bill Buckhurst's site-specific production of *Sweeney Todd*, which took place in a working pie shop in London (2015) and a recreation of a shop in New York (2017) – far from either a mainstream theatre or opera house. It is no longer sensible to develop expectations of a musical from its original production, therefore, as when a musical is staged again (and again and again) its expected performance style stays in constant flux, no matter where it is performed.

Revision and reinvention

This chapter has so far explored the ways in which musicals find new success in revival with new actors, direction, design, choreography, orchestrations, venue and so on. While the original performance style and visual elements are altered in the above examples, the written text is typically not; the characters still sing the same songs in the same moments. That said, there exists a dominant trend of musicals being rewritten and revised for a contemporary audience. Despite, or perhaps because of, featuring new songs and a heavily revised book, Stephen Fry and Mike Ockrent's 1985 version of *Me and My Girl* (1937), for instance, ran for over eight years in the West End, and for three years on Broadway, and is now the licensed edition of the show. This updated version avoids the problems faced by other musical comedies of the 1930s, and earlier, where the comedy no longer 'lands'. Similarly, Asian American playwright David Henry Hwang revised Rodgers and Hammerstein's *Flower Drum Song* (1958) for a 2002 Broadway production to tackle the show's problematic racial politics and history of casting non-Asian performers in Asian roles. In these cases, Kirle's notion of musicals being 'unfinished' or 'works-in-process' can be taken literally. Through careful revision and alteration, several musicals have been reproduced with enough sameness to elicit nostalgia for the original production, yet with enough originality to satisfy and interest new audiences.

In 1971, for example, as other Broadway musicals were being revived, Otto Harbach and Frank Mandel's original book for *No, No, Nanette* (1925) was revised by director Burt Shevelove and choreographer Donald Saddler. With nearly fifty years having passed since the original production, the musical's dialogue had aged far more quickly than its upbeat score (though more of composer Vincent Youman's songs were added). As a result, *No, No, Nanette* became an upbeat and somewhat nostalgic version of an earlier dance show, which later travelled America and generated several international productions. Similarly, Cole Porter's popular classic *Anything Goes* (1934) has been revised three times since the 1930s, with two subsequent versions (1962 and 1987) available for licensing. While the basic plot and characters remain the same in both revised versions, there are several songs that appear in one version, but not in the other (or in the unlicensed original). 'You're the Top' and 'Blow, Gabriel, Blow', for instance, have been take-home hits since 1934, whereas 'Goodbye, Little Dream, Goodbye' was only added in 1987. Subsequently, the exact song list and dialogue of the musical, both of which have been revised by different artists, depend on which version a company chooses to perform – something unknown to audiences who simply purchase tickets because of the musical's recognizable title.

In more extreme cases, however, multiple elements of a musical are revitalized to create what might best be described as a 'new' musical. *Crazy for You* (1992), for example, with a book by Ken Ludwig, is a reworking of George and Ira Gershwin's *Girl Crazy* (1930), with a revised plot and several additional songs from the Gershwin brothers' back catalogue. Part-revival, part-jukebox musical, this production won the 1992 Tony Award for 'Best Musical' given its reliance on predominantly new material and a new title. The production team consisted of British director Mike Ockrent, of *Me and My Girl* fame, American choreographer Susan Stroman (who later married Ockrent), and opened in London the following year to transatlantic success. That said, many other, often heavily revised, productions are not identified as such by the device of changing the title. The 2016 revival of *Half a Sixpence* (1963), for instance, which transferred from Chichester Festival Theatre to the West End, featured a new book, new music and new lyrics. The original work was based on a 1905 novel by H. G. Wells, adapted by Beverley Cross with music and lyrics by David Heneker, to provide a star vehicle for pop star and tap dancer Tommy Steele (who featured in twelve of the fifteen numbers). Retaining the basic narrative arc, Julian Fellowes (book), George Stiles (music) and Anthony Drewe (lyrics) wrote new versions of many of the songs, including the hit of the show 'Flash, Bang, Wallop', and added new songs and dialogue that gave the other characters more impact. With entirely new orchestrations, the mixture of old and new material was given a single musical identity that eradicated potentially uneasy transitions between the work of several different writers. As noted in Chapter 3, this was something Stiles, Drewe and Fellowes had also done when creating the stage version of Disney's *Mary Poppins* in 2005. Although the new version of *Half a Sixpence* is currently licensable as *KIPPS – The New 'Half A Sixpence' Musical*, thus providing a new brand identity, it initially played in London with the same title as the popular stage and screen musical that has continued to be performed (predominantly by amateur companies) since the 1960s.

Despite these multiple versions potentially confusing audiences by applying the same title to vastly different works, these issues become culturally significant when reviving (or revising) problematic representations of race (and sometimes gender). Warren Hoffman writes, for instance, that 'what is being relived and nostalgized is not only the show itself but what the show represents and the racial context of its time period' (2014, p. 169). *The King and I* (1951) and *Miss Saigon* (1989), for example, plus previously discussed works like *Flower Drum Song* (1958) and *The Mikado* (1885), contain problematic representations of race and have exhibited tropes of 'yellowface' performance throughout their performance history. Consequently, many revivals undergo, what Hoffman terms, 'plastic surgery', wherein new writers, or the production's director, work to eradicate the worst excesses of racism. In several recent productions of *The Mikado*, therefore, the presentation of Japanese characters has been recontextualized and thus distanced from the operetta's now racist roots. San Francisco-based company, Lamplighters Music Theatre, for example, set their 2014 production in Milan, Italy, during the Renaissance (Tran, 2016). Initially intending to employ Asian American performers and make the text's Japanese setting more culturally specific, the company ultimately chose to recontextualize the piece entirely to avoid any racial insensitivity. The director, Ellen Brooks, altered every character name, removed all references to Japan and deliberately eradicated any line or reference that could be considered an ethnic slur. In recontextualizing the piece, the operetta took on new meaning in a way that successfully upheld the operetta's iconic score and plot without reverting to ethnic stereotyping. Although several spin-off musicals based on *The Mikado* have similarly featured racist elements, including *The Swing Mikado* (1938) and *The Hot Mikado* (1939), both being set in different times and places and playing on Broadway, the Lamplighters Music Theatre company looked to revise the original text in a way that could still entertain audiences over a century since its creation.

KEY CONCEPT: Yellowface performance

Just as blackface minstrelsy is a practice that is now considered racist (see Chapter 2), the portrayal of Asian characters by white actors in make-up, often with offensive costumes and vocal inflections, is also racist. Typically relying on, and perpetuating, Asian stereotypes, yellowface performance can be evidenced across twentieth-century Hollywood cinema (including Mickey Rooney as Mr Yunioshi in *Breakfast at Tiffany's* [1961]) and, in some cases, musical theatre. In 1989, for example, Jonathan Pryce, a white British actor, originated the role of the Engineer, a Eurasian pimp, in *Miss Saigon*. Using heavy make-up and prosthetics to alter his skin tone and the shape of his eyes, Pryce's portrayal was celebrated by many British critics but criticized by Asian American playwright David Henry Hwang and actor B. D. Wong, among others, who wrote public letters of protest. The controversy over Pryce's casting intensified when producer Cameron Mackintosh sought to cast Pryce in the 1990 Broadway transfer of the show. Actor's Equity in New York urged Mackintosh to take the opportunity to cast an Asian actor in a leading role, though this ruling was criticized by Actor's Equity in Britain and several major newspapers as a violation of artistic freedom and integrity. When *Miss Saigon* finally opened in New York in 1991, Pryce recreated his role, now with softened make-up, and the production ran for a decade. That said, the lasting effects of this controversy inspired Hwang's play *Yellow Face* (2007), the casting of Asian actors in future productions of *Miss Saigon*, and much greater awareness of issues of casting and race in theatre. Many long-running musicals now cast performers of any race, no matter the role, in a practice sometimes problematically referred to as 'colour-blind' casting, whereas musicals such as *Hamilton* (2015) use 'colour-conscious' casting to comment on the lack of racial diversity in, typically, all-white stories. This progression is also evident in Hwang's 2018 musical *Soft Power*, which features a score by Jeanine Tesori, in which Asian actors exocitize America in whiteface to comment on the long-standing tradition of the reverse.

In terms of reviving classic American musicals, less strident choices are often made to eliminate any racist elements. The 1999 Broadway revival of *Annie Get Your Gun* (1946), for instance, featured a revised book by Peter Stone that depicted the action as a 'show-within-a-show' to disguise the musical's racist depiction of Native Americans. Set in a Big Top travelling circus, the action took place within a picture frame, which informed the audience that they were seeing something in the past in a way that, hopefully, softened their responses by distancing them from the action. Similarly, the number 'I'm an Indian Too' was cut, rather than reframed, in this (and several other) recent productions.

Meanwhile, several directors created a series of realistic and more character-focused productions of American Golden Age musicals in the mid-2000s. This trend started in Britain in the 1990s, of course, as discussed in Chapter 6, and included Trevor Nunn's 2001 production of Rodgers and Hammerstein's *South Pacific* (1949) at the National Theatre. Here, Nunn reinstated some racist epithets from the original production that had been removed during rehearsal, as they were deemed to further emphasize the troubling politics of the Second World War, but which remain contentious choices. For example, Nellie, who struggles to accept the love of a man whose children are mixed race, exclaimed 'Colored!' in Nunn's production, unlike in earlier versions where, as actress Kelli O'Hara claims, 'they didn't need any of that. The audience knew what the problem was' (Lunden, 2008). O'Hara played Nellie in Bartlett Sher's 2008 revival of *South Pacific* at New York's Lincoln Center, in which both cut and drafted material was reinstated by Sher. Also, in 2008, Barack Obama, the soon-to-be first black president, ran for office. As critic Frank Rich noted, in response, 'in a year when war and race are at center stage in the national conversation, this relic turns out to have a great deal to say' (quoted in Lovensheimer, 2010, p. 1). As America illustrated its ever-changing attitudes towards race in the political arena, Broadway audiences flocked to see a production that challenged (or at least recognized) home-grown racism, as in lyrics like 'you've got to be taught / to hate and fear' – a message written by Hammerstein six decades earlier. While the production's socio-cultural context seemed to emphasize the musical's politics, Sher envisioned certain scenes and songs with a more critical eye to further highlight such politics. For instance, the number 'Happy Talk', often recognized as a chirpy showtune, was staged to suggest that Bloody Mary is trying to sell or prostitute her daughter, Liat, to Lieutenant Cable (Lovensheimer, 2010, p. 171). Unlike Bloody Mary's attempts to promote romance in the 1958 film version, Sher provides a sinister interpretation of this moment by having Bloody Mary attempt to profit from her daughter's innocence (and virginity) by making her dance for an American naval officer. Consequently, Sher exaggerated the musical's historically controversial aspects by retaining various past revisions and adding draft material to further emphasize this reading. The production, in turn, spoke to the American political landscape and provided a simultaneously cynical and nostalgic theatregoing experience.

CASE STUDY: *West Side Story* (1957)

Music: Leonard Bernstein. Lyrics: Stephen Sondheim. Book: Arthur Laurents.

Based on William Shakespeare's iconic play, *Romeo and Juliet*, *West Side Story* explores the tensions between two warring gangs in 1950s New York. Maria, a member of the Puerto Rican 'Sharks', falls in love with Tony, a white 'Jet', and their forbidden romance plays out against a rivalry fuelled by racial hatred. After Tony kills Maria's brother, Bernardo, in 'The Rumble', the couple are further driven apart by Anita, Maria's friend and Bernardo's girlfriend, and Chino, whom Maria is promised to. In the final scene, Chino shoots Tony, who dies in Maria's arms, as she sings their haunting love theme, 'Somewhere'. In turn, these narrative tensions are reflected stylistically through a blend of musical styles (be-bop/Jazz for the Jets, Latin American rhythms for the Sharks), a violent narrative told using balletic choreography and a semi-symphonic and operatic score.

The musical has been revived several times, often retaining Jerome Robbins's choreography and Bernstein's orchestrations, and was most recently revived on Broadway in 2020 by radical Belgian theatre director, Ivo van Hove. It was adapted into a major film version in 1961, with Natalie Wood as Maria, which won ten Academy Awards (including Best Picture). A new film adaptation, directed by Steven Spielberg, was released in 2021.

Perhaps the most significant example of the revisal trend, and the closing case study of this chapter, is the 2009 Broadway production of *West Side Story* (1957). As an iconic musical built on a multitude of conflicts, *West Side Story* spoke directly to its cultural context when first performed in 1957 (as introduced in Chapter 6). Due to the major demographic shift that had occurred post–Second World War, with over half a million Puerto Ricans living in New York during the 1950s, the musical depicts (and was written during) a time of great ethnic tension. Unlike many other Golden Age musicals, which were set in a nostalgic past (e.g. *Oklahoma!*), *West Side Story* presents a cramped city of immigrants, all living on top of each other in tenement buildings. In March 2009, these conflicts and contradictions – all of which highlight the differences between the warring gangs – were enhanced by having the Sharks, the Puerto Rican-born gang, sing in Spanish. The new Spanish lyrics by Lin-Manuel Miranda, who had just won a Tony Award for *In the Heights* (2008), provided a sense of authenticity and further distanced the gangs from one another, adding to the already complex dramaturgy. The 'Tonight (Quintet)', for instance, scored to be an intricate collage of vocal and musical styles, distanced audiences even further with some of the characters singing in Spanish, others in English – a situation with which many Americans might be familiar. Similarly, Maria very rarely sings in Spanish, her mother tongue, in an attempt to integrate and perhaps to show her devotion to the English-speaking Tony. While she sings 'I Feel Pretty' (now 'Me Siento Hermosa') in Spanish, while gossiping with her Puerto Rican friends, she commits her love to Tony in English, in the song 'Somewhere', hence using the dominant language of the country in which she wishes to assimilate. Maria's acceptance of English is most noticeable in her duet with Anita, 'Un Hombre Asi/I Have a Love', in which Anita chastises Maria in Spanish and Maria responds in English (perhaps a deliberate attempt to have the character demonstrate her new identity, while simultaneously representing racial conflicts within families). Despite the interesting dramaturgical moments these revisions produced, they were considered too distancing for audiences and removed five months into the revival's Broadway run (except for the Shark's Spanish lyrics in 'Tonight (Quintet)'). What was intended to be an 'experiment' in authenticity was removed in favour of the white, American and tried-and-tested original. *West Side Story* has a long history of stereotyping the Sharks, in particular, whether through inauthentic casting, make-up, costuming and more, and these issues continue to be faced by all production teams looking to reinvent the piece for a contemporary audience.

Conclusion

This chapter has explored how popular musicals – from *Gypsy* to *West Side Story* – remain fluid and unfinished in performance. Musicals are regularly brought back to life in ways far removed from their original productions, responding to shifting cultural contexts, aesthetic choices and/or the revisions of authors and creative teams. The ephemerality of live performance makes this possible, meaning musical theatre can respond to a multitude of factors and, as we have seen, constantly does. Musicals come and go; they are rarely filmed or published as scripts or scores in full (particularly in Britain), though segments or selections do tend to be available, and past musicals tend only to be accessible through a series of paratexts (a cast recording, a film version, a streamed performance etc.). Musical theatre 'past' thus can only become musical theatre 'present' through revivals. Some producers look for sure-fire hits and audience pleasers in troubled times, while others capitalize on nostalgic memories and associations. Some directors seek to honour past productions, and others critique contemporary politics. Altogether, the expanding archive of revivals and revisals is extremely diverse. That archive is likely to continue to grow and diversify as directors continue to take a 'journey to the past' in search of new artistic opportunities and new ways to comment on the contemporary world.

This final history is also notably transatlantic. This book has demonstrated that the history of musical theatre is one of movement, transition and interaction. Just like the history of opera and dramatic theatre (plays), musicals are revived in multiple contexts and, whether revised or not, alter to suit such contexts around the world. Despite the dominance of American influence suggested in multiple 'Broadway histories' of musical theatre, the form undeniably develops internationally. The journey from *Oklahoma!* as a Broadway landmark in 1943 to Daniel Fish's experimental 2019 Broadway production (in which audiences are served chilli and cornbread and the dream ballet is performed by a single dancer) is not simply an American history. *Oklahoma!* is a landmark work because of its major productions in London, several international cities and a plethora of amateur productions, plus film and television adaptations and cast recordings. Like the complex web of historical interactions outlined in the introduction, which we referenced as an underground or subway train map, every major musical transcends the country or city in which it is first performed and, certainly in the twenty-first century, can be recognized as a transatlantic and global text. Musical theatre is neither British nor American, but a complex history of interaction between two major centres and the rest of the world.

Tasks

Propose a new revival of a classic British or American musical. How did the musical respond to its original performance context(s)? What alterations might you make so that the 'text' reflects contemporary sensibilities and contexts? How might you advertise and promote this production to a modern audience?

Imagine you are casting a new revival of a classic British or American musical. If casting performers from minority ethnic groups has the power to shift the production 'into a new and profound realm of representation and semantics' (Liu, 2019, p. 203), then who might you cast to deliberately challenge white, English language or heterosexual normativity? How might this alternative casting choice have the potential to shift the representation? How might the new depiction of these roles be interpreted by audiences?

Discussion topics

The term 'revival' is typically applied to musical theatre, rather than dramatic works by acclaimed playwrights like Sophocles, William Shakespeare and Anton Chekhov (see Lundskaer-Nielsen, 2008, pp. 109–19). Why do directors 'stage' Shakespeare but 'revive' Rodgers and Hammerstein? Why are musicals considered 'dead', in need of reviving, while classic plays remain in constant health? What does this terminology say about the cultural significance of musical theatre in relation to other art forms and genres?

Warren Hoffman argues that 'the practice of rewriting shows is a dicey one. While perpetrating stereotypes is obviously wrong, revising shows to make them acceptable for the current age feels like whitewashing history' (2014, p. 201). What do you think? What are the most appropriate ways to revisit problematic, though still popular, musicals?

Further reading – conceptual

Kirle, B. (2005) *Unfinished Show Business: Broadway Musicals as Works-in-Process*. Carbondale: Southern Illinois University Press.

Lovensheimer, J. (2019) 'Recreating the Ephemeral: Broadway Revivals since 1971'. In: J. Sternfeld and E. L. Wollman (eds) *The Routledge Companion to the Contemporary Musical*. London and New York: Routledge, 58–66.

Rugg, R. A. (2002) 'What It Used to Be: Nostalgia and the State of the Broadway Musical'. *Theater* 32/2: 44–55.

Further reading – case study

Browne, S. (2016) '"Everybody's Free to Fail": Subsidized British Revivals of the American Canon'. In: R. Gordon and O. Jubin (eds) *The Oxford Handbook of the British Musical*. New York: Oxford University Press, 361–80.

Eisler, G. (2011) 'Encores! and the Downsizing of the Classic American Musical'. *Studies in Musical Theatre* 5/2: 133–48.

Liu, S. (2019) '"Before the Parade Passes By": All-Black and All Asian *Hello, Dolly!* As Celebration of Difference'. In: J. Sternfeld and E. L. Wollman (eds) *The Routledge Companion to the Contemporary Musical*. London and New York: Routledge, 196–205.

Bibliography

Abbate, C. and Parker, R. (2012) *A History of Opera: The Last 400 Years*. Milton Keynes: Penguin Random House.

Adler, S. (2011) 'Box Office'. In: Knapp, R., Morris, M. and Wolf, S. (eds) *The Oxford Handbook of the American Musical*. Oxford and New York: Oxford University Press, 351–64.

Adler, S. (2020) '*Big River*: A New Road to Broadway'. In: Sternfeld, J. and Wollman, E. L. (eds) *The Routledge Companion to the Contemporary Musical*. London and New York: Routledge, 418–26.

Adler, S. (2004) *On Broadway: Art and Commerce on the Great White Way*. Carbondale: Southern Illinois Press.

Alridge, D. P. and Stewart, J. B. (2005) 'Introduction: Hip Hop in History: Past, Present, and Future'. *The Journal of African American History* 90/3, 190–5.

Anderson, B. (2006 [1983]) *Imagined Communities: Reflections on the Origins and Spread of Nationalism*. 2nd edn. London and New York: Verso.

Anderson, L. (1997) *Mammies No More: The Changing Image of Black Women on Stage and Screen*. Lanham: Rowman & Littlefield.

Associated Press (1993) 'A Rougher, Pared-Down "*Cabaret*" Revival'. 20 December, *Associated Press*. Available at: https://www.csmonitor.com/1993/1220/20172.html. [Accessed 15 May 2020].

Baker, R. A. (1990) *Marie Lloyd: Queen of the Music-Halls*. London: Robert Hale.

Baker, R. (1994) *Drag: A History of Female Impersonation in the Performing Arts*. London: Cassell.

Barthes, R. (1977) *Image, Music, Text*. Trans. Stephen Heath. London: Fontana Press.

Becker, T. (2014) 'Touring the Empire: Theatrical Touring Companies and Amateur Dramatics in Colonial India'. *The Historical Journal* 57/3, 699–725.

Bennett, S. (2005) 'Theatre/Tourism'. *Theatre Journal* 57/3, 407–28.

Bennett, S. (2020) '*The Lion King*: An International History'. In: Sternfeld, J. and Wollman, E. L. (eds) *The Routledge Companion to the Contemporary Musical*. London and New York: Routledge, 445–53.

Billington, M. (2015) 'Gypsy Review – "Imelda Staunton Gives One of the Greatest Performances I've Even Seen in a Musical"'. *The Guardian*, 16 April 2015.

Available at: https://www.theguardian.com/stage/2015/apr/16/gypsy-review-imelda-staunton-momma-rose-stephen-sondheim-jonathan-kent-peter-davison. [Accessed 16 June 2020].

Block, G. (2004 [1997]) *Enchanted Evenings: The Broadway Musical from Show Boat to Sondheim*. Paperback edn. Oxford and New York: Oxford University Press.

Bradley, I. (2004) *You've Got to Have a Dream: The Message of the Musical*. London: SCM Press.

Brantley, B. (2003) 'Theatre Review: New Momma Takes Charge'. *The New York Times*, 2 May. Available at: https://www.nytimes.com/2003/05/02/movies/theater-review-new-momma-takes-charge.html. [Accessed 16 June 2020].

Brantley, B. (2006) 'The Day the Musical Died'. *The New York Times*, 21 May. Available at: http://query.nytimes.com/gst/fullpage.html?res=9400E7DD123EF932A15756C0A9609C8B63&pagewanted=all.

Brantley, B. (2008) 'Fish Out of Water in the Deep Blue Sea'. *The New York Times*, 11 January. Available at: https://www.nytimes.com/2008/01/11/theater/reviews/11merm.html. [Accessed 25 July 2022].

Browne, S. (2016) '"Everybody's Free to Fail": Subsidized British Revivals of the American Canon'. In: Gordon, R. and Jubin, O. (eds) *The Oxford Handbook of the British Musical*. New York: Oxford University Press, 361–80.

Browne, S. (2018) 'Girl Talk: Feminist Phonocentrism as an Act of Resistance in the Musical *Hair*'. *Studies in Musical Theatre* 12/3, 291–303.

Browne, S. (2019) '"Dedicated to the Proposition … ": Raising Cultural Consciousness in the Musical *Hair*'. In: Whitfield, S. (ed.) *Reframing the Musical: Race, Culture and Identity*. London: Red Globe Press, 167–8.

Bunch, R. (2015) 'Oz and the Musical: The American Art Form and the Reinvention of the American Fairy Tale'. *Studies in Musical Theatre* 9/1, 53–69.

Burston, J. (2009) 'Recombinant Broadway'. *Journal of Media & Cultural Studies* 23/2, 159–69.

Bush, J. J. (2004) *Our Musicals, Ourselves*. Hanover and London: Brandeis University Press.

Carlson, M. (2001) *The Haunted Stage: The Theatre as Memory Machine*. Ann Arbor, MI: University of Michigan Press.

Carter, T. (2007) *Oklahoma! The Making of a Broadway Musical*. New Haven and London: Yale University Press.

Chernow, R. (2004) *Alexander Hamilton*. New York: Apollo.

Cohen, P. (2010) '"Scottsboro Boys" Is Focus of Protest'. *ArtsBeat, New York Times Blog*, November 7. Available at: https://artsbeat.blogs.nytimes.com/2010/11/07/scottsboro-boys-is-focus-of-protest/. [Accessed 25 July 2022].

Cook, S. C. (2009) 'Pretty like the Girl: Gender, Race and *Oklahoma!*' *Contemporary Theatre Review* 19/1, 35–47. DOI: 10.1080/10486800802547260

Daboo, J. (2018) *Staging British South Asian Culture.* London: Routledge.

Davis, T. C. and Postlewait, T. (eds) (2004) *Theatricality.* Cambridge University Press.

Döhl, F. (2020) 'The Third Biggest Market: Musical Theater in Germany since 1990'. In: Sternfeld, J. and Wollman, E. L. (eds) *The Routledge Companion to the Contemporary Musical.* London and New York: Routledge, 427–36.

Donatella, G. (2018a) 'Being in "The Room Where It Happens": *Hamilton*, Obama, and Nationalist Neoliberal Multicultural Inclusion'. *Theatre Survey* 59/3, 363–85.

Donatella, G. (2018b) 'Feeling Yellow: Responding to Contemporary Yellowface in Musical Performance'. *Journal of Dramatic Theory and Criticism* 32/2, 67–77.

Edney, K. (2010) 'Integration through the Wide Open Back Door: African Americans Respond to *Flower Drum Song* (1958)'. *Studies in Musical Theatre* 4/3, 261–72.

Eisler, G. (2011) 'Encores! and the Downsizing of the Classic American Musical'. *Studies in Musical Theatre* 5/2, 133–48.

Enbutsu, S. (2001) 'Playing "The Mikado" in the "Town of Titipu"'. *The Japan Times,* 28 January. Available at: https://www.japantimes.co.jp/culture/2001/01/28/stage/playing-the-mikado-in-the-town-of-titipu/. [Accessed 20 June 2022].

Everett, W. A. (2017) 'George Edwardes: The Guv'nor of Late Victorian Musical Theatre'. In: MacDonald, L. and Everett, W. A. (eds) *The Palgrave Handbook of Musical Theatre Producers.* London: Palgrave Macmillan, 53–63.

Felperin, L. (2015) '*Gypsy:* Theatre Review'. *The Hollywood Reporter,* 16 April. Available at: https://www.hollywoodreporter.com/review/imelda-staunton-gypsy-theater-review-789195. [Accessed 16 June 2020].

Freshwater, H. (2009) *Theatre Censorship in Britain: Silencing, Censure and Suppression.* Basingstoke: Palgrave Macmillan.

Ganzl, K. (2018) 'The Black Crook or How to Invent History'. *Kurt of Gerolstein,* 20 June. Available at: https://kurtofgerolstein.blogspot.com/2018/06/the-black-crook-or-how-to-invent-history.html. [Accessed 25 July 2022].

Garard, J. (1994) 'Disney's Beauty and the Beast'. *Variety,* 19 April. Available at: https://variety.com/1994/legit/reviews/disney-s-beauty-and-the-10)beast-2-1200436613/. [Accessed 25 July 2022].

Gardiner, J. E. (2015) 'Monteverdi's Orfeo: "A Brilliant and Compelling Fable to the inalienable Power of Music"'. *The Guardian*, 3 August. Available at: https://www.theguardian.com/music/2015/aug/03/monterverdi-orfeo-john-eliot-gardiner-the-inalienable-power-of-music. [Accessed 19 June 2020].

Gardner, L. (2008) 'The Amazing Mr Musicals'. *The Guardian*. Available at: https://www.theguardian.com/stage/2008/jan/24/theatre.musicals. [Accessed 8 February 2019].

Gennaro, L. (2011) 'Evolution of Dance in the Golden Age of the American Musical'. In: Knapp, R., Morris, M. and Wolf, S. (eds) *The Oxford Handbook of the American Musical*. Oxford University Press, 45–61.

Gilbert, D. (2015) 'A New Musical Rhythm Was Given to the People'. In: *The Product of Our Souls: Ragtime, Race and the Birth of the Manhattan Musical Marketplace*. New York: University of North Carolina Press, 16–46.

Gilbert, H. and Tompkins, J. (1996) *Postcolonial Drama: Theory, Practice, Politics*. London: Routledge.

Gilbert, H. and Tompkins, J. (2010) 'Re-acting (to) Empire'. In: Gale, M. B. and Deeney, J. F., with Rebellato, D. (eds) *Routledge Drama Anthology and Sourcebook: From Modernism to Contemporary Performance*. London and New York: Routledge, 656–66.

Gilroy, P. (2002) *The Black Atlantic: Modernity and Double Consciousness*. London and New York: Verso.

Gordon, R., Jubin, O. and Taylor, M. (2016) *British Musical Theatre since 1950*. London: Bloomsbury.

Goron, M. (2016) *Gilbert and Sullivan's 'Respectable Capers': Class, Respectability and the Savoy Operas, 1877–1909*. London: Palgrave Macmillan.

Grant, B. K. (2018) 'Foreword'. In: Rodosthenous, G. (ed.) *Twenty-First Century Musicals: From Stage to Screen*. London: Routledge, xv–xvi.

Griffin, G. and Iball, H. (eds) (2007) 'Forum "Gagging": Forum on Censorship'. *Contemporary Theatre Review* 17/4, 516–56.

Grover, N. (2015) *Kinky Boots* (Review). *Time Out London*, 22 September. Available at: https://www.timeout.com/london/theatre/kinky-boots. [Accessed 15 May 2020].

Harbert, E. (2018) '*Hamilton* and History Musicals'. *American Music* 36/4, 412–28.

Harvie, J. (2005) *Staging the UK*. Manchester and New York: Manchester University Press.

Hayashi, A. E. (2020) '"You Tube Musicals! You Tubesicals!" Cultivating Theater Fandom through New Media'. In: J. Sternfeld and E. L. Wollman (eds) *The Routledge Companion to the Contemporary Musical*. London and New York: Routledge, 374–83.

Heffer, S. (2010) 'America Is the Acceptable Face of Cultural Imperialism'. *The Telegraph*. 24 July. Available at: https://www.telegraph.co.uk/comment/columnists/simonheffer/7908380/America-is-the-acceptable-face-of-cultural-imperialism.html. [Accessed 25 July 2022].

Herrera, B. E. (2015) *Latin Numbers: Playing Latino in Twentieth Century US Popular Performance*. Ann Arbor, MI: University of Michigan Press.

Hillman, J. (2007) 'Goyim on the Roof: Embodying Authenticity in Leveaux's *Fiddler on the Roof*'. *Studies in Musical Theatre* 1/1: 25–40.

Hillman-McCord, J. (2017) 'Digital Fandom: *Hamilton* and the Participatory Spectator'. In: Hillman-McCord, J. (ed.) *iBroadway: Musical Theatre in the Digital Age*. Houndmills: Palgrave Macmillan, 119–44.

Hodge, R. (2018) 'This Performance Contains: Trigger Warnings in Theatre'. *The Theatrical Board*, 27 November. Available at: https://www.thetheatricalboard.com/editorials/rebeccatw. [Accessed 4 March 2022].

Hoffman, W. (2014) *The Great White Way: Race and the Broadway Musical*. New Brunswick: Rutgers University Press.

Holdsworth, N. (2010) *Theatre & Nation*. Basingstoke and New York: Palgrave Macmillan.

Houchin, J. H. (2003) *Censorship of the American Theatre in the Twentieth Century*. Cambridge: Cambridge University Press.

Houchin, J. H. (2016) 'Freedom of Speech and *Hair*: The Legal Legacy'. In: O'Leary, C., Santos, S. D. and Thompson, M. (eds) *Global Insights on Theatre Censorship*. London and New York: Routledge, 234–44.

Hutcheon, L. with O'Flynn, S. (2012) *A Theory of Adaptation*. 2nd edn. London and New York: Routledge.

Jackson, S. (2010) 'When "Everything Counts": Experimental Performance and Performance Historiography'. In: Canning, C. M. and Postlewait, T. (eds) *Representing the Past: Essays in Performance Historiography*. Iowa City: University of Iowa Press, 240–60.

Johnston, J. (1990) *The Lord Chamberlain's Blue Pencil*. London: Hodder & Stoughton.

Kantor, M. (dir.) (2004) *Broadway: The American Musical* [DVD]. London: Granada Media.

Kenrick, J. (2017) *Musical Theatre: A History*. 2nd edn. London: Bloomsbury Methuen Drama.

Kim, H. (2016) 'Celebrating Heteroglossic Hybridity: Ready-to-Assemble Broadway-Style Musicals in South Korea'. *Studies in Musical Theatre* 10/3, 343–54.

Kirle, B. (2005) *Unfinished Show Business: Broadway Musicals as Works-in-Process*. Carbondale: Southern Illinois University Press.

Knapp, R. (2005) *The American Musical and the Formation of National Identity.* Princeton: Princeton University Press.

Knapp, R. (2006) *The American Musical and the Performance of Personal Identity.* Princeton and Oxford: Princeton University Press.

Knapp, R. (2009) '"How Great Thy Charm, Thy Sway How Excellent!": Tracing Gilbert and Sullivan in the American Musical'. In: Eden, D. and Saremba, M. (eds) *The Cambridge Companion to Gilbert and Sullivan.* Cambridge: Cambridge University Press, 201–15.

Knapp, R. (2020) 'Saving Mr. *[Blank]*: Rescuing the Father through Song in Children's and Family Musicals'. In: Ruwe, D. and Leve, J. (eds) *Children, Childhood, and Musical Theater.* London and New York: Routledge, 59–79.

Kotis, G. and Hollman, M. (2003) *Urinetown.* [Libretto] London: Nick Hern Books.

Kruger, M. (2000) 'English Pantomime: Reflections on a Dynamic Tradition'. *South African Theatre Journal* 14, 146–73.

Kruger, M. (2003) 'Pantomime in South Africa: The British Tradition and the Local Flavour'. *South African Theatre Journal* 17, 129–52.

Lamb, A. (1986) 'From Pinafore to Porter: United States–United Kingdom Interactions in Musical Theater, 1879–1929'. *American Music* 4/1, 34–49.

Lee, H. (2017) 'Between Broadway and the Local: Arts Communication International (ACOM), Seol & Company, and the South Korean Musical Industry'. In: L. MacDonald, and W. A. Everett (eds) *The Palgrave Handbook of Musical Theatre Producers.* London: Palgrave Macmillan, 441–8.

Lewis, C. (2019) 'The Gender Problem "Tootsie" Can't Dress Up'. *American Theatre*, 7 May. Available at: https://www.americantheatre. org/2019/05/07/the-gender-problem-tootsie-cant-dress-up/. [Accessed 1 July 2020].

Lewis, C. (2021) 'One Step Forward, Two Steps Back: Broadway's Jagged Little Journey toward Nonbinary Inclusion'. *The Brooklyn Rail.* April 2021. Available at: https://brooklynrail.org/2021/04/theater/One-Step-Forward-Two-Steps-Back-Broadways-Jagged-Little-Journey-Toward-Nonbinary-Inclusion. [Accessed 1 March 2022].

Lewis, H. D. (2018) '"With a Bit of Rock Music, Everything Is Fine": *Mamma Mia!* and the Camp Sensibility on Screen'. In: Rodosthenous, G. (ed.) *Twenty-First Century Musicals: From Stage to Screen.* London and New York: Routledge, 121–34.

Linton, D. and Platt, L. (2014) 'Dover Street to Dixie and the Politics of Cultural Transfer and Exchange'. Platt, L. Becker, T. and Linton, D. (eds) *Popular Musical Theatre in London and Berlin 1890–1939.* Cambridge: Cambridge University Press, 170–86.

Linton, D. (2021) *Nation and Race in West End Revue: 1910–30*. Palgrave Macmillan.

Liu, S. (2019) 'Before the Parade Passes By: All-Black and All Asian *Hello, Dolly!* As Celebration of Difference'. In: J. Sternfeld and E. L. Wollman (eds) *The Routledge Companion to the Contemporary Musical*. London and New York: Routledge, 196–205.

Lloyd, W. I. (2015) 'Odds & Ends'. *Broadway.Com*, 27 February. Available at: https://www.broadway.com/buzz/179752/odds-ends-kelly-clarkson-eyes-broadway-lena-halls-next-gig-stark-sands-big-tv-role-more/. [Accessed 15 May 2020].

Lockitt, M. (2020) 'Chart-Toppers to Showstoppers: Pop Artists Scoring the Broadway Stage'. In: J. Sternfeld and E. L. Wollman (eds) *The Routledge Companion to the Contemporary Musical*. London and New York: Routledge, 120–9.

Lonergan, P. (2015) *Theatre & Social Media*. Houndmills: Palgrave Macmillan.

Lott, E. (2013) *Love & Theft: Blackface Minstrelsy and the American Working Class*. 20th-Anniversary edn. New York: Oxford University Press.

Lovelock, J. (2019) '"What about Love?": Claiming and Re-Claiming LGBTQ+ Spaces in 21st Century Musical Theatre'. In: Whitfield, S. (ed.) *Reframing the Musical: Race, Culture and Identity*. London: Red Globe Press, 187–209.

Lovensheimer, J. (2010) *South Pacific: Paradise Rewritten*. New York: Oxford University Press.

Lovensheimer, J. (2019) 'Recreating the Ephemeral: Broadway Revivals since 1971'. In: J. Sternfeld and E. L. Wollman (eds) *The Routledge Companion to the Contemporary Musical*. London and New York: Routledge, 58–66.

Lowerson, J. (2005) *Amateur Operatics: A Social and Cultural History*. Manchester: Manchester University Press.

Lunden, J. (2008) 'In Revival, "South Pacific" Still Has Lessons to Teach'. *NPR*, April 3. Available at: https://www.npr.org/2008/04/03/89309296/in-revival-south-pacific-still-has-lessons-to-teach?t=1624616426464. [Accessed 25 July 2022].

Lundskaer-Nielsen, M. (2008) *Directors and the New Musical Drama: British and American Musical Theatre in the 1980s and 90s*. London: Palgrave Macmillan.

MacDonald, L. (2017) 'Connection in an Isolating Age: Looking Back on Twenty Years of Engaging Audiences and Marketing Musical Theatre Online'. In: Hillman-McCord, J. (ed.) *iBroadway: Musical Theatre in the Digital Age*. Houndmills: Palgrave Macmillan, 17–42.

MacDonald, L. and Everett, W. (eds) (2017) *The Palgrave Handbook of Musical Theatre Producers*. Basingstoke: Palgrave.

MacKinnon, K. (2003) *Representing Men*. London: Hodder and Stoughton.

Macpherson, B. (2016) 'Some Yesterdays Always Remain: Black British and Anglo-Asian Musical Theatre'. In: Gordon, R. and Jubin, O. (eds) *The Oxford Handbook of the British Musical*. New York: Oxford University Press, 673–96.

Macpherson, B. (2018) *Cultural Identity in British Musical Theatre, 1890–1939: Knowing One's Place*. London: Palgrave Macmillan.

Magee, J. (2018) 'Miranda's Les Miz'. *Studies in Musical Theatre* 12/2, 213–21.

Marks, P. (2002) 'If It's a Musical, It Was Probably a Movie'. *The New York Times*, April 14. Available at: https://www.nytimes.com/2002/04/14/movies/if-it-s-a-musical-it-was-probably-a-movie.html. [Accessed 25 July 2022].

Masters, T. (2010) 'Bon Anniversaire! 25 Facts about Les Mis'. *BBC News*, 1 October 2010. Available at: https://www.bbc.co.uk/news/entertainment-arts-11437196. [Accessed 9 January 2019].

McMasters, J. (2016), 'Why Hamilton Is Not the Revolution You Think It Is'. *HowlRound*, 23 February. Available at: http://howlround.com/why-hamilton-is-not-therevolution-you-think-it-is. [Accessed 15 May 2020].

McMillin, S. (2006) *The Musical as Drama*. Princeton: Princeton University Press.

Miller, H. D. (2011) *Theorizing Black Theatre: Art versus Protest in Critical Writings, 1898–1965*. Jefferson: McFarland.

Miller, S. (1997) '*Assassins* and the Concept Musical'. In: Gordon, J. (ed.) *Stephen Sondheim: A Casebook*. London and New York: Routledge, 187–204.

Miller, S. (1999) *Rebels with Applause: Broadway's Ground-Breaking Musicals*. Portsmouth, NH: Heinemann Publishing.

Mizejewski, L. (1999) *Ziegfeld Girl: Image and Icon in Culture and Cinema*. Durham and London: Duke University Press.

Morra, I. (2009) 'Constructing Camelot: Britain and the New World Musical'. *Contemporary Theatre Review* 19/1, 22–34.

Nancy, S. (2013) 'The Singing Body in the *Tragédie Lyrique* of Seventeenth- and Eighteenth-Century France: Voice, Theatre, Speech, Pleasure'. In: Symonds, D. and Karantonis, P. (eds) *The Legacy of Opera: Reading Music Theatre as Experience and Performance*. Amsterdam: Rodopi, 65–78.

Napolitano, M. (2014) *Oliver!: A Dickensian Musical*. New York: Oxford University Press.

Negrón-Mutaner, F. (2004) *Boricua Pop: Puerto Ricans and the Latinization of American Culture*. New York: NYU Press.

O'Connell, S. (2016) 'From "Sal Tlay Ka Siti" to "I Am Africa": Parody, Politics, and Musical Representations of Cultural and National Identity in *The Book of Mormon*'. In: Shaw, M. E. and Welker, H. (eds) *Singing and Dancing to*

The Book of Mormon: Critical Essays on the Broadway Musical. Lanham: Rowman & Littlefield, 113–27.

O'Leary, C. (2016) 'Introduction: Censorship and Creative Freedom'. In O'Leary, C., Santos Sánchez, D. and Thompson, M. (eds) *Global Insights on Theatre Censorship*. London and New York: Routledge, 1–24.

Oja, C. J. (2009) '*West Side Story* and *The Music Man*: Whiteness, Immigration, and Race in the US during the Late 1950s'. *Studies in Musical Theatre* 3/1, 13–30.

Patinkin, S. (2008) *No Legs, No Jokes, No Chance: A History of the American Musical Theater*. Evanston: Northwestern University Press.

Paulson, M. (2017) 'The Battle of "Miss Saigon": Yellowface, Art and Opportunity'. *The New York Times*. Available at: https://www.nytimes.com/2017/03/17/theater/the-battle-of-miss-saigon-yellowface-art-and-opportunity.html. [Accessed 8 February 2019].

Platt, L. (2004) *Musical Comedy on the West End Stage, 1890–1939*. London: Palgrave Macmillan.

Postlewait, T. (2009) *The Cambridge Introduction to Theatre Historiography*. Cambridge: Cambridge University Press.

Raben, J. (1998) '*The Mikado* in Japan', Gilbert and Sullivan Archive. Available at: https://www.gsarchive.net/mikado/html/mikado_japan.html. [Accessed 25 July 2022].

Rebellato, D. (2009a) '"No Theatre Guild Attraction Are We": *Kiss Me, Kate* and the Politics of the Integrated Musical'. *Contemporary Theatre Review* 19/1, 61–73.

Rebellato, D. (2009b) *Theatre & Globalization*. Houndmills: Palgrave Macmillan.

Reddick, G. (2011) 'The Evolution of the Original Cast Album'. In: Knapp, R., Morris, M. and Wolf, S. (eds) *The Oxford Handbook of the American Musical*. New York: Oxford University Press, 179–93.

Reinelt, J. (2006) 'The Limits of Censorship'. *Theatre Research International* 32/1, 3–15.

Rich, F. (1991) 'THEATER/1991'. *The New York Times*, December 29. Available at: https://www.nytimes.com/1991/12/29/theater/year-arts-theater-1991-throw-away-those-scripts-some-greatest-moments-were.html. [Accessed 25 July 2022].

Riis, T. (1986) 'The Experience and Impact of Black Entertainers in England, 1895–1920'. *American Music* 4/1, 50–8.

Rodosthenous, G. (2017) 'Introduction'. In: Rodosthenous, G. (ed.) *The Disney Musical on Stage and Screen: Critical Approaches from 'Snow White' to 'Frozen'*. London: Bloomsbury, 1–14.

Rothstein, M. (1991) 'Theater: Sondheim's *Assassins*: Insane Realities of History'. *The New York Times*. Available at: https://archive.nytimes.com/www.nytimes.com/books/98/07/19/specials/sondheim-assassins.html [Accessed 14 May 2020].

Rugg, R. A. (2002) 'What It Used to Be: Nostalgia and the State of the Broadway Musical'. *Theater* 32/2, 44–55.

Rush, A. (2017) 'Oh, What a Beautiful Mormon: Rodgers and Hammerstein, Intertextuality and *The Book of Mormon*'. *Studies in Musical Theatre* 11/1, 39–50.

Rush, A. (2021a) '#YouWillBeFound: Participatory Fandom, Social Media Marketing, and *Dear Evan Hansen*'. *Studies in Musical Theatre* 15/2, 119–32.

Rush, A. (2021b) '*Hamilton – An American Musical*: The Very Model of a Modern Major (British) Megamusical'. In: Lodge, M. J. and Laird, P. R. (eds) *Duelling Grounds: Revolution and Revelation in the Musical Hamilton*. New York: Oxford University Press, 215–29.

Russell, S. (2007) 'Re-Act: The Performance of Discipline on Broadway'. *Studies in Musical Theatre* 1/1, 97–108.

Sáez, E. M. (2018a), 'Bodega Sold Dreams: Middle-Class Panic and the Crossover Aesthetics of *In the Heights*'. In: Gallego, C. and González, M. (eds) *Dialectical Imaginaries: Materialist Approaches to U.S. Latino/a Literature*. Ann Arbor, MI: University of Michigan Press, 187–216.

Sáez, E. M. (2018b) 'Blackout on Broadway: Affiliation and Audience *In the Heights* and *Hamilton*'. *Studies in Musical Theatre* 12/2, 181–97.

Sanders, J. (2006) *Adaptation and Appropriation*. London and New York: Routledge.

Sater, S. and Sheik, D. (2007) *Spring Awakening*. [Libretto] New York: Theatre Communications Group.

Savran, D. (2004) 'Toward a Historiography of the Popular'. *Theatre Survey* 45/2, 253–65.

Savran, D. (2011) 'Class and Culture'. In: Knapp, R., Morris, M., and Wolf, S. (eds) *The Oxford Handbook to the American Musical*. New York: Oxford University Press, 239–50.

Savran, D. (2014) 'Trafficking in Transnational Brands: The New "Broadway-Style" Musical'. *Theatre Survey* 55/3.

Schneider, R. (2014) *Theatre and History*. Basingstoke: Palgrave Macmillan.

Sebesta, J. (2003) 'From Celluloid to Stage: The "Movical," *The Producers*, and the Postmodern'. *Theatre Annual* 56, 97–112.

Shellard, D. Handley, M. and Nicholson, S. (2004) *The Lord Chamberlain Regrets: A History of British Theatre Censorship*. London: British Library.

Sibley, J. and Lassell, M. (2007) *Mary Poppins: Anything Can Happen if You Let It*. New York: Disney Editions.

Sondheim, S. and Lapine, J. (1987) *Into the Woods*. [Libretto] New York: Theatre Communications Group.

Southern, E. (1997 [1971]) *The Music of Black Americans: A History*. 3rd edn. New York and London: W. W. Norton and Company.

Steger, M. B. (2017) *Globalization: A Very Short Introduction*. 4th edn. Oxford: Oxford University Press.

Stempel, L. (2010) *Showtime: A History of the Broadway Musical Theater*. New York: W. W. Norton.

Sternfeld, J. and Wollman, E. L. (2011) 'After the "Golden Age"'. In: Knapp, R., Morris, M. and Wolf, S. (eds) *The Oxford Handbook to the American Musical*. New York: Oxford University Press, 111–24.

Sternfeld, J. (2006) *The Megamusical*. Bloomington: Indiana University Press.

Sternfeld, J. (2009) '*Damn Yankees* and the 1950s Man: You Gotta Have (Loyalty, an Escape Clause, and) Heart'. *Studies in Musical Theatre* 3/1, 77–83.

Sternfeld, J. (2017) 'Revisiting Classic Musicals: Revivals, Films, Television and Recordings'. In: Everett, W. A. and Laird, P. R. (eds) *The Cambridge Companion to the Musical*. 3rd edn. Cambridge: Cambridge University Press, 406–22.

Stiehl, P. (2017) 'The Digital-Age Musical: Sighting/Siting Musicals Defined by High-Tech Content, Themes, and Memes'. In: Hillman-McCord, J. (ed.) *iBroadway: Musical Theatre in the Digital Age*. Houndmills: Palgrave Macmillan, 43–72.

Stilwell, R. (2011) 'The Television Musical'. In: Knapp, R., Morris, M. and Wolf, S. (eds) *The Oxford Handbook of the American Musical*. New York: Oxford University Press, 152–66.

Swain, J. P. (1990) *The Broadway Musical: A Critical and Musical Survey*. Oxford University Press.

Symonds, D. (2015) *We'll Have Manhattan: The Early Work of Rodgers and Hart*. New York: Oxford University Press.

Symonds, D. (2016) 'The American Invasion: The Impact of *Oklahoma!* and *Annie Get Your Gun*'. In: Gordon, R. and Jubin, O. (eds) *The Oxford Handbook of the British Musical*. Oxford and New York: Oxford University Press, 225–48.

Thierens, S. (2017) 'Stage Entertainment's Global Success'. In: MacDonald, L. and Everett, W. A. (eds) *The Palgrave Handbook of Musical Theatre Producers*. Basingstoke: Palgrave, 520–8.

Titrington-Craft, E. 'Musical of the Month: Little Johnny Jones'. *NYPL*, 21 July 2012. Available at: https://www.nypl.org/blog/2012/07/21/musical-month-little-johnny-jones. [Accessed 6 May 2020].

Tran, D. (2016) 'Building a Better "Mikado," Minus the Yellowface'. *American Theatre*. Available at: https://www.americantheatre.org/2016/04/20/building-a-better-mikado-minus-the-yellowface/. [Accessed 8 February 2019].

Traubner, R. (1983) *Operetta: A Theatrical History*. London: Victor Gollancz Ltd.

Valencia, B. D. (2017) 'Charles Frohman: King of the Star-Makers'. In: MacDonald, L. and Everett, W. A. (eds) *The Palgrave Handbook of Musical Theatre Producers*. London: Palgrave Macmillan, 53–63.

Viagas, R. (2016) '*The Black Crook*, the "First" Broadway Musical Is Headed Back to NY'. *Playbill.com*. Available at: http://www.playbill.com/article/the-black-crook-the-first-broadway-musical-will-return-to-new-york. [Accessed 18 July 2019].

The Walt Disney Company (2022) 'Stories Matter'. Available at: https://storiesmatter.thewaltdisneycompany.com/. [Accessed 4 March 2022].

Warner, M. (1995) *From the Beast to the Blonde: On Fairy Tales and Their Tellers*. London: Vintage.

Wells, E. (2016) 'After *Anger*: The British Musical of the Late 1950s'. In: Gordon, R. and Jubin, O. (eds) *The Oxford Handbook of British Musicals*. Oxford University Press, 273–89.

Whitfield, S. (ed.) (2019) *Reframing the Musical: Race, Culture and Identity*. London: Red Globe Press.

Williams, J. (2017) 'Immigrant Discourse and Mixtape Authenticity in the Hamilton Mixtape'. *American Music* 36, 487–506.

Wolf, M. (1997) *Nine* (Review). *Variety*, 9 January. Available at: https://variety.com/1997/legit/reviews/nine-4-1117436787/. [Accessed 8 February 2019].

Wolf, S. (2002) *A Problem Like Maria: Gender and Sexuality in the American Musical*. Ann Arbor, MI: University of Michigan Press.

Wolf, S. (2008) 'Defying Gravity: Queer Conventions in the Musical *Wicked*'. *Theatre Journal* 60/1, 1–21.

Wolf, S. (2011) *Changed for Good: A Feminist History of the Broadway Musical*. New York: Oxford University Press.

Wolf, S. (2012) 'The 2003/2004 Season and Broadway Musical Theatre as a Political Conversant'. In: Spencer, J. (ed.) *Political and Protest Theatre after 9/11: Patriotic Dissent*. London and New York: Routledge, 19–37.

Wolf, S. (2020) *Beyond Broadway: The Pleasure and Promise of Musical Theatre across America*. New York: Oxford University Press.

Woll, A. (1989) *Black Musical Theatre: From Coontown to Dreamgirls*. New York: Da Capo Press.

Wollman, E. (2002) 'The Economic Development of the "New" Times Square and Its Impact on the Broadway Musical'. *American Music* 20/4, 445–65.

Wollman, E. (2013) *Hard Times: The Adult Musical in 1970s New York City*. New York: Oxford University Press.

Wollman, E. (2017) *A Critical Companion to the American Stage Musical*.
London and New York: Bloomsbury Methuen.

Womack, M. (2009) "'Thank You for the Music": Catherine Johnson's Feminist
Revoicings in *Mamma Mia!' Studies in Musical Theatre* 3/2, 201–11.

Zoglin, R. (2016) 'Broadway Shuffle'. *Time*, 23 May, 42–5.

Index